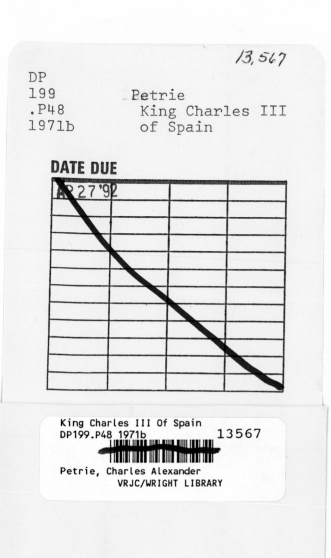

KING CHARLES III OF SPAIN

By the same author

Don John of Austria
The Drift to War, 1900–1914
The Edwardians
Great Beginnings in the Age of Queen Victoria
The Jacobite Movement
King Alfonso XIII and His Age
Philip II of Spain
The Victorians

KING CHARLES III
OF SPAIN

AN ENLIGHTENED DESPOT

SIR CHARLES PETRIE

THE JOHN DAY COMPANY
New York

The John Day Company,
257 Park Avenue South,
New York N.Y. 10010
an Intext publisher

Published in Great Britain by
Constable & Company Ltd.,
10 Orange Street London WC2

Library of Congress Catalogue Card Number: 71–141792

Printed in Great Britain

By gracious permission
this life of the Greatest of the Spanish Bourbons
is dedicated to the latest

H.R.H. DON JUAN CARLOS
Prince of Spain

CONTENTS

ILLUSTRATIONS

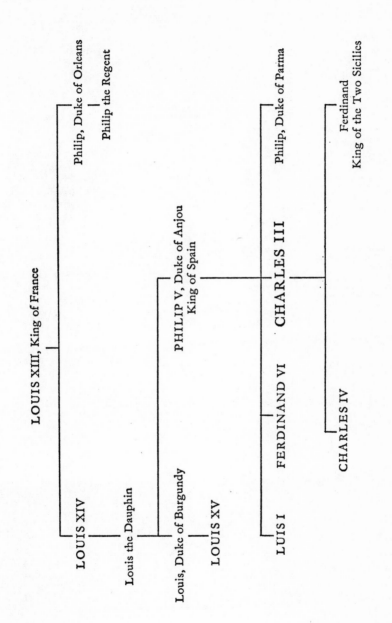

FOREWORD

THE eighteenth century was for Europe the age of intellectualism, the sowing of the revolutionary seeds which were to culminate in the form of nineteenth-century democracy, but if it was the age of intellectualism it was also the age of kings. Nations had by then reached their maturity, and kings had emerged triumphant from their struggles with the Church and the territorial nobility, so that '*L'Etat, c'est moi*', if the words had ever been uttered in the sense in which they are so often quoted, would have been no empty boast. That it was sometimes the royal confessor or the royal mistress who ruled behind the throne made no outward difference, for the power was the king's, and the favourites, whether they wore cloth or silk, who might exercise it temporarily, were themselves subject to the king's caprice.

The history of the three hundred years which elapsed between the discovery of America and the outbreak of the French Revolution is one of monarchical government by hereditary dynasties, and it was the era of benevolent despotism: of these benevolent despots Charles III of Spain was an outstanding example. The view of their duties held by the great monarchs of the period – and neither before nor since have so many able men and women occupied thrones – was that the nations over which they ruled were personified in themselves, but that if their subjects were in duty bound to obey them, they, too, had their obligations towards those they governed. If everything for, and nothing by, the people came to be the watchwords of governments it was hardly surprising, for when authority was for a time relaxed such outbreaks as those which took place all over Europe in the middle of the seventeenth century proved that the only alternatives were monarchy or chaos.

The difficult means of communication, the general ignorance, and the widespread ferocity of manners rendered popular government impossible, so that unless the head of the state made his power felt, the country concerned merely became a prey to the contending ambitions and jealousies of the nobility and a few rich burghers, with a Fronde as the inevitable result. Industry and commerce, although practised to a far greater extent than during the Middle Ages, were still in their infancy, with the consequence that the middle class, which was to be the backbone of representative democracy in the nineteenth century, was few in numbers and weak in influence. In effect, no other form of government but hereditary monarchy was possible, and so long as it proved itself efficient it held the field.

Furthermore, at the same time that the power of the monarchy had been going up, that of its rivals had everywhere been going down. Not only had the ranks of the English, French, and Spanish nobility been heavily depleted by the civil and foreign wars of the fourteenth and fifteenth centuries, but the increasing employment of gunpowder had made fighting itself more expensive; and when, in addition, there came the enormous increase in the cost of living as a result of the discovery of America, the day when a great noble could overshadow his sovereign was clearly passing. Similarly the power of the Church declined after the Popes left Rome for Avignon; it was still further reduced by the Great Schism; while the Reformation ushered in a period in which, both in Catholic and Protestant countries, the clergy have always been subordinated to the secular authority – not least in Spain itself. Meanwhile the increase of trade automatically raised the revenue from the customs duties, and as this went to the king, the latter was soon possessed of a new power that none of his predecessors had known, namely that of the purse.

As a general rule the benevolent despotism in its earlier days worked through the old medieval institutions. It lasted three centuries if we take as its commencement the discovery of America and as its close the outbreak of the French Revolution. In the sixteenth century the old representative assemblies which had survived from the Middle Ages still continued to meet fairly regularly, though the masterful men and women who occupied the thrones of Western Europe during this period left Parliament, States-General, and Cortes with little save the appearance of authority; and in point of fact these bodies performed no more important function than the confirmation of royal decisions, as can be seen in the progress of the Reformation in England. The seventeenth century saw the monarchies begin to discard the old forms under cover of which they had hitherto been content to work: the States-General never met again after 1614 until the throne itself was tottering in 1789, and though the Cortes was still summoned from time to time as a matter of form it enjoyed no real power: only in England, where special conditions obtained, did Parliament gain ground, and there were many occasions when matters might so easily have taken a different course.

By the eighteenth century new problems were arising which called for new machinery, though the old medieval assemblies were still for the most part left intact, but the actual work of administration was carried out by councils or boards, each with its own special duties, with the royal council, over which the monarch usually presided in person, at their head: in Spain practically the whole administration of the empire was vested in the Councils of Castille and of the Indies. This system had grown up at the end of the fifteenth and the beginning of the sixteenth centuries when governments found themselves saddled with new responsibilities: the easiest course was obviously to constitute a fresh *ad hoc* authority, and the body thus created soon showed a natural tendency to enlarge the sphere of its activities, and so to increase its own importance. Some may see a parallel with the conditions obtaining in many countries today.

The weakness of these new bodies through which the benevolent despotism worked was that they did not really provide a satisfactory connecting-link between central and local government, and that at a time when municipal life, which had been so flourishing during the Middle Ages, was showing a marked tendency to decay. As we shall see in the following pages, Charles III was taken completely by surprise by the rioting in 1766, which he would certainly not have been had there been any intermediaries between him and his subjects to tell him what was afoot.

Not the least claim which the benevolent despotism – and here the Spanish Bourbons were certainly no exception – has upon the gratitude of posterity is the favour that it showed to literature and art, an attitude which has not been displayed either by democracy or by the dictators who have succeeded them. A Voltaire and a Diderot found nothing incongruous in accepting the bounty of

a Frederick or a Catherine. It is true that in a number of instances
the taste of the royal and princely patrons left a good deal to be
desired, for there were very few who possessed that of Charles I
of England; but with the solitary exception of the House of
Hanover – and even there we must exclude George IV in some
degree – there was not a dynasty in Europe which did not display
at any rate an outward interest in the affairs of the mind. In this
way the benevolent despotism passed on the legacy of the
Renaissance almost down to modern times, for the divorce
between letters and politics is in many cases quite recent.

Of the benevolent despots of the eighteenth century Charles III
of Spain was outstanding, and he had no need to fear comparison
even with such contemporaries as Frederick of Prussia, Joseph of
Austria, and Catherine of Russia. In these circumstances it is the
more remarkable that there is no biography of him in the English
language – only a prize essay written by the late Sir Joseph
Addison at the beginning of the present century. Yet he has
always been remarkably well documented in Spanish – the classic
work of course being the six volumes of Manuel Danvila y
Collado published in Madrid in 1891 – and of recent years there
have been several notable additions to the bibliography concerning him upon which I have drawn freely in the following pages.
In France there are the two volumes of François Rousseau which
appeared as long ago as 1907. Charles was brought into contact
with Great Britain, admittedly hostile contact, on many occasions,
and Spain played a prominent part in the War of American
Independence, while such problems of today as the possession of
Gibraltar and the Falkland Islands were to the fore in his reign:
I have therefore felt that a study of Charles and his times in the
English language was long overdue, and this book is the result
of that belief.

The number of those to whom I am indebted for encouragement, advice, and information on various points is legion. In
particular I wish to express my thanks to the Spanish ambassador
in London, the Marqués de Santa Cruz, who has made many
valuable suggestions; I am more indebted than I can express to
the Rev. Thomas Corbishley, s.j., and Canon de Zulueta for
guidance over the vexed question of the expulsion of the Jesuits
from Spain; the Director of the Spanish Institute in London,
Professor Don Carlos Clavería, and his staff have been more than

kind in the loan of books; and in the same connection I would also like to thank Mr. S. C. Holliday, Chief Librarian of the Royal Borough of Kensington and Chelsea. None of them, I may add, is in any way responsible for the opinions expressed in these pages.

CHARLES PETRIE

THE INHERITANCE

ON 10th August 1759 Charles of Bourbon, who had already been Duke of Parma, and was the reigning King of the Two Sicilies, succeeded his half-brother, Ferdinand VI, as King of Spain and the Indies at the age of forty-three. In appearance he was not impressive, for he was short in stature, lean, and round-shouldered, with a sunburnt complexion and bad teeth from which we are told that he suffered severely in those days of primitive dentistry. As he grew older his Bourbon nose became his most prominent feature, but his eyes were bright, and signified a man with an intelligence above the ordinary. His expression was genial, and he was always dignified, with a simplicity of manner which could on occasion belie him. By contrast with many an eighteenth-century monarch the tastes of the new occupant of the Spanish throne were frugal in the extreme: he realized the importance of exercise to one who was engaged in a predominantly sedentary occupation, and he took it in the form of hunting and shooting, which he regarded as a physical necessity: otherwise his recreations were fishing, billiards, and carpentry. Serious music made no appeal to him, though he was eventually to build one of the largest of contemporary opera-houses. In religious matters Charles was a man of sincere piety, though that did not prevent him from expelling the Jesuits from his dominions, and he was a model of filial virtue.

As a king he was the perfect type of the benevolent despot of the eighteenth century, as he proved in Parma, Naples, and Madrid. He had done much to improve the Two Sicilies, and in Spain his care for his subjects' good was to have even greater scope. By his ministers, notably Aranda, Squillacci, Campomanes, and Floridablanca, he was ably supported, and as an enlightened monarch Charles had no need to fear comparison with such of his contemporaries as Frederick the Great and Joseph II. Unfortunately, like Joseph II, he was a good deal of a doctrinaire, and in more than one instance he tried to force upon Spain reforms which, however excellent in themselves, were alien to the national genius, and so took no root. Indeed it must be admitted that in many ways Charles was the prototype of innumerable Spanish liberals of more recent times, and in particular of those who were responsible for the country's two essays in republicanism. It is difficult to resist the conclusion that although the new King of Spain was thoroughly imbued with the ideas of the French Encyclopaedists, he was not always sufficiently acquainted with the outlook of the ordinary Spaniard.

From his birth in Madrid on 20th January 1716 he was the centre of much political intrigue, for although his father, Philip V, was by now firmly established on the Spanish throne on which he had finally been seated by the Treaty of Utrecht, as former Duc d'Anjou he had aspirations to the crown of France which was then worn by Louis XV, who was only a child and a delicate one at that. The character of Philip V[1] is not easy to determine. His mother was a Wittelsbach, and from her he inherited that melancholy, at times almost amounting to madness, and that indulgence in long periods of seclusion, which have marked some members of the family from generation to generation down to the present day. On his father's side he was a Bourbon, and he possessed to the full their terrible sexual appetite. Miss Nancy Mitford, in her charming study of Madame de Pompadour, has reminded her readers that when Madame de Maintenon was seventy-five and Louis XIV was seventy she told her confessor that it tired her very much to make love with him twice a day.[2] In this respect Philip was truly his grandfather's grandson. The continual physical possession of a woman was a necessity to him, but, unlike Louis XIV, he combined with a character incredibly sensuous a conscience abnormally scrupulous. His conscience was unconvinced by his grandfather's example that the strictest principles may be mitigated by a somewhat easy practice, and he refused to take a mistress, with the result that the first separation from his wife during his Italian campaign in 1702 put a severe

---

[1] The best modern biography is that of Señor Don Luciano de Taxonera: *Felipe V*. Barcelona. 1956.

[2] Mitford, Nancy: *Madame de Pompadour*, p. 185. London. 1954.

strain upon both his physical and mental health. This meant that he must be married early, and that he must remain married; if one wife died, another would have to be found with as little delay as possible. Such uxoriousness could only have one result, namely that Philip was at the same time the tyrant and the slave of the woman he married. However many wives had died, he would have married more, and he would have been a model of troublesome attachment to all of them. He was at once the most affectionate and the least considerate of husbands.

Unlike most of his Bourbon relatives, but like the Stuarts, Philip was one of those men who mature early, and who later belie the promise of their youth. Soon after his first arrival in Madrid he insisted, against the advice of his ministers, upon going in person to Naples and Sicily, and thus becoming personally acquainted with those who were still his Italian subjects: Philip II, he declared, had lost the United Provinces because he had not gone there himself. 'If I lose territories,' he declared, 'it shall not be for that reason.' Three years later, when his cause in the Peninsula itself seemed desperate, he rallied the people of Castille to the defence of his crown by a display of energy which caused him to become known to them as *el animoso*, or 'the spirited'. Yet in later life he would for long periods at a time withdraw himself from his subjects' gaze at San Ildefonso in a manner reminiscent, as has been suggested, of the Wittelsbachs of the nineteenth century.

More important than the King was his first wife, Maria Luisa of Savoy, who, although she was only twenty-five at the time of her death in 1714, did much by her charm and ability to save his throne. In 1703, when the War of the Spanish Succession was at its height, it seemed as if Andalusia was at the mercy of the British, and it was due to her dauntless resolution and example that the province rose in arms against the Habsburg claimant, the Archduke Charles; nor did she hesitate to stand up to Louis XIV himself, of whom her husband was in considerable awe. By him she had four sons – half-brothers of the future Charles III: two of them died as children, but the other two lived to become kings of Spain with the titles of Luis I and Ferdinand VI.

For reasons already mentioned it was desirable that on his first wife's death Philip should marry again at the earliest possible moment, and with the somewhat reluctant consent of Louis XIV a bride was found for him in Elizabeth Farnese, the daughter of Odoardo, eldest son of Ranuccio II, Duke of Parma, by Dorothea Sophia, daughter of Philip William, Elector Palatine, and sister of the widowed queen of Charles the Bewitched, the last Habsburg King of Spain. The chief architect of this marriage was Giulio Alberoni, later the famous Cardinal of that name. The Spanish scene in the early eighteenth century abounded in bizarre figures, but none of them was more remarkable than Alberoni. From the beginning his career had proceeded along somewhat unorthodox lines for one who was to become a prince of the Church, for he was the son of a gardener in Piacenza, and he had originally come to the Peninsula as a sort of clerical buffoon to the Duc de Vendôme. His jokes were more racy than decent, and he was also an excellent cook, while time was to show that his ability was as undoubted as his character was unattractive. When Vendôme died, Alberoni contrived to get himself made the representative of the Duke of Parma in Madrid, where it soon occurred to him that if he could marry his master's daughter to Philip there would surely be no heights to which he could not himself aspire. His machinations were successful, and on 16th September 1714 Philip and Elizabeth were married by proxy at Parma.

The eighteenth century, more than any other in the Christian era, was notable for its remarkable women, and among the most remarkable was the new Queen of Spain. Illustrious blood, both spiritual and temporal, flowed in her veins, for the Farnesi owed their fortunes to the marriage of a bastard daughter of the Emperor Charles V to the son of a bastard of Pope Paul III. Their territory of Parma and Piacenza had been in its origin, and had again latterly become, a buffer state between Papacy and Empire. It was indeed recognized as a Papal fief, but it had been detached from that group of municipalities which had been crystallized into a state under the rule of the Dukes of Milan; it was therefore always liable to the revival of Imperial claims when it should suit the policy of Vienna to make them.

Elizabeth was born on 25th October 1692, and so was twenty-one at the time of her marriage. The Prince of Monaco, in a letter to Torcy, the French Foreign Minister, drew a flattering picture of her as she passed through his dominions on her way to meet her husband in Madrid:

4

She is of medium height and has a good figure: the face long, rather than oval, much marked with small-pox; there are even some scars, but all this is not disagreeably prominent. Her head is nobly set on her shoulders; she has blue eyes, which, without being large, are as sparkling as can be; she can say everything with them. The mouth is rather large, beautified by admirable teeth, which are often disclosed by the pleasantest of smiles. Her voice is charming. Her conversation with everyone is gracious, and is said to be prompted by the heart. She is passionately fond of music; sings and paints very prettily; can ride and hunt; Spanish is the only language which she does not know. Lombard heart and Florentine head; her will is extremely strong.[1]

Elizabeth's aunt, the widow of Charles II, met her at Pau. The older woman had not been popular in Spain, nor, it must be confessed, anywhere else, for she seems to have been one of those unhappy, middle-aged ladies whom nobody wants, and whom each relation would gladly foist off upon another: ultimately, however, she appears to have found happiness in the arms of a French commercial traveller whom she secretly married. However this may be, she doubtless had much sound advice to give her niece upon the duties and responsibilities of a Queen-Consort of Spain.

That the Prince of Monaco did not err in his estimate of Elizabeth's will was proved even before she reached Madrid. On 23rd December she arrived at Jadraque, where that very formidable lady the Princesse des Ursins, who had long been the dominant factor in Spanish politics in the interests of Louis XIV, had to receive her as chief lady-in-waiting. The Princesse was determined to establish an ascendancy from the beginning, and when Alberoni made his appearance some three hours before the Queen she burst out to him, 'Well, when is the Queen going to arrive? She treats the King very cavalierly, making him wait like this, tramping by night like a prostitute. You represented her to me as a heroine, but upon my word she is a poor creature, from her appetite downwards. I am told that she eats nothing but garlic and hard-boiled eggs.' When the Queen did arrive the Princesse remained at the top of the stairs, which she made no effort to descend, alleging that her legs were swollen: she took

[1] cf. Baudrillart, Mgr.: *Philippe V et la Cour de France*, vol. I., p. 603. Paris. 1890–1901.

Elizabeth into her room, where she was heard to say 'You have treated the King, Madame, very cavalierly, for you have shown little attention to his impatient desire to see you.' She followed this outburst by seizing the Queen by the wrist and turning her round like a marionette, exclaiming at the same time, 'My word, Madame, you are very badly made.' Up to this point Elizabeth had said nothing, but she now called out, 'Count Alberoni, take this mad woman away, who dares to insult me,' which was accordingly done, and the Princesse was placed under arrest. When Philip heard of this incident he of course took the part of his wife, and so the woman who had governed Spain for so long, and had on occasion even defied Louis XIV, was driven into exile through a snowy winter's night over the bleakest uplands in Europe. Undoubtedly one of the cleverest women of her age, she had been outmanoeuvred by a chit of a girl and by the son of a gardener, though it can hardly be denied that at the end her arrogance contributed in no small measure to her fall.[1]

Such were the parents of the future Charles III, but when he was born it appeared far from likely that he would ever sit upon the Spanish throne. Apart from his father there were two lives between it and him, namely those of his half-brothers, and he was merely the Infante Don Carlos. For the first seven years of his life he was entrusted to the care of a Spanish governess of the most rigid principles, whose main idea seems to have been to inculcate in him a blind obedience to his parents and to the teaching of the Catholic Church. After that age he was given his own apartments in the Escorial, where he was attended by a train of tutors, in all probability more remarkable for their quantity than their quality. All the same, he acquired a working knowledge of Latin, Italian, German, and French, as well as a certain amount of history both sacred and profane. The young prince's director of studies was the Conde de San Esteban, and under his supervision Don Carlos was taught the rudiments of military tactics, naval science, geometry, and fortification, while his predilection for outdoor exercise, notably hunting and shooting, was wisely encouraged.

Whatever views his tutors may have entertained on the subject of education in the abstract, it is not without interest to note that, like his contemporary benevolent despots in Berlin, Vienna, and

[1] *Bellardi*, MS.: Ambrosiana, 173.

6

St. Petersburg, Don Carlos was brought up to believe that his country and people belonged to him, and that he had to serve his people to the best of his ability. The maxim of them all may have been 'L'Etat, c'est moi', yet this was nevertheless to the benefit of the state, since it imposed upon them the duty to look after it as well as they would look after themselves. None of them saw or feared that the ideas which they were encouraging were in due course to threaten their own position, and to make the landslide to democracy inevitable.

While Don Carlos was under instruction in the Escorial, events were taking place which were vitally to affect not only his future but that of his country and of Europe as a whole. Louis XIV, who had dominated the international scene for so long, had ended his reign in September 1715, little more than two years after the Treaty of Utrecht, which had brought the War of the Spanish Succession to an end by establishing his grandson on the Spanish throne. With his death there ensued a somewhat confused period in the history of international relations: the allies of decades became enemies almost overnight, while sworn foes found themselves acting together against their erstwhile friends. This state of affairs continued until disputed successions in Poland and Austria brought about a redistribution of forces more or less along the traditional lines, that is to say Britain and the Habsburgs against the House of Bourbon, with the lesser Powers inclining to one party or the other, not without occasional changes of side. This was the scene which faced Don Carlos while he was ruling in Parma and Naples, though it was changing again by the time that he returned to Madrid on the death of his half-brother.

Spain had fared worse by the Treaty of Utrecht than any other of the participants in the war to which it had put an end. She had, it is true, been relieved of the *damnosa hereditas* of the Netherlands with which Charles V had burdened his son, Philip II, but she had lost Naples, the Milanese, and Sardinia to the Emperor, Gibraltar and Minorca to Great Britain, and Sicily to the Duke of Savoy. No Spaniard regretted the Netherlands, but it was otherwise with the rest of the lost provinces, and from Philip downwards there was a general determination to regain them as soon as possible. In these circumstances it was not unnatural that the first threat to the new order should have come from Spain, and to this several causes contributed. Philip V was by no means enamoured of the progress of events in France, and being on the worst possible terms with the Regent there, namely the Duc d'Orléans, he was prepared to listen to desperate counsels. In any event he was by now completely dominated by his wife, who wished to see her sons on Italian thrones since Luis and Ferdinand, the heirs to the Spanish crown, were her husband's children by his first marriage.

Nevertheless these various aspirations would have been of little practical importance had it not been for the work accomplished by Alberoni in the regeneration of Spain. He had certainly not let the grass grow under his feet since he had been instrumental in bringing about the marriage of Philip and Elizabeth, for he had become the principal minister, and in 1717 he was made a Cardinal. What is more, he had succeeded in creating a fleet, and in July 1717 he suddenly put the weapons he had forged to the test. A Spanish expedition sailed from Barcelona to Cagliari, and by the end of November all Sardinia was in Philip's hands. From this moment Alberoni's ambitions knew no bounds, and he began to meditate nothing less than the wholesale revision of the Utrecht settlement. He aimed at overthrowing both the French regency and the House of Hanover by a combination of Sweden, Russia, and Prussia, while he endeavoured to rouse the Hungarians against the Emperor. An expedition was got ready to restore James III to his throne, and in 1719 a few Spanish troops did actually land in Scotland.[1] These projects had the not unnatural result of bringing together those whom they threatened, and on 2nd August the Quadruple Alliance was concluded in London between Great Britain, France, Austria, and the United Provinces to curb the ambitions of Alberoni and his master.

This coalition disposed of greater force than any that Philip and Alberoni could bring against it, although Spanish troops were in possession of Sardinia and the larger part of Sicily. The British fleet had the superiority in the Mediterranean, while in the west another British squadron captured Vigo: a French army invaded Spain under the command of the Marshal Duke of Berwick, to whose victory at Almansa in the War of the Spanish Succession Philip largely owed his crown, and in due course Fuenterrabia and San Sebastian fell into his hands. With the

[1] For an account of this expedition cf. Petrie, Sir Charles: *The Jacobite Movement*, pp. 285-303. London. 1959.

8

Spanish army facing Berwick was the Queen of Spain, and she encouraged the soldiers by appearing on horseback, pistols at the saddle-bow, dressed in a blue habit embroidered with silver. Her dresses were made not in Madrid but in Paris, and the French commander-in-chief placed no obstacle in the way of their delivery to her through his lines. By the end of 1719 the Spanish position was desperate, and on 26th January of the following year Philip had to give way. He surrendered Sardinia to Savoy, and renounced all claim to Sicily, but Don Carlos took the first step to a throne, for the victors acknowledged his presumptive succession to Tuscany and Parma, where the reigning dynasties were on the verge of extinction.

By this time Alberoni was in exile, and his dismissal was effected in a truly Churchillian manner. One morning the King on leaving Madrid handed to the Secretary of State a decree ordering the Cardinal to quit the capital in eight days and Spain within three weeks, to take no further part in politics, and not to appear at court or anywhere that the King and Queen might happen to be. After begging in vain for a last interview Alberoni left Madrid for Barcelona, but was stopped at Lerida, where his papers and, according to some authorities, a large sum of money were taken from him. He then took refuge in the territory of the Republic of Genoa, whence all attempts to extradite him failed.

It might have been assumed that Alberoni's career was now finished, but it is notoriously difficult to keep an ambitious ecclesiastic down, of whatever denomination. The Cardinal accordingly lay low in Genoese territory until the death of Clement XI in 1721, when he duly put in an appearance at the Conclave which elected his successor, while three years later he actually seems to have been seriously considered in some quarters as a possible occupant of the Chair of St. Peter himself, though his candidature would certainly have been quashed by the Spanish veto. Benedict XIV made him Vice-Legate of Romagna, and his tenure of this office was marked by an unsuccessful attempt to incorporate the Republic of San Marino in the Papal States. Finally, he retired to his native Piacenza, where he died in 1752, a rich man, at the age of eighty-eight. Alberoni was never unpopular with the mass of the Spanish people, who were grateful to him for what he had done for their country, however unpleasing may have been some of his personal characteristics,[1] and when the Spanish troops occupied Piacenza in the War of the Austrian Succession he was treated by the soldiers with the most profound respect.

The Spain of those days was a veritable paradise for adventurers, and within a few years of Alberoni's dismissal another and much more picturesque fortune-hunter appeared in the person of the Baron de Ripperdá, who, indeed, owed his earlier advancement to the fallen Cardinal. Unlike his predecessor, there was nothing to be said against him on the score of his birth, for he came of a noble family, originally Spanish, which had settled in the Low Countries, and he was born in the lordship of Groningen about 1665. Even before he entered the Spanish service Ripperdá's career had been varied, for, having been educated by the Jesuits, he then became a Protestant, and he managed to combine a military career in the Dutch service with the study of political economy. In due course his knowledge of this subject caused him to be selected as his country's representative at Madrid. From that moment his rise was extremely rapid, for he became a naturalized Spanish subject, returned to the bosom of the Catholic Church, and on the fall of Alberoni he was made Superintendent-General, with his headquarters at Segovia, where he lived in a style of considerable magnificence, conveniently close to the royal residence at San Ildefonso.

That Ripperdá was a man of very considerable ability cannot be denied, but his ambitions were boundless, and it was not long before he felt that even Spain was too restricted a field, and nothing less would satisfy him but the reputation of a great international statesman. Nor was he long in making an opportunity to appear in this rôle. The relations between Vienna and Madrid had been strained ever since the War of the Spanish Succession, and Alberoni's activities had certainly done nothing to improve them, but Ripperdá now managed to persuade the Queen that she could best advance the cause of her children by a direct appeal to the Emperor, since nobody else was showing much desire to do anything for them. The moment was not ill-timed, for Charles VI was on the worst of terms with his British ally, partly owing to her opposition to his favourite project, the

[1] cf. *The Duke of Berwick and His Son, Some Unpublished Letters and Papers, passim.* London. 1951.

Ostend East India Company, and partly owing to the German policy of George I as Elector of Hanover, which favoured the Hohenzollerns too much for the Habsburg taste. All the same, the Emperor's terms were high, and Philip seems to have been somewhat reluctant to come into too close contact with the man with whom he had contended for the Spanish throne; so that nothing might have come of the negotiation had not the French Regent, by now the Duc de Bourbon, chosen that particular moment (March 1725) to send back the Infanta, who was to have been the bride of Louis XV. This insult threw Philip into the arms of the Emperor, and at the end of the following month the Treaty of Vienna was signed. By this, and a further arrangement, Charles promised that two of his three daughters should marry the Infantes Don Carlos and Don Felipe, and that if he himself should die before the eldest, Maria Theresa, became marriageable, she should wed Don Carlos. Other clauses stipulated the division of the spoils in the event of a successful war with Britain and France, while Spain guaranteed to the Emperor the privileges of the most favoured nation, and an opening for the Ostend Company in the Indies.

The Treaty of Vienna marked Ripperdá's apogee, and he was made a duke and a grandee, but his triumph was to be temporary, for as in the case of the schemes of Alberoni, in the face of this threat the Western Powers once more drew together, and there came into existence the Alliance of Hanover between France, Britain, and Prussia. It professed to be merely defensive, but it provided for the maintenance of the balance of power, threatened by the prospective marriage of Don Carlos and Maria Theresa. This was a very real threat, for his elder half-brother, Luis, was dead, and there was only the Prince of Asturias, the future Ferdinand VI, between him and the Spanish throne. If he succeeded, and married Maria Theresa, the empire of Charles V would be re-created, a prospect which was by no means relished either in London or Paris on political or economic grounds.

In actual fact Ripperdá's house of cards speedily collapsed, for the alliance between Spain and the Emperor proved a most unhappy partnership, for when the Spaniards laid siege to Gibraltar their ally did nothing to assist them. Meanwhile the progress of events in France was tending to bring the Bourbon

Powers together, for the marriage of Louis XV to a Polish princess considerably diminished any prospects of succession to the French throne which Philip might still entertain, while the dismissal of the Duc de Bourbon removed one who had become anathema to the Spanish King and Queen; so in May 1727 an agreement was reached by which the Emperor promised to suspend the Ostend Company for seven years, and the Spaniards raised the siege of Gibraltar.

Ripperdá now followed Alberoni into retirement, but his fall, if less sudden than that of the Cardinal, was more dramatic, and it is worth recording for the light which it throws upon the political scene in which Don Carlos, now eleven, was being educated. It was some time before the Queen could face the prospect of dispensing with Ripperdá's services, though Philip had become disillusioned earlier, for with all his hypochondriac melancholy he was neither deficient in judgement nor in love of his people, while more than once the minister, relying on the Queen's support, had gone too far with his master. His garrulity and indiscreet remarks were also a contributory cause of his downfall, and on one occasion he publicly declared, 'I know that the Spanish nation hate me; but I despise their attempts while I am protected by the Queen, to whom I have rendered the most important service.' It is small wonder that the British ambassador, Stanhope, should have written to the Duke of Newcastle, 'The King is extremely agitated and uneasy, and has daily disputes with the Queen, who does nothing but cry from morning to night.' Finally, means were taken to overcome her infatuation, and she was persuaded that other ministers could be found no less capable of realizing her pet projects than Ripperdá, but without his vanity and indiscretion.

The first stage in his fall was his removal from the superintendence of the finances, but this was palliated with the pretence of relieving him of a part of the burdens of administration. Ripperdá, however, had too much political experience not to realize that this was the beginning of the end, so he immediately applied for permission to retire from all his other offices; this request was at first refused, but on 14th May 1726, as he was leaving a meeting of the Council, he received an official notification of the acceptance of his resignation together with the information that he had been granted an annual pension of three thousand pistoles on account of his past services. The news of his fall soon spread all over Madrid, and before long his house was besieged by an angry mob. 'I have never in my life', wrote Liria in his diary, 'seen such universal joy as that which everybody displayed when Ripperdá fell.' In these circumstances the fallen minister seems to have lost his head, which is not altogether surprising in view of the fact that he had for some time been selling State secrets to the British and Dutch governments, a piece of treachery which he feared might now come to light.

He accordingly sought asylum at the Dutch legation, but his fellow-countrymen knew him too well to wish for closer relations; so from there he proceeded to the British embassy, where he was much better received, and he disclosed all the secrets of the Spanish government to Stanhope, who duly passed them on to London. It could hardly be expected that Philip would allow his late minister to insult him from the cover of a foreign embassy in his own capital, and he demanded Ripperdá's immediate surrender; this Stanhope declined, so Ripperdá was removed from the British embassy by force, and taken under a strong guard to Segovia. Stanhope protested against the violation of his diplomatic immunity, but as the ex-minister's conduct was in itself unjustifiable, the British government took no further action in the matter, doubtless being influenced in its attitude by the fact that it had already extracted the maximum benefit from his disclosures.

With all his weaknesses Philip was a humane man and he lived in a humane age, or he might have made Ripperdá answer for his treachery with his life; instead he was allowed to make his escape with the aid of a maidservant whom he had seduced. By way of Portugal he reached England, where he was received at the Foreign Office in secret but with respect: nevertheless he saw no future for himself in London, so he passed into the United Provinces, where he became a Protestant once more. He was not, however, to be left in peace for long, since the Spanish government was demanding his extradition; so, with the aid of the Moorish minister at The Hague, he departed to Morocco with letters of introduction to the Sultan, Ahmad Dhahabi, who received him well, and under whom he served in an expedition against Ceuta, whereupon Philip deprived him of his rank of duke and grandee. Finally, on the deposition of the Sultan, he obtained the protection of the Pasha of Tetuan, where he eventually died in November 1737. So ended the chequered career of Ripperdá, one of the most extraordinary in a century of extraordinary careers.[1]

Meanwhile Don Carlos, whose future was the subject of so much intrigue, was passing from boyhood to adolescence. He learned to dance, an important accomplishment for royalty in those days, with grace, and he had a good seat on a horse. To the studies mentioned on an earlier page he now added an interest in mechanics, and he was becoming acquainted with what was going on in literary circles in Madrid. In this he was much influenced by his parents, who were not only liberal patrons of the arts, but helped and encouraged Spanish literature as actively and far more judiciously than had Philip IV. To them is due the foundation of the National Library, the Royal Academy, the Royal Academy of History, and many other learned societies which placed Spanish scholars at no disadvantage with those of other countries.

The royal example was widely followed, and it was not unusual to find members of the high aristocracy, such as the Conde de Fernan Nuñez, founding primary schools for both sexes on their estates, for he established 'a house of education for poor orphan girls, in which they should be brought up to be good mothers of families, not being required to take the veil, wear monastic dress, or do anything appertaining to the education of nuns'. Women, it may be added, especially the women of the aristocracy, helped a great deal in this revival of culture; they, too, founded primary schools, and furthered the spread of knowledge in every possible way. Most important of all were the Sociedades Economicas de Amigos del Pais, which were founded by private enterprise, but were much encouraged by the State. They united all those who were open to new ideas and were inspired by a desire for the regeneration of Spain, while to their initiative was due the creation of classes for artisans, the holding of literary and scientific discussions, and investigations of an industrial or agricultural character. The young prince was thus brought up in an atmosphere where culture very definitely had a prominent place. In women he would not appear to have taken any particular interest, though

[1] cf. Coxe, W.: *Memoirs of the Kings of Spain of the House of Bourbon*, vol. II, pp. 321 et seq. London. 1813.

his letters show that he was devoted to his governess, the Marquesa de Montehermoso.[1]

In spite of political alarums and excursions it was a very well-ordered household in which Don Carlos was brought up, for his father's day, like that of his great-grandfather, Louis XIV, was most regular. The King and Queen had light refreshments in bed at eight, after which Philip got up and attended to business for two and a half hours. They then heard Mass and had dinner, afterwards spending an hour together, when Philip went hunting: on his return there was another light meal, followed by the further despatch of affairs of State until supper, which was at eight o'clock. Both the King and Queen took an early dislike to Madrid, and at first they spent much of their time at Aranjuez; but in those days the place was considered unhealthy, and Alberoni warned Elizabeth that if any mishap befell her stepsons while they were there public opinion would hold her responsible for their death. For four years in the middle of Philip's reign the court was absent from Madrid, and the country was administered from Seville. Indeed, there seemed a fate against residence in Madrid, for when the King and Queen had made up their minds to pass the winter of 1734–1735 there, and the palace was being warmed against their coming, it was destroyed by fire on Christmas Eve. The real home of Philip and Elizabeth, at any rate in their later days, was San Ildefonso, where they built the palace of La Granja on the model of Versailles, and it is hardly surprising that it should have been their favourite residence, for it is surely one of the most attractive palaces in Europe. There, in due course, they were buried, not at the Escorial like their Habsburg predecessors.

Don Carlos followed his parents in their wanderings, and it was well that this should have been the case. As he was the son of a French father and an Italian mother, the Spanish blood in his veins was very thin, and he was shortly to leave Spain for Italy, not to return until in middle age as her sovereign. What he knew of the country he acquired during these early and impressionable years. In particular at Seville he made the acquaintance of a Franciscan, Sebastian de Jesus Sillero, who exercised a very considerable and most beneficial influence over him; but then all his

[1] cf. Ferrer del Rio, Antonio: *Historia del Reinado de Carlos III en España*, vol. I, pp. 196–197. Madrid. 1856.

life Don Carlos was an excellent judge of character, a quality in which members of royal families as a rule are singularly deficient.

His family circle cannot have been disagreeable. Philip could hardly be described as a wit, but from time to time he gave evidence of a sense of humour which he may well have inherited from his ancestor, Henry of Navarre. On one occasion when relations with France were particularly strained, the government issued an order giving French subjects a choice between naturalization and expulsion from the country. Shortly afterwards, the Queen went into her husband's apartments to find his boxes and portmanteaux open and his wardrobes empty. In astonishment she asked what all this meant. 'Why,' replied the King, 'have not all Frenchmen been ordered to leave Spain? Well, then, I am French, and so I am getting ready to be off.' The order was, needless to say, immediately rescinded. Philip also had the merit of being readily accessible. The Duke of Liria, for example, considered that he should have been promoted brigadier, and in an audience told the King so to his face, adding, 'I cannot imagine why Your Majesty holds the views you do concerning me; they are not opinions worthy of a great King.' Liria goes on to say, 'The King listened to me attentively', and that evening he received the coveted promotion.[1]

The Queen, as we have already seen, was an uninhibited extrovert, and she made no secret of the fact. She accompanied her husband on his hunting and shooting expeditions, and the Court News informed the public that 'on Thursday last the Queen in gentleman's attire went hunting, and killed two stags and a boar; and shot from horseback at a rabbit running, leaving it stone dead, to the admiration of the King and bystanders on seeing Her Majesty's extraordinary agility and skill.' It was clearly a tolerant age, for no Queen of Spain in more recent times would have cared to affront public opinion by appearing in male attire. Don Carlos was his mother's favourite, and all the evidence goes to show that he returned her affection, but, as will be shown in due course, he refused to be guided by her when political matters were involved.

Of his elder half-brother, Luis, he can have known very little, for he was only eight when Luis died. From January to August 1724, Luis had actually been King of Spain during the short-lived abdication of his father, who, however, resumed the

[1] MS. Diary.

throne on the young monarch's death. Very different estimates of his character have come down to us, but it must be remembered that he was only seventeen, and he was doubtless somewhat wild in his boyhood; but Liria, who knew him well, and who could be a stern critic, described him as 'a prince endowed with every kind of virtue and good quality. . . . He was discreet, and applied himself to business which he easily grasped. . . . This adorable prince would have made a model monarch.'[1] Of his popularity with his subjects there can be no doubt whatever.

Of his sister-in-law, the wife of Luis, Don Carlos must have heard much, and it was not likely to raise her sex in his estimation. She was the daughter of the Regent Duc d'Orléans, and she had inherited much of his ability, but his household was a bad school for a young girl, and her behaviour, if not her morals, left everything to be desired. An Englishman who met her at dinner at Vincennes left a most unflattering description of her when he wrote, 'She was fat, not seventeen, gluttonous, ate with both hands; the two men attendants carried her off swinging in their arms, like a fat spirit in *Henry VIII*; her feet did not touch the ground till she landed in the third room, and then she fell a-boxing them: she never reads or works, seldom plays cards, and cuts her hair like an English schoolboy.'[2] Perhaps the last word on this singularly unattractive young lady was the remark of her grandmother, 'She is the most disagreeable person that I have ever seen.' As Dowager Queen, after the death of her husband, her behaviour was no better, and her continued presence in Spain caused such a scandal that, contrary to what had been the usual practice, she was sent back to her own country with a pension, of which she was before long deprived owing to her way of life.

On the death of Luis, and the resumption of the crown by his father, Ferdinand, who was three years older than Don Carlos, became Prince of Asturias, but the relations between the two half-brothers can more conveniently be considered at a later stage in their lives when one was ruling in Madrid and the other in Naples.

The Spain in which Don Carlos was brought up was a country in a state of transition, for the substitution of the Bourbons for

[1] MS. Diary.
[2] *H.M.C.C.*, vol. VI, Report 7, App. 248c.

the Habsburgs soon proved to be a good deal more than a mere change of dynasty. Inspired by the court, there was a determined attempt to imitate the classical example of France, but the only result was that the period of the earlier Bourbons is one of the most barren in Spanish historical and artistic annals. The Spaniard does not take kindly to foreign models, whether in literature or politics, and the eras when his leaders thrust them upon him are invariably jejune. He will, like the Irish, consent to be guided by a foreigner, of whom he at once proceeds to make a good Spaniard, like the Emperor Charles V or El Greco, but he revenges himself upon a foreign system by rendering it a farce, as was later to be the fate of the Constitution of 1876.

One unfortunate result of the French influences which proceeded from the court was that among cultured people there came about a revulsion against the authors of the sixteenth and seventeenth centuries, especially in the theatre, though the works of Lope de Vega, Calderón, and other dramatists were still played, and greatly enjoyed by the mass of the population. This break, for it was nothing less, with the old tradition, combined with the new formalism imported from the other side of the Pyrenees, was the reason why none of the writers of the eighteenth century endeavoured to follow up the glories of their predecessors, so the picaresque novel, religious drama, and the plays of cloak and sword ceased to be cultivated at all. Painting also fell into great decay, for French and Italian influences, in the decadent style, became paramount, and remained so until the end of the century, when the glories of Spanish art were revived by Goya. In one respect the advent of the Bourbons certainly caused a revolution, and that was in matters of dress, though whether the changes were for better or worse must be a matter of opinion now as it was to contemporaries. The fashion was radically changed by the introduction of short knee-breeches, coats, coloured waistcoats, shirts with collars, frilled fronts and embroidered or laced cuffs, cloaks etc. for the men; and for the women, short, very full skirts, close-fitting shoes, bodices with a great tucker, all very brilliant in colouring, and made of silk where the wealthier classes were concerned. Curled and powdered wigs also became the order of the day, plaited for men, and three-cornered hats or complicated horn combs for the women.

Don Carlos was not, however, destined to remain in the land

of his birth much longer, for in January 1731 Antonio, the last
Farnese Duke of Parma, died, and the question at once arose how
far the seemingly endless treaties, pacts, and agreements of the
last few years were to prove binding. Antonio's widow fancied
herself pregnant, but nobody shared her illusion, and Imperial
troops at once occupied Parma and Piacenza. For a space it looked
like war, as Philip and Elizabeth were determined to seat Don
Carlos on the vacant ducal throne, and in that case the ensuing
hostilities would assuredly have assumed European dimensions.
This by no means suited Great Britain, then governed by Walpole,
whose policy it was to let sleeping dogs lie, for he was under no
illusions but that if his country became involved in a major war
there was every chance of a Jacobite rising, as, indeed, was to
happen in 1745: accordingly he took the lead in arranging a
compromise.

Fortunately for the peace of Western Europe, the Emperor
Charles VI was generally willing to retire from strong positions
for the sake of phantoms, and he proved to be so in the present
instance. His great desire at the moment was to persuade the
Powers to guarantee the Pragmatic Sanction, by which the succes-
sion to his dominions was to be secured to his daughter, Maria
Theresa, and Walpole determined to take full advantage of this
paternal solicitude. In return for a British guarantee of the
Pragmatic Sanction the Emperor agreed *inter alia* to allow 6,000
Spanish troops into the duchies of Parma and Piacenza, though
Walpole insisted by the insertion of an important secret clause
upon a promise that Maria Theresa should not marry a Bourbon.
In effect, the persistence of the Queen of Spain had been amply
rewarded: the arrangements made at Utrecht had been modified
through her pertinacity, the Austrian hold on Italy weakened,
and a Spanish dynasty introduced into Parma. Moreover, her
success had been secured in the face of overwhelming difficulties
both at home and abroad. When she arrived in Spain the country
was weakened by civil war, was a satellite of France, and was of
little account in Europe, whereas by 1731 she was once again a
powerful nation, whose policy was independent and whose
alliance was valuable.

These matters having all been settled, Don Carlos, now aged
fifteen, prepared to leave his native land which he was not to see
again for nearly thirty years. On 20th October 1731 he took

leave of his parents at Seville, knelt before them, and asked for their blessing. Philip thereupon made the sign of the cross upon his son's head, and presented him with a jewelled sword which he had himself received from Louis XIV, while the Queen gave him an enormous diamond ring. The young prince then commenced his journey to Italy with a suite of some two hundred and fifty people, as befitted his new importance. He travelled by land as far as Antibes, stopping on the way at Valencia and Barcelona, and while he was on French soil he was treated as a son of France by order of Louis XV. At Antibes an Anglo-Spanish squadron and three Tuscan galleys awaited him, and four days later, after a stormy Christmas at sea, he landed at Leghorn on December 27th, to be greeted by the comforting news that the Austrians had peacefully evacuated Parma and Piacenza.

On this news a sigh of relief must have gone up from the chancelleries of Europe at the pacific settlement of a problem which at one time had seemed only too likely to lead to war, for the settlement of 1731 appeared to assure them some years of tranquillity. The dreaded union of France and Spain did not appear likely to take place, for there was now a Dauphin, and in any event the two countries were not on good terms. The settlement of the question of the Italian duchies had been effected without the co-operation of France, whose influence was momentarily lessened, while the growth of the House of Bourbon, which had recently been a cause of alarm at Vienna no less than in London and The Hague, seemed to have received a decided check. On the other hand the friendship between Britain and Spain, and between Spain and the Emperor, appeared likely to continue. Colonial disputes had been peacefully adjusted, and affairs in the Italian Peninsula offered no opening for hostile manifestations. Unhappily all this was soon to prove but the calm that preceded a storm.

II

DUKE OF PARMA

WHATEVER the future might hold, the present promised well for Don Carlos, for he found himself not only Duke of Parma and Piacenza but also heir to the Grand Duchy of Tuscany. The Medici were following the Farnesi into extinction, for the reigning Grand Duke, Gian Gastone – a man of ability, but a homosexual with an evil reputation[1] – was childless, and the Powers, without the formality of consulting him, had decided that his heir was to be Don Carlos. Faced with this situation there was nothing to be done but to accept it with the best grace possible, so he tolerated Spanish garrisons in the Stato dei Presidi,[2] and agreed to share the guardianship of the young prince with his grandmother, the Dowager Duchess of Parma. So when Don Carlos landed at Leghorn he was greeted by the ministers of the Grand Duke as heir presumptive, for even on so important an occasion Gian Gastone could not be persuaded to leave the Pitti Palace, while San Esteban proclaimed to all that he had come in the rôle of a son to the last of the Medici.

The new Duke of Parma, as he was to be called until he ascended the throne of the Two Sicilies, created an excellent impression from the beginning, but he had not long arrived in Italy before he developed smallpox, and this fell disease had during the past generation exacted such a heavy toll in the Bourbon family, including the late King of Spain, Luis I, that

[1] cf. Acton, Harold: *The Last Medici, passim.* London. 1932.
[2] This comprised the towns of Orbetello, Talamone, Monte Argentaro, Porto Ercole, and Porto Santo Stefano, with Porto Longone on the Island of Elba, which Philip II had in 1557 obliged Cosimo I of Tuscany to leave in Spanish hands as pledges for his loyalty, and they provided Spain with a ready means of access to the Italian peninsula should Genoa ever be closed to her. They thus possessed considerable strategic, but no other, importance.

there was naturally general alarm. He was still only a boy, and everything possible was done to amuse him, for according to Sir Horace Mann, 'his pages used to fix little hooks to fine threads or wires that hung down unobserved in different parts of the room, which were all fastened to a sort of bell-rope within his bed; which hooks, when properly baited by the sly pages, with the wigs of his courtiers, he with a sudden jerk drew them up to the top of the room'.[1] The Duke himself from his early years was no great lover of formality, and he generally wore his own hair, which at this period of his life was black, only putting on a white wig on the most important occasions.

Owing to this illness, from which he soon recovered, he did not make his formal entry into Florence until 9th March 1732, and a very magnificent affair it was with guns firing, a *Te Deum* in the Duomo sung by eight choirs of three hundred musicians, fireworks exploding from the tower of the Palazzo Vecchio, and crowds rejoicing in the streets. The new heir presumptive to Tuscany was received in the Pitti Palace by the Grand Duke and his sister, but in separate rooms, on such bad terms were they with each other. As usual Gian Gastone was in bed, and Charles had an early exercise in restraint when he was confronted by a valetudinarian resembling a bloated turkey-cock under a ponderous wig. All the same the Grand Duke rose to the occasion, and after signing his last will and testament, in which he declared the Duke of Parma his successor, he remarked that he had just got a son and heir by a stroke of the pen, which was more than he had been able to do by more normal methods during thirty-four years of married life. He also took kindly to the younger man, and treated him with fatherly kindness.

The festivities in Florence lasted for some time, but in the summer they were carried on to the accompaniment of sterner business, which also served to give Charles a personal insight into the intricacies of Italian politics. On St. John the Baptist's Day, 24th June, Gian Gastone allowed him to receive the homage of the Tuscan Senate and provinces, which was a very colourful scene, for Charles, who was now styled Grand Prince of Tuscany, sat on a raised platform in front of the Palazzo Vecchio, and before him were elevated and dipped banners carried by men on

[1] cf. Acton, Harold: *The Bourbons of Naples*, vol. I, p. 14. London. 1956.

horseback.[1] The ceremony was welcomed by the Florentines, who had few opportunities for rejoicing under their present Grand Duke or his father, a gloomy bigot, but a very different view was taken in Vienna. The Emperor had old feudal claims on Tuscany, and he protested strongly that Charles should have waited for the Imperial investiture, as well as for a special dispensation in view of the fact that he was still a minor. The Emperor's protest was referred to Madrid, but Philip told his son and Gian Gastone to take no notice of it – in any event the Spanish troops were already installed at all strategic points.

The Duke spent the summer in Tuscany becoming acquainted with those who had been allotted to him as his future subjects, and making the most favourable impression upon them. In October he moved on to his duchy, and he received as warm a welcome in Parma and Piacenza as he had done in Florence. The Emperor, needless to say, was as annoyed at the Parmesan demonstrations as he had been by the Tuscan, and he was particularly angry when he heard that the slogan *Parma Resurget* was blazoned across the front of the ducal palace, but there was nothing he could do about it. Both now and until his father's death fourteen years later Charles was politically under the influence of his parents, and when they told him to take no notice of the growlings in Vienna he followed their advice.

For the rest, time passed pleasantly enough for the young Duke, who was able to combine his love of sport with an apprenticeship to statecraft. His letters to his father and mother reflect his contentment with his circumstances, and he told them that Colorno, the summer residence of the Farnesi, was far superior to their new palace at San Ildefonso, while the fertile plains of Parma appealed to his taste more than the hills of Tuscany, thereby, Mr. Harold Acton maintains, showing himself a true child of the eighteenth century.[2] He also met Alberoni once again, though it is more than doubtful if he remembered him. The old statesman was now living in retirement in Piacenza, and he obviously welcomed the opportunity of giving the young prince what he considered to be good counsel. These halcyon days were not, however, destined

[1] This gathering was an annual event, and was the last survival of the old democratic Florence, when the peasants seized the Sala Regia of the Palazzo Vecchio and were allowed to dance there, being lavishly regaled with sweets.
[2] *The Bourbons of Naples*, vol. I, p. 16. London. 1956.

to last for long, for in February 1733 there died Augustus II of Poland, who was also Elector of Saxony, and this raised another of those succession problems of which the eighteenth century was so prolific.

The natural successor to the vacant throne was Stanislaus Leszczynski, who was duly elected by the Seym. He and his supporters looked to France for help, and that on several grounds. In the first place his daughter Marie had married Louis XV, and in the second it was the traditional policy of France to maintain the independence of Poland, as of Sweden and Turkey, as a check upon the House of Habsburg. The French government was accordingly not slow to champion a cause so peculiarly its own. Four million livres were sent to Warsaw to be distributed among those Polish magnates whose support of Stanislaus might otherwise prove somewhat lukewarm, while in a circular letter, addressed to all its representatives abroad, it declared that, as the Emperor, by massing troops on the Silesian frontier, had sufficiently revealed his intention of destroying the liberties of Poland by interfering with the free election of her King, His Most Christian Majesty could not regard with indifference the political extinction of a Power to whom he was bound by all the ties of honour and friendship, but would do his utmost to protect her against her enemies.

These were brave words, but they took no account of the new factor which had arisen in eastern Europe, namely Russia. Pressure could always be applied to the western possessions of the Emperor to compel him to moderate his ambitions elsewhere, but the remote position of the Tsar and his dominions rendered him unsusceptible to such methods. Russia and Austria had no desire to see a revival of French influence in Warsaw, and they therefore brought forward as their candidate the son of the dead King, also named Augustus. A Russian army entered Poland to give effect to this policy, and before long Stanislaus was besieged in Danzig, while the rest of the country was in the hands of his rival and of the Russians. A French expeditionary force arrived too late to change the course of events, and in January 1736 Stanislaus finally renounced his rights. France was unwilling to waste any more men or money on her ally, more particularly as she was finding ample compensation for her reverses on the Vistula in the triumphs of herself and the Spaniards in Lombardy and on the Rhine. 'Must we', asked Cardinal Fleury, 'ruin the King to aid his father-in-law?' There could be no doubt about the answer, but the traditional French influence in Poland had received its death-blow.

The repercussions of the War of the Polish Succession in Italy were not long in making themselves felt, for if France could do little to hamper the operations of Russia, she could attack Russia's ally, the Emperor. War was declared in October 1733, and an offensive and defensive alliance made with the King of Sardinia. As we have seen, by this time the ties of friendship between Madrid and Vienna had been broken, and in an outbreak of war in Italy the Queen of Spain saw the opportunity of further advancement for her children. Accordingly, on November 7th the two Bourbon Powers signed the Treaty of the Escorial. Louis and Philip pledged themselves and their posterity to eternal friendship. They guaranteed each other's possessions both in Europe and overseas, and Charles was confirmed in his duchy as well as being promised the reversion of Tuscany on the death of Gian Gastone; in addition he was to have Naples and Sicily. France further pledged her aid to Spain if the latter were attacked by Great Britain. Finally, 'all earlier treaties made between France and Spain, and between Their Majesties and other Powers, shall no longer have effect between France and Spain'. Such was the first of the three Family Compacts between Paris and Madrid which were to play so great a part in the history of the eighteenth century.

There was, however, one little fly in this Franco-Spanish ointment, and that was the Treaty of Turin which France had previously concluded with Charles Emmanuel III of Sardinia, by which the latter was promised Milan. Spain refused to ratify the treaty when the Family Pact was concluded, for Charles Emmanuel and Elizabeth Farnese profoundly mistrusted one another, and with very good reason.

British neutrality having been secured by a promise of abstention from any attack on the Austrian Netherlands, it was clear that the main French effort would be made on the Rhine and in Italy. For the former command the Marshal Duke of Berwick was selected, and for the latter Marshal Villars, in spite of the fact that he was eighty-two. In December 1733 the Spanish government followed the example of its French ally, and declared war on the

Emperor. The plan of campaign was for Villars in collaboration with Charles Emmanuel to conquer Lombardy, which was duly accomplished, while the Conde de Montemar, who had landed at Leghorn at the head of thirty thousand Spaniards, was to guard the line of the Po against a possible Austrian descent from the eastern Alps. All went well at first, but Charles Emmanuel refused to co-operate with Montemar unless Philip first of all signed the Treaty of Turin, so the Spanish general received orders from Madrid to take no further notice of him, and to make preparations for the conquest of Naples.

These events brought the young Duke of Parma into the centre of the stage. On 20th January 1734 he became eighteen, so he declared himself to be of age, 'free to rule and administer our States independently', though in actual fact he was still very much under the control of his parents. At the same time he was made titular commander-in-chief of the Spanish army in Italy, and he received an enthusiastic letter from his mother bidding him conquer the Two Sicilies, 'which elevated into a free kingdom, will be yours. Go forth and win: the most beautiful crown in Italy awaits you.' Charles needed no prompting. Montemar joined him in Parma to discuss the details of the coming campaign, and when these had been settled he left the duchy under the regency of his grandmother, not, however, before he had taken with him many of the Farnese family treasures. He then spent a fortnight in Florence, where he took a sad farewell of the Grand Duke, who was under no illusions but that this latest turn of events meant that the future of Tuscany was once more in the melting-pot. On 5th March Charles was at Perugia, where the army he was to lead into Naples was waiting for him.

The fact that Perugia was on Papal territory and that Clement XII raised no objection to its use by the Spanish troops as their base was eloquent testimony to the general belief that they would meet with little opposition when they moved south. Spanish rule in Italy had never been so unpopular as is often stated by Anglo-Saxon historians. In the sixteenth century at any rate the ordinary Italian knew quite well that the alternative was to become an Ottoman vilayet. Independence was either a memory of the past or a dream of the future – it was certainly not practical politics – and the French were much more disliked than the Spaniards; nor was what the Italians had seen of the Austrians since the Treaty of Utrecht likely to endear them to the inhabitants of the provinces allotted to them at that settlement. Above all it was obvious that the Emperor would not be able to make any effective resistance to the forces which Charles could muster against him, and in these circumstances people, not least Italians, like to be on the winning side. The defence of the Imperial interests was entrusted to three pro-Habsburg Italians. The Viceroy was the Conte Giulio Visconti, who early lost his head and his nerve, and burst into tears in front of his officers. The army was under the command of Marshal Giovanni Caraffa, but it was barely seven thousand strong: while Admiral Pallavicini had only three frigates and four galleys to defend Naples against the extremely well-found Spanish fleet.

Such being the case it is in no way surprising that Charles's progress was as rapid as that of his French namesake at the end of the fifteenth century. Montemar took full advantage of the weakness and confusion of his opponents, and he gave them no time to recover from their unpreparedness: indeed he moved at a pace which would have done credit to Napoleon himself. There was no sort of resistance on the part of the civil population or of the Austrian forces in the field. A few isolated forts here and there did hold out for a few days – Pescara, Gaeta, and Capua were the only places to give the Spaniards much trouble – but in general the hostilities were marked by the utmost courtesy on both sides, and we are told that the Castel dell'Oro was bombarded 'with the utmost humanity'. Charles followed the armies south, but in a more leisurely fashion, and during his journey he was even able to get some fishing in the Garigliano.

One weapon, however, was used, though still in its infancy, and that was propaganda. The *austriacanti* declared that the Spaniards, mindful of the loss of the Two Sicilies at the Treaty of Utrecht, would descend upon southern Italy animated by a spirit of revenge, and the Emperor himself issued a proclamation in which he expressed his 'certainty of final victory over an enemy that broke laws human and divine in attempting to usurp the kingdom which Divine Providence had entrusted to his care', and he went on to tell his subjects that they might 'rest assured that I shall ever be mindful of the troubles and sacrifices which the hostile invasion may cause you'. On their side the Bourbons were no less active, for on 14th March 1734 a proclamation was issued at Monterotondo 'in the name of Don Carlos, by the grace of God Infante of Spain, Duke of Parma, Piacenza, and Castro etc., Hereditary Grand Prince of Tuscany and Generalissimo of the armies of His Catholic Majesty in Italy'. This contained a dispatch from Philip explaining his desire to recover his two lost kingdoms and save them from the excessive violence, oppression, and tyranny of their Austrian masters. His sole aim was to restore Naples to happiness and prosperity, and he was ready to let bygones be bygones. With this end in view he had authorized the Duke of Parma to grant dispensations and free pardons both general and particular, to confer privileges, and to abolish every tax invented by the insatiable greed of the Imperial government. Nor was this all, for the Spanish troops were ordered to go out of their way to be conciliatory where the Italian population was concerned, and so to erase the memory of the reputation for arrogance which their predecessors in the sixteenth and seventeenth centuries had rightly or wrongly earned. Charles himself set the example in affability and courtesy.

On 10th May he made his state entry into Naples, where he met with the same rapturous welcome as that with which he had been greeted in Florence, and the blood of San Gennaro testified the saint's approval by obligingly liquefying out of season. Charles proceeded by way of the Porta Capuana through the Via Tribunali to the cathedral, where he dismounted, and was duly blessed by the Cardinal Archbishop; he then went on to the royal palace where he dined in public. The illuminations and festivities continued for three days, and the excitement became the more intense as a result of the rumours that were going round in respect of what the future might have in store: the Venetian resident even reported to the Serenissima that many people believed that Charles would proclaim himself King of Italy. These doubts were put at rest on 15th May, when it was announced that Philip had renounced all his rights in the Two Sicilies to his son, so once more Naples had become the capital of an independent state. Ten days later the Austrian field army was decisively defeated by the Spaniards at Bitonto.

There were, however, a few places that continued to resist both on the mainland and in Sicily. Pescara held out for a mere thirty-eight days, but Capua did not surrender until 24th November, while the citadels of Messina, Trapani, and Syracuse each sustained a siege of nearly six months. It cannot be said that the Spaniards pressed their advantage, and they behaved with a courtesy which was surely excessive. At Capua, for instance, Marshal Traun sent word to the Spanish commander that he even lacked oil for the Blessed Sacrament, whereupon he received two pack-saddles of oil, fifty pounds of wax candles, fifty pounds of chocolate, another fifty of coffee, and a hundred lemons, besides other provisions.

The siege of Gaeta was attended by Charles in person, and there he may well have met his first Englishman in the person of his namesake, Prince Charles Edward Stuart, the 'Bonnie Prince Charlie' of later years, who was now fourteen. His father had placed him under the guardianship of the former Duke of Liria, now the second Duke of Berwick, and he made the most favourable impression upon all with whom he came in contact. In a letter[1] Berwick wrote of his 'pleasure of seeing the Prince adored by officers and soldiers. . . . His manner and conversation are really bewitching. . . . The King of Naples is much taken with his polite behaviour, and there is not the least necessity of suggesting to him what is proper for him to do or say.' Certainly the two young men took a liking to one another, and when they were on board the galley from Gaeta to Naples after the siege the Stuart prince's hat fell into the sea, and when the sailors were about to rescue it Charles called out, 'Never mind, it floats towards England, and the owner will soon go to fetch it; and that I may have something to fetch, too, mine shall accompany it': whereupon he threw his own hat into the sea, and there were general shouts of 'To England'. When this incident was repeated to George II he was not at all amused, especially as Charles Edward was everywhere treated as if he were the son of a reigning monarch. It was the first, but by no means the last, time that the new King of the Two Sicilies was to come into conflict with the British government.

During the rest of that summer and autumn Charles made a leisurely tour of his dominions. He did this on horseback and in an informal manner. His habit was to dine in public in the places he visited, afterwards taking his gun and shooting a few birds. His courtesy charmed his subjects whenever he came into contact with them, and his consideration for others became proverbial.

[1] Quoted by Ewald, A. C.: *The Life and Times of Prince Charles Stuart*, pp. 28–29. London. 1883.

On one occasion, for example, he took shelter from a downpour of rain in a poor hut, where he found a young woman who had recently given birth to a boy. He told her that he wished the infant to be called after him and to become his godson, at the same time giving her a hundred gold doubloons: furthermore, the boy was to receive twenty-five ducats a month until the age of seven, when he was to go to the royal palace for employment. In Sicily the King behaved in the same easy way, though he was duly crowned in Palermo cathedral with much pomp and circumstance.

Meanwhile the same outstanding successes had not attended the Bourbon armies in the north, where it was in any case easier for the Emperor to reinforce his troops. One of the chief handicaps experienced by the Franco-Spanish High Command was the attitude of Charles Emmanuel, who would neither fight a decisive battle himself nor lend his artillery for a siege. In consequence he was suspected both in Versailles and Madrid of being ready, for a sufficient bribe, to change sides, and aid the Emperor to evict the Bourbons from Italy. Nor were the relations between the French and Spanish troops in the field any too happy. Of the allied armies the Spaniards unquestionably displayed the best military qualities, and they were most effectively supported by their government. The French fought well, but their discipline was not what it had been in the days of Louis XIV, and, as always, it deteriorated when they were in Italy. In any event the war itself was unpopular in France, where it was believed to be the result of a low marriage, for the match between Louis XV and Marie Leszczynska was regarded in this light.

Cardinal Fleury had never been an enthusiastic supporter of the war, and he neglected no opportunity of bringing it to an end, but it was not until the summer of 1739, in consequence of yet another Treaty of Vienna, that all the Powers concerned were again at peace. Substantial modifications were made in the Utrecht settlement (with the approval of Great Britain and the United Provinces) in so far as this affected Italy. Charles obtained the Two Sicilies and the Stato dei Presidi, but he had to surrender Parma to the Emperor in exchange, while Charles Emmanuel received the benefit of some frontier rectifications. Not less important were the clauses relating to Lorraine and Tuscany. The French government, assuming that Francis of Lorraine would marry Maria Theresa, and ultimately be elected Emperor, declared that an Emperor holding Lorraine and Bar would be a standing menace to the security of France. It was agreed, therefore, that Stanislaus should renounce his claim to Poland, and should be indemnified with Lorraine and Bar, which were to revert to France on his death: the Duke of Lorraine, in his turn, was to succeed Gian Gastone in the Grand Duchy of Tuscany. The preliminaries of this treaty were signed as early as October 1735, but nearly four years elapsed before it was finally ratified.

So ended the War of the Polish Succession, and after two decades of shifting alliances the alignment of the principal Powers was roughly what it had been in the later years of Louis XIV. France and Spain were allied against the Emperor, and the House of Savoy was throwing its weight first into one scale and then into the other: all that was required was for Britain to range herself on the side of the Habsburgs, and it was not long before this development, too, took place.

III

THE TWO SICILIES

A SPANISH sovereign was no novelty in the Kingdom of the
Two Sicilies. Naples had been in the possession of an illegitimate
branch of the Aragonese Royal House for several generations
until its absorption in the Spanish monarchy in the early years of
the sixteenth century, while Sicily had belonged to Aragón itself.
This state of affairs had been temporarily interrupted by the Treaty
of Utrecht, which had handed Naples over to the Emperor, while
Sicily was given to the Duke of Savoy: in 1720, as we have seen,
Sicily passed into the hands of Vienna. These periods of Austrian
and Savoyard rule were, however, too brief to have made any
lasting impression upon either the Neapolitans or the Sicilians,
and their condition when Charles became their ruler was to all
intents and purposes what it had been when they were administered from Madrid.

In Naples the Viceroy, at least in theory, had been supposed to
consult the Collateral Council, while the old Neapolitan Parliament with its three estates, was still summoned to vote supplies.
In the city of Naples the municipal administration was conducted
by district councils called *piazze*, five for the nobles and one for
the people, each of which chose an *eletto* to transact business with
the Viceroy: actually, the country was so divided against itself
that this machinery never functioned properly. The memories of
the old feuds between Ghibelline and Guelf, and between Aragón
and Anjou, prevented any common action on the part of the
aristocracy, while the people were too fickle to remain united long
enough to achieve any one object. At the same time it must be
admitted that a good deal of money was spent by the Viceroys
upon public works, and the military element was not supreme in
Naples as it was in Milan. The real trouble was financial, chiefly
due to the fall in the value of money, which necessitated the

trebling of taxation between 1558 and 1620, while the cumbrous and wasteful Spanish fiscal system was a further disadvantage.

In some ways Sicily was in a happier position, in spite of the fact that it suffered from many of the disadvantages to which Naples was subject. It retained its medieval constitution, and consequent independence in political life, which enabled it to resist the bureaucratic tendencies of Spanish rule. Moreover, the memory of the Sicilian Vespers was sufficiently fresh to make any foreign ruler cautious, so Parliament continued to make laws and vote taxes, and the nobles to retain their feudal authority. The towns were specially active and independent, and the export of corn made them wealthy. The rivalry between them, particularly between Palermo and Messina, was bitter, and for their own ends it was short-sightedly encouraged by the Spaniards, who eventually allowed it to go so far that it ultimately led to the most dangerous Italian revolt which they had to face in the seventeenth century.

The enthusiasm with which Neapolitans and Sicilians alike greeted Charles cannot disguise the fact that they had by no means always been patterns of loyalty to Spain in the past. It was in Naples that Madrid encountered the most opposition, and it was there that took place one of the most famous insurrections in history, namely that led by Masaniello. This revolt had, however, been preceded by several earlier disturbances, for Philip III was hardly seated on his father's throne when, in 1600, the peasants of Calabria rose at the bidding of a mystic called Campanella, but the movement was suppressed. In 1631 there were riots in Naples itself owing to the rise in the cost of living, but these, too, were put down. By 1646 the expense of Spanish participation in the Thirty Years' War made it necessary to impose fresh taxation upon Naples, and the Viceroy put a gabelle upon fruit, the staple article of Neapolitan diet.

This provoked an explosion, and Masaniello, a fishmonger, became the symbol, rather than the leader, of the agitation which followed. The Viceroy had but few troops at his disposal, and being himself of a timid nature he conceded all the demands of the insurgents. The consequence of this was mob law both in town and country, and in the ensuing anarchy Masaniello, whose arrogance had become insufferable, was murdered. At this point

Don John of Austria, the illegitimate son of Philip IV, arrived with a fleet, but the bombardment of Naples, far from inducing the insurgents to surrender, drove them to abandon the last pretence of loyalty to the Spanish throne, and to proclaim a republic. With the French winning victories in the Low Countries, and Portugal and Catalonia in revolt, Spain was in no position to coerce Naples, and she must have lost that kingdom had the Neapolitans not been so fickle, or had they received adequate support from Paris. Henri, Duc de Guise, did, indeed, come to Naples, where he passed as the heir of the Angevins, and at first he met with an enthusiastic reception; but he could get no serious assistance from Mazarin, who rightly distrusted him, and he was not long in quarrelling with the Neapolitans, who wanted him to be a kind of Stadtholder on the Dutch pattern, while he was determined to be a real king.

In these circumstances all who had anything to lose saw that the only hope of restoring order lay in the re-establishment of Spanish rule, and the revolt soon afterwards collapsed. The Spaniards returned without conditions, and when a new Viceroy reduced the gabelles the Neapolitans allowed him to hang the leading rebels without protest. The Duc de Guise did make another attempt in 1654, but received no support. For the remainder of the reign of Philip IV, save for a severe outbreak of plague in 1656, and during the whole of that of his son, the history of Naples was uneventful: indeed, there was a definite revival of prosperity owing to the energy of the Viceroys of this period in reforming taxation and suppressing brigandage. It was doubtless the memory of those days, contrasted with the severity of the Austrian rule which followed, that did much to account for the enthusiasm with which Charles was received in 1734.

In Sicily the most serious rising against Spanish rule took place in 1674, and it was to no small extent due to the rivalry between Palermo and Messina, for the latter had been allowed a monopoly of silk, and when this was cancelled there were riots. The Viceroy thereupon declared that this amounted to a revolt, which he was determined to crush, but the people of Messina retaliated by fortifying their town and invoking the aid of France. In 1675 Louis XIV sent troops to Sicily, but although they could easily have conquered the whole island, in actual fact they did very little, for Louis regarded the expedition merely as a method of distracting

Spanish attention from the other theatres of war, and as soon as the Messinesi awoke to this they refused to obey his generals. All the same the struggle dragged on until 1678, when the French evacuated Sicily. Madrid proved extremely moderate in its hour of victory, though all the privileges of Messina were taken away. So long as Charles II lived the Sicilians gave no further trouble to Spain, and when they were separated from the Spanish monarchy by the Utrecht settlement they were extremely dissatisfied.

In Naples, as has already been mentioned, there had been little change during the short period of Austrian rule, and what change there was had been for the worse. Charles VI had displayed a touching, if misplaced, partiality for the Spaniards who had supported him in his struggle with Philip V, and who were now in exile in the Austrian capital; there was a tendency to govern Naples through them by a system of remote control. This resulted in a diminution of the power of the Viceroy, and the encouragement of direct appeal to Vienna. At the same time the local authorities, including the Collateral Council, recovered some of their decayed powers, with the result that there was a recrudescence of disorder, corruption and injustice, which suited the aristocracy very well, and it was from this class that the *austriacanti* were almost exclusively drawn. The Imperial government, to give it its due, did make some attempts at reform. It wished to recover the alienated taxes, to codify the laws, and to reorganize the Communes, but it was too far away to be effective, and its good intentions were thwarted by the opposition of local vested interests.

At the other end of the social scale the condition of the mass of the Neapolitan population beggars description, though it was only relatively worse than that of the lower orders in London, Madrid, and Paris. In size and appearance the city had for long remained the Naples of that great Spanish Viceroy, Don Pedro de Toledo, at the beginning of the seventeenth century, though by this time the whole space enclosed by his walls was built over, and two little forts, the Torretta, had been erected as a protection against the Barbary corsairs. It became the fashion to extol not only the beauty of the Bay, but also that of the city itself. Fynes Moryson as early as 1594 had been enraptured with the gardens both in Naples and outside, which in his vivid imagination rivalled those of the Hesperides. The new street, the Toledo, was deservedly admired, and Evelyn was loud in its praise. 'The building of the city', he wrote, 'is for its size the most magnificent in Europe, the streets exceeding large, well-paved, having many vaults and conveyances under them for the sulliage, which renders them very sweet and clean, even in the midst of winter', while he also found the inhabitants 'merry, witty, and genial, also very musical', all of which he attributed to the excellent quality of the air.

It says a great deal for the Neapolitan that he should have been 'merry, witty, and genial' considering the housing conditions in the poorer quarters down towards the port, which were not materially improved until the cholera outbreak in the eighties of the last century. The narrow alleys, in some of which, like the Orefice, it was barely possible for two persons to walk abreast, the tall, gaunt houses that must have reminded many a Catalan of his own cities, damp and dirty, yet crowded from cellar to roof, were doubtless built with the laudable object of keeping out the sun, but which certainly bred disease. The filth lay stinking and rotting in heaps, where dogs, cats, and children innocent of clothing and with the morals of animals – it was said that a virgin over twelve was a definite rarity – scavenged eagerly. The women were glad to possess a single garment to cover their nudity, while on parts of the quays the beggars lay naked all day long.

The *lazzaroni* would beg with a persistence worthy of the Orient, and there was nothing they would not do for a few coins, even to the lethal use of a knife. In normal circumstances they were patient and good-tempered so long as their very simple needs were supplied, and they would forget all their miseries at the sight of a good carnival car, in the scramble for a few gold coins, or the capture of a packet of macaroni in a scuffle. Another diversion much in favour was the excitement of a hanging in the Piazza del Mercato or a breaking on the wheel in the Pennino. The plaintive notes of a Neapolitan song had the same effect, and there was a wistful melancholy that was continually making itself felt, even among the fisher girls dancing the tarantella on the flat roofs of the cottages away in the villages around the Bay by the light of the moon.

The Neapolitan quickly passed from one extreme to another: from a state of nervous excitement if the blood of San Gennaro was slow in melting to one of murderous fury at some fancied outrage on the part of a foreign soldier: equally he could be set roaring with laughter by the *lazzi* of Pulcinella in a booth on the Piazza del Castello. It has been well said that 'the mob of Naples was far the most alive, interesting and powerful, if also the most poverty-stricken, in Italy, while its mobility made it the most difficult to control'.[1] Exact figures are difficult to obtain, but it would appear reasonable to suppose that in the seventeenth century the population rose from roughly some two hundred thousand to about half a million. This was not due to what is known as a natural increase, but to immigration from the provinces where conditions were much harder, and also to the fact that the nobles spent much of their time and their money in the capital. Taxes, too, were lower in Naples, and crime was less easily detected, while there alone, certainly not in the country-side, were to be found brilliant displays, a superficial gaiety, and even a rudimentary organization for the relief of the poor. The Viceroy took no pleasure in this increase of population for it made the mob more difficult to control, and the Masaniello outbreak showed what could happen if it was really roused.

The nobles were another class of the Neapolitan community that hardly made for stability. The stronger Viceroys had managed to keep them in control, and during the Thirty Years' War they had supplied the Spanish cause both with men and money. During the troubles of Masaniello's rebellion they had as a whole remained loyal to Spain, but in the period of relative peace which marked the reign of Charles II they had no real outlet for their energies, so they became idle and a nuisance. They crowded into Naples as, indeed, they were encouraged to do by the government, which, like Louis XIV, much preferred a nobleman wasting his substance at court to plotting on his estate in the country. Many of them kept *bravi*, and carried matters with a very high hand. The Caraffa tyrannized over the upper city, plundering and murdering almost unchecked, while the Caracciolo, Minutolo, and Capecelatro behaved in the same way in S. Giovanni a Carbonara. One member of the Caraffa family, being out of humour, had three men killed and two badly wounded in three days. The Viceroys did their best to curb these excesses, and if the normal methods of bringing the culprits to justice failed

[1] Collison-Morley, L.: *Italy after the Renaissance*, p. 46. London. 1930.

detachments of troops were quartered on their estates. Such being the case it is not surprising that some of these turbulent aristocrats should, when the change of dynasty came, have preferred as their master an absent Habsburg in Vienna to a resident Bourbon in Naples. Unhappily no commercial middle class existed to counter-balance the excesses of the upper and lower classes.

In such a state of society it was only to be expected that there should be a great deal of duelling, and nowhere in Italy were there more duels than in Naples. The government did its best to dis-courage the custom by imposing a heavy fine and five years' im-prisonment for the first offence and death for the second, but these deterrents had little effect. Whole clans were involved in duels about the most absurd trifles, and on one occasion the refusal to return a stolen lap-dog to its owner resulted in a duel with six combatants on each side, one of whom was killed. By the time that Charles acquired the kingdom, however, it had become more customary for the principals only to fight, and this greatly reduced the death-rate.

Of what may perhaps be described as more normal crime there was plenty. Coining and clipping were specially frequent, and in 1662 four men were hanged and thirty-six sent to the galleys for coining new money before it was issued. Certainly this species of crime paid so long as it was undetected, and one coiner before he was hanged, drawn, and quartered admitted to having been mak-ing false money for eighteen years, during which time he had coined no less than 40,000 ducats: priests and monks, it may be added, were often convicted. Presumably as an added deterrent criminals were taken to the place of execution in a cart decorated with the implements of their trade, and wearing false coins pinned on their breasts, but owing to the chronic shortage of rowers as many as possible were sent to the galleys.

In seventeenth-century Naples resort was had to violence not in the last but in the first resort. In 1617 Don Lucio Coppola was shot by a Carmelite friar in the Church of S. Spirito in a quarrel about some prostitutes, one of whom had taken refuge there. The punishment in some cases seems to have been made to fit the crime, as when a man was first flogged and then sent to the galleys for putting dogs' flesh in sausages, for while he was being lashed a dog's head was put in his mouth and another in his hand. One Viceroy may be said to have pushed this policy to extremes, for when a couple of sellers of antidotes who had quarrelled about their wares appealed to him, each was given a glass of poison. One of them, thanks to his antidote, duly brought his poison up, while his rival died. The victor was thereupon rewarded with a gold chain, and granted a number of privileges.

The country roads were no safer than the streets of the capital, and, as else where, the highwaymen were no respecters of persons; the Duca di Tocco was robbed of his plate and his baggage on the way to his estate in the Abruzzi. Usually grandees of his type were exempt from such misfortunes either because they were well guarded or because they had a private understanding with the gentlemen of the road. Brigandage was by no means confined to the laity, and the Abate Cesare Ricciardi made his living out of robbing the Rome mail. Eventually, strong measures were taken by the Viceroy, and troops were employed to clean up the roads. Among the highwaymen captured and hanged was the Abate, whose rotting head was sent to Naples as a trophy. Many of his fellow-criminals were strung up on gibbets or trees by the road-side, to the annoyance of travellers, who found their mouldering remains definitely repulsive. Sacrilege was held in peculiar detestation, as is shown in the case of the barber of Aversa who stole the pyx, and scattered the wafers on the floor. He was, needless to say, hanged, but the spot where the wafers fell was railed off, and an inscription put up recording the crime.

All over Europe it was the golden age of the prostitute, and nowhere more so than in Naples. It is recorded that one Viceroy made a visit to the upper parts of the city with the idea of confining these ladies in a special quarter as was done elsewhere, but he soon realized that if he tried to shut up all the courtesans of Naples he would have to enclose half the town. All the same, they were not allowed to frequent the fashionable promenade to Posilipo, either in a carriage or a barge, because the wives of the aristocracy resented their presence. Their cheek was colossal, and two of them managed to gate-crash a reception at the Viceroy's palace: but this was going too far, for they were detected and flogged, while the porter who had admitted them was sent to the galleys.

In religious matters both Neapolitans and Sicilians were devout to the point of superstition. When Spain had sought to introduce the Inquisition into the kingdom, it had been frustrated on the grounds that it would be regarded by every Neapolitan as a personal insult, for Naples had been Christian before Rome. Nowhere in Italy were the pomp and ceremonial of the Catholicism of the Counter-Reformation understood or more popular than in Naples, though to what extent this was due to religious belief, and to what to the love of display, it might be indiscreet to enquire. The Viceroy always set an example in these matters, and if he chanced to meet the host being carried through the streets he would himself join in the procession and humbly follow it to its destination. Even actors and actresses had to watch their steps, and Benedette Croce, in his *Teatri di Napoli*, describes a regulation drawn up during the period of Spanish rule in which the actors undertook to confess three times a year —at Easter, Christmas, and the Assumption of the Virgin—and not to gamble among themselves. If a comrade heard one of his company blaspheme he was to denounce the offender at once. The feasts of the Church were celebrated with a splendour even more glorious than that which accompanied a vice-regal *fête*, and the Jesuits led the way. Religion apart, it was for the mass of the population a welcome distraction from the sordid circumstances in which they lived.

Above all it was the age of the baroque. Modern Naples has lost so much of its brilliant colouring in the endeavour to come to terms with the twentieth century that it is not easy today to realize how closely the baroque once reflected its life. Goethe bore witness to this when he noted with delight how everyone who possibly could decorated himself with flowers or ribbons, that chests, furniture, and even carts were in his time painted with brilliant colours, and that it all seemed natural under such a sky. A civilization of display and squalour, of brutality and ceremony, of gorgeous clothes and filthy rags, found its expression in the baroque, which was also the art of the Counter-Reformation, the art which in the hands of the Jesuits became not only the symbol of the revived Catholicism, but also an important means of promoting the triumph of the Church. Both in the Two Sicilies and in Spain the Church was in various ways to play no unimportant part in the life of Charles, and from his first arrival in Naples he began to learn a good deal about its working.

IV

THE MAKING OF A KING

CHARLES was now firmly established in his new kingdom, but
until the death of his father in 1746 he was very much an appren-
tice to kingship: indeed to many contemporaries the old days of
the Spanish Viceroys had returned, the only difference being that
the King of Spain's representative was not some great nobleman
but his own son. Orders were issued from Madrid, as often as not,
it was generally believed, by Elizabeth as by Philip, and they were
obeyed in Naples: nor is this in any way surprising, for Charles
was still only in his early twenties, and he found that the attrac-
tions of the council-chamber palled before those of the chase: he
did attend the deliberations of his counsellors, but at this stage
of his life his attendance was merely perfunctory, and of the future
benevolent despot the benevolence was more noticeable than the
despotism. The next step was to find him a wife.

Like most young men and women of the day he had little or no
say in this. The French were very desirous that he should marry
one of their princesses, but apart from the fact that the oldest
available was barely ten, Elizabeth Farnese was not unnaturally
prejudiced against a French mate in view of her experience with
the wife of Luis I, and her comment on the suggestion was that a
scalded cat fears cold water. When Charles was consulted he said
that he was entirely in his parents' hands, and the bride they
selected for him turned out to be Maria Amalia, daughter of
Augustus III, King of Poland and Elector of Saxony, the successful rival of Stanislaus Leszczynski in the recent War of the Polish
Succession. The marriage could not take place at once, for the
prospective Queen of the Two Sicilies was under thirteen, and a
dispensation had to be obtained. This did not arrive until
December 1737, and even then there was a further delay, as it was
not until the following May that the marriage took place in

Dresden by proxy, with the bride's brother, the Electoral Prince of Saxony, representing Charles. Maria Amalia then made the journey south, and on 19th June her husband met her at Portella, on the frontier between Naples and the Papal States. The young bride advanced with the intention of kneeling as was customary in those days, but Charles picked her up, took her into his coach, and drove off with her to Fondi.

In spite of the fact that neither party had really been consulted the marriage turned out most successful, as was more often the case than is commonly supposed. There was a considerable disparity of age, for Charles was twenty-one and Maria Amalia was just under fourteen, but he was in many ways young for his years just as she seems to have been old for hers. Of the King's devotion to her when she was alive, and to her memory after she was dead, there can be no question. He was irreproachable in his morals and conduct, and during a long widowerhood he never gave the slightest encouragement to licentiousness by his own example. If, however, he was severe to himself, he was, as is not infrequently the case, equally severe to others, for he showed no indulgence to the foibles of youth, and he rigidly exacted from his own children the same continence which he observed himself.

The new Queen was a typical Saxon, being tall, fair, and with blue eyes; she was also inclined to be hot-tempered on occasion. She had been well educated, for she knew French and Italian as well as Latin, and she shared her husband's devotion to open-air pursuits. Unfortunately, not long after her arrival in Naples she developed smallpox, and this left its marks upon her. Of contemporaries, Sir James Gray, the British envoy, was most uncomplimentary, for he considered the King and Queen to be the ugliest couple in the world, but as he was not posted to Naples until 1753 he did not see them in the first flush of their youth.[1]

Matrimony diverted Charles even more from affairs of state, and for the next few years he was very definitely under tutelage, which considering his youth and circumstances is not surprising. His chief adviser was at first his old tutor, the Conde de San

---

[1] He may also have been affected by the tendency of so many British diplomatists, both past and present, to decry everybody and everything in the countries to which they are accredited.

Estebán, who had accompanied him to Parma, where his name became italianized as Santo Stefano. He was omnipotent at court, and was the channel through which the Queen Mother's wishes were conveyed to her son and his Neapolitan ministers. Santo Stefano filled his office as chief councillor of state with considerable dignity. He was also extremely tactful, and fully realizing the strength of the *austriacanti* among the Neapolitan nobles, he went out of his way to conciliate them by appealing to their vanity. In pursuance of this policy he appointed one hundred and fifteen of them to be gentlemen-in-waiting to the King, and of these no less than fifty were given gold keys which ensured admittance to every part of the palace, while the remainder were not allowed to pass beyond the fourth antechamber. Unhappily his wife and daughter were not gifted with the same discretion, and they carried matters at court with so high a hand that a clash was inevitable as soon as Queen Amalia appeared in Naples.

The Secretary of State was another Spaniard who had come to Italy with Charles, namely the Marqués de Monte Alegre, who was a good deal of an intriguer, but possessed a certain amount of ability, and was shortly to succeed Santo Stefano as chief minister.

By far the most outstanding of the royal counsellors was the Minister of Justice, Bernardo Tanucci, a blunt and rugged man, who had none of the courtly graces of Santo Stefano or Monte Alegre. He had been born in 1698 at Stia in the upper valley of the Arno, and was educated at Pisa University, where he early became professor of law. He was, indeed, only thirty-two when the Spanish government applied to the Grand Duke of Tuscany for a jurist to confute the Emperor's claims of investiture to Siena, and he had been recommended. It was in this way that he became acquainted with Santo Stefano, who formed a high opinion of him, and Tanucci was duly appointed legal adviser to Charles as Duke of Parma. He marched south with the Bourbon army during the conquest of Naples, and when Santo Stefano formed his administration Tanucci was included in it as Minister of Justice.

The Neapolitan judicature at this time was a veritable sink of iniquity, and Tanucci set to work with a will to cleanse the Augean stables. So successful was he, that with pardonable exaggeration the Tuscan envoy reported on him to Florence as 'the man who in a few hours has restored law and order to this city and to most of the kingdom, so that one does not hear of a brawl, let alone a murder'. This enforcement of the law early brought him into conflict with the nobles, who had shown little respect for it in Austrian days. Prince Michele Imperiali di Francavilla, for example, had a judge exiled to Ischia because he gave judgement against him, but when he tried to behave in the same way under the new regime he soon found that times were changed. His retainers were concerned in a murder, whereupon he was ordered by Tanucci to arrest them, and hand then over to justice. Instead of doing this he rode to Naples to complain to the King, but Charles refused to see him, and in an interview with Tanucci he was told to obey orders or remove himself from Naples. In the last stages of exasperation he sought to make another appeal for a royal audience, but died of apoplexy on the steps of the palace. The incident did not pass unnoticed by his fellow-aristocrats.

It was not only with the laity that Tanucci made himself unpopular, for he antagonized the clergy even more, and it may well be that in his school Charles first imbibed those anti-clerical ideas which were to come to fruition when he, as King of Spain and the Indies, took action against the Jesuits. At the same time he always remained a devout Catholic, and he never questioned the teaching or doctrines of Catholicism. The Church in politics was another matter, and there he was not prepared to accept dictation from Rome. Clement XII, who occupied the Chair of St. Peter from 1730 to 1740, was, according to the Venetian ambassador accredited to the Holy See, 'more distinguished by the qualities of a gentleman and magnificent prelate than by the talent and power required for sustaining the ponderous burden of the Papacy'.[1] His relations with Charles had been strained from the beginning, for the Pope wavered between the Emperor and Spain in the War of the Polish Succession, in spite of the fact that he had made no opposition to the advancing Bourbon army on its march to Naples; and as he was constitutionally averse to taking important decisions he referred the matter to a committee of cardinals who decided in favour of the Habsburgs. Unfortunately by the time this verdict was pronounced Charles was already in effective possession of the Two Sicilies, and Clement was accordingly placed in an extremely difficult position. Charles had been

[1] cf. Ranke, L.: *History of the Popes*, vol. III, p. 415. London. 1913.

eager for a papal legate to attend his coronation, but in view of the cardinals' decision, this wish could not be granted. It had been customary since Angevin times for the Neapolitan monarch on St. Peter's Day to present the Pope with a white palfrey and seven thousand gold ducats, not, at any rate latterly, as the payment of tribute to a feudal lord, but as evidence of papal recognition. In 1735 both Charles and the Emperor each presented a palfrey, though only the latter's gift was accepted. In a short time, however, force of circumstances compelled Clement to give way, but the insult rankled in the King's mind.

In the case neither of Charles nor of Tanucci had religion anything to do with their attitude towards the clergy, for if the minister was not as devout as his master he was sufficiently so to detest Voltaire and to have his works burned. What aroused the hostility of both was the excessive number of clerics, their ever-increasing property, their immunity from taxation and their separate jurisdiction, which were detrimental to the economics of the kingdom. Charles was not the only monarch who felt this way, for in 1737 the Venetian ambassador wrote home:

> I cannot deny that there is something unnatural in the sight of all the Catholic sovereigns placing themselves in hostility to the court of Rome, and the altercations are now so violent that there can be no hope of any reconciliation by which that court would not be injured in some vital part. Whether this proceed from the diffusion of more enlightened ideas, as many people think, or from a disposition to oppress the weaker party, it is certain that the sovereigns are making rapid progress towards depriving the Roman see of all its secular prerogatives.[1]

An improvement, however, took place, at any rate between the Holy See and Naples, when Clement XII was succeeded by Benedict XIV. He was a very different man from his predecessor, and another Venetian diplomatist, Francesco Veniero, reported on him to the Serenissima as follows:

> He was exalted rather by his own rare virtues, by the peculiar events of that conclave, and by its extraordinary protraction, than by any actual desire on the part of the cardinals who elected him. It was the work of the Holy Spirit alone. . . . The pontiff, endowed with a

[1] Aluise Mocenigo IV, *Relatione di Roma*, 16 Aprile 1737.

sincere and upright mind, would never practise any of those arts which are called 'Romanesque': the same open character which he displayed without reserve as prelate, he continued to exhibit as Cardinal Lambertini, and may be safely said to have shown no other as Pope.

Benedict XIV came from Bologna, and his speech was flavoured by a good-humoured facetiousness, while he did not abandon the somewhat broad witticisms associated with his native city merely because he had become Vicar of Christ. He was not long in grasping the position of the Holy See in respect of the European Powers, and he early discerned what it was possible to retain and what must be abandoned. Such being the case, one of the first acts of his pontificate was to conclude a Concordat with Naples which permitted the taxation of some ecclesiastical property, and limited clerical jurisdiction and immunities, besides restricting the number of clergy in the kingdom. A mixed tribunal of ecclesiastical and secular judges was to settle controversies arising from the Concordat.

By this time there had been a change of government in Naples, or perhaps it would be more accurate to describe it as a palace revolution, for the new Queen had not long arrived before she began to take exception to the power of Santo Stefano, and even more to the arrogance of his wife and daughter. They even failed to show her proper respect, and spoke of her as a child, which, needless to say, soon reached her ears. To what extent she was able to influence her husband is a moot point, but she certainly did not rule him entirely, and an ambassador reports hearing him say to her on one occasion, 'Madam, cease meddling in these affairs.' Where Santo Stefano was concerned he probably shared his wife's views, and among the minister's enemies was now included Monte Alegre, whose wife had become a lady-in-waiting to Elizabeth Farnese, and was in consequence able to exercise considerable influence in Madrid. However this may be it was not long before both the King and Queen wrote to Spain urging Santo Stefano's recall, which he endeavoured to thwart by submitting his resignation, believing, like innumerable politicians both before and since, that he was indispensable. Like most of them he was wrong, and in August 1738 he was dismissed with a golden handshake of two thousand gold doubloons for his return journey.

46

Santo Stefano was succeeded as chief minister by Monte Alegre, who held that office for the next eight years. He was, as a foreigner, no more popular than his predecessor had been, but as long as he retained the confidence of the Queen of Spain his position was unassailable. What did change under the new regime was the position of the King himself. Charles was a late developer, but under the ministry of Monte Alegre he began to develop: he not only continued to attend the meetings of the Privy Council regularly, but he showed an increasing interest in the business that was transacted at them.

For the rest, the King's life was very much of a routine, and a routine dictated by his sporting activities. The first three months of each year were spent at Caserta, with alternate visits to Torre di Guevara, Bovino, and Venafro. Holy Week was invariably spent at Naples; spring and part of the summer there and at Portici. In mid-September Charles sailed to Procida for the pheasant-shooting, and there the birds were so carefully preserved that no cats were allowed on the island; then back to Portici, with a visit to Ottaiano for the partridges; All Saints in the capital; then to Persano for more game.

The easy terms upon which Charles was with his servants are illustrated by a letter to him from a gamekeeper who had promised not to marry before the King had done so, but since this had now happened he asked for permission to take a wife; in the meantime his whole family were 'praying for the continued good health of the King and Queen with abundant offspring for the major consolation of his realm and most faithful vassals'.

Charles had inherited the desire of Louis XIV to be superbly housed, and he was never so happy as when surrounded by architects, painters, and builders. His principal erections were the palaces at Portici, Capodimonte, and Caserta, and it is said that when he chose Portici as a residence he was warned that it was dangerously near Vesuvius, to which he replied that 'God Almighty, the Immaculate Virgin, and San Gennaro, will tend to that'. It was also near Herculaneum, and the King took a great interest in the excavations there. The city had been discovered in Austrian days, and Charles continued the work which had then been begun, though with the primitive means at the disposal of the excavators it is little short of a marvel that so much of Herculaneum survives today. On the other hand the King was very simple in his manners and clothes. State functions bored him even in these early years, and it was almost martyrdom to him to be called upon to wear new clothes: indeed it was said that they were often laid out for a week alongside his old ones until he had become accustomed to them, and condescended to put them on.

This peaceful interlude in his life came to an end with the death of his namesake, the Emperor, on 20th October 1740, for on 16th December the Prussians invaded Silesia, and the War of the Austrian Succession began. This event gave particular pleasure to Elizabeth Farnese to whom the settlement of 1738 was not a peace but a mere truce, and she welcomed the news of the death of Charles VI as giving her a pretext for renewing the war she had so unwillingly abandoned for the last five years. To justify its renewal she caused her husband's government to put forward a claim that the right of the Spanish Habsburgs to succeed on the extinction of the Austrian male line had been transferred, with the crown of Spain and the Indies, to Philip V. Strictly interpreted this would have re-created the empire of Charles V, but it was generally understood to refer only to Italy, and to represent the first stage in an attempt to carve out there an establishment for Charles's younger brother, Philip.[1]

Before long, nearly all the Powers were engaged in the struggle – or rather struggles, for there were three of them, namely that of Great Britain against Spain which had already been going on for the past twelve months; that of Frederick the Great to retain Silesia; and that of the Elector of Bavaria to obtain the heritage of Charles VI. Nevertheless, some little time elapsed before all the Powers appeared as principals: France, for example, did not officially declare war on Great Britain and Austria until 1744 – the year, significantly enough, after the death of the pacific Fleury – although three years before that Louis XV had sent one of his marshals across Europe masquerading as an auxiliary of Bavaria. The War of the Austrian Succession was, indeed, often marked by the ironical, not least in the coincidence that on the very day when the Elector of Bavaria was being crowned as the Emperor Charles VII, his ancestral capital, Munich, was capitulating to the Austrians to avoid being sacked.

There were three main theatres of war, namely Central Europe,

[1] cf. Lodge, Sir Richard: *Studies in Eighteenth Century Diplomacy, 1740–1748*, pp. 37–38. London. 1930.

Flanders and west Germany, and Italy, but it is only with the last-named that the biographer of Charles III is concerned. The struggle there assumed the time-honoured form of a contest between the Bourbon and Habsburg dynasties, with the House of Savoy taking its wares to the best market. In the present instance this proved to be the Austrian, for the danger to her Italian possessions compelled Maria Theresa, the daughter and heir of Charles VI, to come to terms with the 'Prussia of Italy'.

The first reaction of the Neapolitan government was not to get involved if at all possible, and Charles declared his neutrality, but in December 1741 a considerable Spanish force under the Conde de Montemar landed at Orbetello, and Philip ordered his son to send an army to operate in conjunction with it. There was clearly nothing to be done except to obey, so twelve thousand Neapolitans marched north, while their master fondly hoped that his declaration of neutrality would continue to be respected in London and Vienna. He was soon to be very rudely undeceived.

For some weeks warnings from various sources had been reaching Monte Alegre to the effect that the British government was by no means impressed by this declaration of neutrality, and that it was contemplating naval action in the matter, but he paid no attention to what he was told. Accordingly he was completely taken by surprise when on 18th August 1742 a British squadron of thirteen men-of-war under a Commodore Martin anchored in full view of Naples without paying the usual compliments in the way of salutes. The city was quite undefended and indefensible except for the odd fort, and the Mediterranean was so deep that the British warships could come up to the very mole. In these circumstances a bombardment could only do immense damage both to lives and property.

Monte Alegre's first step was to get in touch with the British consul, one Edward Allen, and to ask him to find out what were Commodore Martin's intentions, adding that the King would be glad to receive him as a friend. The consul duly went to see the commodore, and a message was read to him which was to be delivered to Charles. It ran as follows:

That, as His Britannic Majesty was in alliance with the Queen of Hungary and the King of Sardinia, and the King of the Two Sicilies, having joined his forces with those of Spain, in declared war with England, to invade the Queen of Hungary's dominions, contrary to all treaties; he, the Commodore, was sent to demand that the King of the Two Sicilies should not only immediately withdraw his troops from acting in conjunction with those of Spain, but that His Sicilian Majesty should in writing, promise not to give them any further assistance of any kind whatsoever. . . . If His Sicilian Majesty refused to comply with this message, the Commodore would make the necessary dispositions to bombard the city and press his demand by the force of arms.

The consul, with a British naval captain, returned to Monte Alegre's office, and was told that the King's opinion would at once be taken. Charles then presided over a stormy meeting of his Council. He was himself in favour of resistance, as he did not wish to be branded as a coward, but the majority was against him, and he gave way. While the matter was being discussed, the British naval officer had been waiting in an ante-room where he assumed a decidedly truculent air, with his watch in his hand. Monte Alegre at once informed him of the decision that had been reached, that the demand would be complied with, and in writing as required; but he asked that he should have an answer, also in writing, to the effect that upon compliance with the Commodore's ultimatum no hostilities would be committed on either side.

The consul and the captain returned to Martin with this message, but the Commodore said that his orders were absolute, and did not authorize him to give any answer; he expected compliance within an hour after the consul had come on shore, whither they had both returned to deliver the reply to Monte Alegre. It was two o'clock in the morning before the consul was back on board, and the Commodore was so far satisfied that he promised to abstain from any immediate hostilities. Later that morning he received a letter written in the exact words he required and upon this the British squadron weighed anchor: at first it only sailed as far as Capri, and another ten days elapsed before it finally left Neapolitan waters.

It is true that in due course the British government disavowed Martin's action, though it refused to acknowledge the neutrality of the Two Sicilies, but the insult to which he had been subjected rankled with Charles for the rest of his life, and influenced his attitude towards Great Britain when he succeeded to the Spanish throne. The immediate reaction both in Madrid and Versailles was extremely unfavourable to him, and he was sternly rebuked by his mother for what she considered to be his pusillanimity. Nevertheless it is in retrospect difficult to see what different line he could have taken, and the moral of the affair is surely the folly of pursuing a foreign policy without the armaments to render it effective.

The appearance of the British squadron off Naples had co-incided with an attempt by the *austriacanti* in the city to make trouble, but they met with no response. Before long, however, it became clear that a definite Habsburg fifth column did exist, though it was almost entirely confined to the aristocracy and the clergy. More than eight hundred people of this way of thinking were arrested owing to the discovery of secret documents at Portella, and one of the ringleaders was an Augustinian monk who operated in Calabria. Another Austrophil priest was a certain Abate Gambari who reaped a handsome profit from the sale of coupons or promissory notes for posts in an Austrian puppet government, and these bore faked seals of Maria Theresa. To deal with these gentry Charles revived an old tribunal called *Giunta d'Inconfidenza*, and put Tanucci at its head. His activity in suppressing disaffection proved extremely effective, and this was done without recourse to any very drastic repressive measures. Here, again, the effect upon the King personally was considerable, for he did not forget the part played by the clergy in the movement against him, and it undoubtedly weighed with him when the time came to investigate the charges against the Jesuits.

In his education as King the incident was an important land-mark: he certainly did not abate his love of sport, but he began to take an active interest in affairs of state. It was abundantly clear that the armed forces required attention, as did the fortifications of the capital. Accordingly new regiments were raised, and by the end of the following year ten had come into existence: nor was the navy neglected, for there was called into being a small force consisting of two men-of-war with sixty-four and sixty guns respectively, two frigates of thirty guns, and six xebes[1] of twenty guns. On land a new mole was built, also a new road

[1] A sailing ship that has a long overhanging bow and stern, and is usually three-masted with a lateen rig, but often carries square sails on the fore-mast.

from the arsenal to Carmine Fort. In all these activities and many others Charles was the moving spirit.

While these events were taking place in the Two Sicilies the fighting in the North of Italy was very confused. In October 1743 Charles's brother, Philip, with a mixed Spanish and French force, occupied Savoy, but it failed to force its way through the Alps, while in the spring of 1744 France came into the conflict as a principal with a declaration of war against Great Britain and Maria Theresa. It was clear that the war was entering upon a new phase, and the Prince of Lobkowitz set out to regain Naples for the Habsburgs. The time had come for Charles to make up his mind where he stood.

Monte Alegre was in favour of adhering to a policy of neutrality in spite of the fact that it was not recognized by Great Britain, but Charles, after a short period of hesitation, and influenced by the pressure put upon him from Madrid, decided that this was no longer possible. In any event the war had taken a turn for the worse from the Bourbon point of view, for the Conde de Gages, who had replaced Montemar, had been driven by Lobkowitz as far as the Neapolitan frontier, and was now appealing to Charles for assistance. This decided the King to intervene, so he allowed the Spanish army quarters in Calabria, and he issued a proclamation to the effect that the Austrians had forced him to take up arms to defend his kingdom. A council of regency was appointed, the Queen was sent to Gaeta for safety, while to show that he had complete faith in his subjects' loyalty all political prisoners were released. This done, Charles took command of an army of twenty thousand men, linked up with Gages and the Spaniards in the Papal States, and eventually confronted Lobkowitz at Velletri, a small town twenty-five miles south-west of Rome.

For six weeks the two armies confronted each other across the valley, the King hoping that a victory for his brother in Piedmont would draw Lobkowitz to the north, while the Austrian general was relying on some diversion on the part of the British Navy. At this point General Maximilian Brown, an Irishman[1] who was serving under Lobkowitz, conceived the idea of a *coup de main* against Velletri which would bring the war to a sudden end by the capture of Charles himself. He talked his superiors into

[1] Son of a Jacobite officer from Limerick, who had left Ireland with Sarsfield.

countenancing the project, and was provided with six thousand picked men to put his scheme into effect. Curiously enough, Velletri was held by his fellow-countrymen in the shape of the Irish Brigade in the Spanish service, consisting of the regiments of Hibernia, Ultonia, and Irlanda.

The attack took place on the night of 11th August 1744, but just before it was made, an Austrian grenadier deserted to warn the garrison at Velletri. When Brown was told of this he dismissed the threat very lightly, merely observing, 'On with the advance: we'll try our luck', and his luck held. When the deserter reached the Spanish outposts he was halted by a picket of Irlanda, but the officer in command, a Lieutenant Burke, knew no German, so he sent the grenadier, who was obviously trying to impart something of importance, back to the town for questioning. At this point the relief arrived under Captain Slattery, and Burke was about to march his detachment off when the Austrian attack broke. The two Irish officers quickly formed up their men, and fired two volleys into the enemy before they were forced back by weight of numbers. Burke was killed, but Slattery managed to make a fighting retreat, and it is said that when Brown called on him to surrender he answered, 'By the breakfast I've just received, I can judge what a fine lunch is being prepared for me.'

About a mile away from the Irish was encamped a Walloon regiment, which at once marched to the sound of the firing, and these four units took almost the whole weight of the enemy onslaught. They all suffered very heavy losses in consequence, but the survivors made a stand at the Nettuno gate, and so held up Brown's entry into Velletri; but the Irish Brigade lost eleven captains and thirty subalterns in the process, while around the gate heaps of red-coated bodies showed how the Irish 'by this generous sacrifice gave the ultimate touch of glory to the memory of their fame and to the honour they had achieved in the said battle'.

Their gallant stand had in fact enabled Charles to escape, with the assistance it is said of yet another Irishman, Maurice Lenihan. However this may be, the King leapt out of bed half-dressed, and got out of a window of the Ginetti Palace where he was staying. As soon as this news reached General Brown he decided to call off the attack, for there was now no object in continuing with it, and the Austrian casualties were proving by no means light. This decision was easier to take than to put into execution, for after his Croats had burst into the town they dispersed all over it, and proceeded to indulge in an orgy of looting, during the course of which they grabbed the bishop's silver and linen from before his very eyes. Meanwhile, Charles had established contact with Gages, and used his troops to fall on the retreating Austrians, who suffered further heavy losses, while the Walloon Guards cleaned up Velletri itself. During the Austrian retreat, which soon degenerated into a rout, Brown was wounded in the face by an Irish soldier.[1]

The battle of Velletri was another notable milestone in Charles's life. By his victory he had not only saved his throne, which was never afterwards seriously threatened, but had finally established his confidence in himself. The King of Sardinia, who could not be accused of partiality, wrote that on this occasion Charles 'had revealed a constancy worthy of his blood, and had acquitted himself gloriously'. There was no serious fighting in that part of Italy during the remainder of the campaigning season, and Charles took the opportunity to visit Rome on his way back to Naples. The victor of Velletri met with the magnificent reception which might have been expected by one in his position, and in his interview with Benedict XIV he raised one or two points connected with Church matters, in particular stressing the need to reduce the number of religious holidays in Naples, which were regarded as excessive by his lay subjects.

One of the casualties of the war was, quite justifiably, Monte Alegre. By his lack of preparation he had left his master exposed to the insult of Martin's ultimatum, and he had given the wrong advice in the all-important matter of neutrality. The Queen was his enemy, and recently he had made a new one in Gages, but all the same it was not until the spring of 1746 that permission for his dismissal arrived from Madrid, and he was recalled to Spain. His place was taken by the Marchese Fogliani, who had from a Neapolitan point of view the advantage of being an Italian, having been born in Piacenza; but although he was an accomplished courtier he was nothing else, being mediocre in the extreme. Fogliani had represented Charles at Genoa and at The Hague, and the Sardinian ambassador summed him up as 'tall, fair, with a long face, an average mind, and a strong bias towards France. He was long-winded and inconclusive, and he was apt to

---

[1] cf. *The Irish Sword*, vol. VIII, pp. 219–220: 'The Hibernia Regiment of the Spanish Army', by Thomas J. Mullen, Jr. Dublin. 1968.

ignore his former promises.' In short, he possessed all the qualities of a successful politician, except the skill to make use of them.

The new minister had barely taken office before an event occurred which was to have the most profound effect upon Charles, his family, and his kingdom, and that was the death of his father. Philip V died in the palace of the Buen Retiro in Madrid on 4th July 1746, and by a codicil in a will made in 1727 he gave directions that he was to be buried, not in the Escorial, but at San Ildefonso, and this was accordingly done. The benefits which he conferred upon Spain have already been discussed, but in one respect he did her an ill service, and that was when he altered the order of the succession to the crown. The *Siete Partidas* of Alfonso X had recognized the right of females to succeed to the throne of Castille and Leon in default of male heirs of an equally near degree of consanguinity, and that this right had also been admitted in practice is proved by the succession of Isabella I. It was recognized, too, in Aragón, for the claim of Charles I was through his mother, Juana the Mad. With the advent of the Bourbons a change was made, and Philip in 1713 introduced the so-called Salic Law, which established the French procedure. The following century was to show that he had sown a fine crop of dragons' teeth.

Philip's death was followed by the involuntary retirement of his widow from public life, and these two events completed the emancipation of their eldest son. Henceforth Charles was his own master, and from that moment his character seemed to change, though we now know that it had been developing for a number of years, and that it had in fact reached maturity. Everywhere it became obvious that he had acquired a greater sense of responsibility and a greater energy, as well as a wider vision. He began to control his ministers, and to take a leading part in their deliberations, while the foreign ambassadors to whom he gave audience were impressed as much by his firmness as by his affability. He hunted and shot as much as ever, but, like Louis XIV, he adhered to a strict time-table: as he told the Sardinian ambassador:

> I rise at five in the morning, read and attend to memorials till eight, when I dress and proceed to the State Council. I hope to make this kingdom flourish again and relieve it from taxes, especially since this

year (1750) I have finished paying all the debts contracted during the last war, and still have 300,000 ducats in savings to put in my treasury. To prove this I have refused the usual voted tax from the Sicilian Parliament, a larger sum than any voted previously, telling them that I had no present need of it, and that they were to save it until it was required. Apart from which I have revoked a tax, and devote all my attention to improving the welfare of my subjects, since I wish to save my soul and go to Heaven.

Nothing in Charles's life, either in Naples or Madrid, was to contradict this statement.[1]

---

[1] cf. Acton, Harold: *The Bourbons of Naples*, vol. I, p. 66. London. 1956.

V

REAL POWER

FERDINAND VI, the new King of Spain and the Indies, was the second and only surviving son of Philip V by his first wife, the heroic Maria Luisa of Savoy. He had been born in 1713 so was a man of thirty-three when he came to the throne, and he was married to Barbara of Braganza, daughter of John V of Portugal. The wits of Madrid said that Queen Barbara had succeeded Queen Elizabeth, and there was something in the jest, but the effect upon the destinies of Spain was very different. Ferdinand was by nature of the most pacific disposition, and his favourite motto was *'Paz con todos y guerra con nadie'*.[1] When he died, and was buried in the Monasterio de las Salesas Reales in Madrid, for like his father he refused to be interred in the Escorial, there were engrossed on his tomb the words, 'Here lies King Ferdinand VI, the best of princes: he died childless, but with a numerous issue of patriotic virtues.' It is true that, like his father, he was much under the influence of his wife, but whereas Elizabeth had encouraged Philip in an aggressive foreign policy in order to place her sons upon Italian thrones, Barbara shared to the full her husband's peaceful intentions. She had no children for whom to provide, and the Portuguese are not a bellicose people, so that her influence was always exercised on the side of peace; with the result that Ferdinand's reign was to be one of the most tranquil in Spanish history, and both King and Queen devoted their energy to promoting the best interests of their country. It was, in effect, the beginning of that benevolent despotism which Charles was to do so much to develop.

Meanwhile the War of the Austrian Succession was pursuing its leisurely course. In Italy it had been marked by a good deal of fighting, but without any decisive victory for either side,

[1] 'Peace with all and war with none.'

57

though on balance Maria Theresa found herself in the better position, for although she had failed to shake Charles in the possession of the Two Sicilies her forces had more than held their ground further north. Thanks to her own energy and courage, and the assistance of Sardinia by land and of Great Britain by sea, the Italian campaigns had left her not merely with her own territory undiminished, but in possession of that of the Duke of Modena as well. That at the peace she had to give up this acquisition, and also to sacrifice Parma and Piacenza, was due to what had happened elsewhere. Italy had to pay the debts of Flanders, where the Maréchal de Saxe had been driving the British, Austrians, and Dutch before him.

As the years passed, there came over the principal combatants a desire for peace, though it must be admitted that friction between allies on both sides had much to do with the growth of such sentiments. Frederick had already withdrawn from the conflict, while French intrigues with Sardinia behind the backs of the Spaniards resulted in a coolness between Paris and Madrid. Now came the accession of Ferdinand VI, who not only took no particular interest in the Italian ambitions of his half-brothers, but was also very definitely a man of peace. Indeed, Maria Theresa, who had at last secured a promise of Russian assistance, alone wished to continue the war, but she was powerless in the face of British opposition. Pelham's government informed the King of Sardinia that its financial aid would come to an end, and unwilling as that monarch was to see another Bourbon established upon an Italian throne, he could not fight without British subsidies. Maria Theresa had no means of bringing pressure to bear on London, and she could do nothing in Italy without the Sardinian army and the British fleet, so she had to give way.

Louis XV, whose arms had lately been crowned with success in the old cockpit of the Low Countries, played a prominent part in the ensuing settlement. He declared that he wished to make peace, not like a merchant, but like a king. All the same, there was a good deal of manœuvring for position before the final pacification was effected. Kaunitz, whose long ascendancy in Austrian counsels was just beginning, endeavoured to open direct negotiations with France, but she was found to be already in communication with Britain, with whom she preferred, if possible, to come to terms. The Congress of Aix-la-Chapelle actually met in March

The Royal Palace, Caserta

Maria Amalia of Saxony, Queen of Spain, by Liani

1748, but, as in the case of so many similar gatherings, most of the real business was transacted privately and directly between the Powers chiefly concerned. Finally, on 18th October, a definite treaty was concluded between Britain, France, and the United Provinces; Spain adhered to it two days later; and before the end of the following month Austria and Sardinia had given their reluctant assent.

The basis upon which the Treaty of Aix-la-Chapelle was concluded was eminently reasonable, for it was a general restitution of conquests, though there were some exceptions. Silesia and Glatz, for example, were guaranteed to Frederick, while the ambitions of Elizabeth Farnese were at last satisfied by the cession to Don Felipe of his brother's old duchies of Parma and Piacenza. Charles Emmanuel of Sardinia, on the other hand, had to content himself with the recovery of Savoy and Nice, which had been occupied during the war by the forces of the Bourbon Powers. For the rest, the Pragmatic Sanction was guaranteed, except in respect of Silesia, Glatz, Parma, and Piacenza; Francis I was recognized as Emperor; the Duke of Modena regained his dominions; and in spite of the protests of Maria Theresa the barrier fortresses on the French frontier were again committed to the proved inefficiency of their Dutch garrisons to whom they had originally been entrusted by the Treaty of Utrecht.

With the coming of peace Charles was able to devote himself to the affairs of his kingdom, which he proceeded to do with conspicuous success. Whether his wife was an asset or a liability to him in this task is not easy to determine. After the birth of her eldest son she was admitted to the Council of State, but she had to listen to its deliberations behind a curtain. This gave her a taste for political intrigue, and it was not long before she was trying to trip up Fogliani as she had done Santo Stefano and Monte Alegre. She was hot-tempered, and was in the habit of boxing the ears of her pages, and of slapping her ladies-in-waiting. Nevertheless Charles was genuinely fond of her, and he tolerated her tantrums.

Maria Amalia would appear to have suffered from two major defects – she had no sense of humour and she had no self-control. On one occasion when she was in an advanced state of pregnancy an order was issued that as soon as she was seized with the first pangs all courtiers were to put on full-dress uniform to celebrate the baptism which, in the case of the members of the Spanish royal family, immediately followed their birth. A certain Spaccaforno was waiting on the King and Queen at dinner, and during the course of the meal upset some gravy. Maria Amalia gave a yell, whereupon Spaccaforno dropped the dish, and rushed out of the room. 'Where are you going, you lunatic?' Charles called after him. 'Sire,' was the reply, 'I was hurrying to change my uniform, for I thought Her Majesty was about to be delivered.' The King burst out laughing, and told him to stop playing the fool; while to his wife he remarked with a twinkle in his eye, 'You see what happens.' Spaccaforno was, it may be added, readily forgiven.

It was during these years that Charles made the acquaintance of Leopoldo di Gregorio, better known as the Marchese di Squillacci. He was a Sicilian of obscure origin, and he had begun his career as an accountant in a commercial firm. According to his critics the less said about his business activities the better, and the more so when he was concerned with army contracts. How much of all this is supposition and how much the King knew must be a matter of conjecture, but he was soon impressed by the Sicilian's industry and initiative, and in 1746 he was put in charge of the customs. From that he was in due course promoted to be Minister of Finance. Squillacci was a little too slick to suit the taste of Fogliani or Tanucci, but nothing could shake the King's confidence in him, and when he succeeded to the Spanish throne he took Squillacci with him—not with the happiest consequences, as will be seen.

Once Charles's confidence had been gained it was very difficult to shake it, for he liked familiar faces just as he liked old clothes. A typical instance was the Duca di Losada with whom he used to play *reversi*.[1] The Duca, like the Queen, would not appear to have possessed much sense of humour, and the King used to chaff him, to which the other replied by relapsing into silence. On these occasions Losada would show his resentment by absenting himself from the palace on the following day, when Charles would send for him, and with a few well-chosen words repair any damage which might have been done.

During these last years of his reign in the Two Sicilies the King's passion for building showed no signs of diminution, but

[1] A card game in which the winner is the player who makes the lowest score.

he built for others besides himself. In particular he formed the design of building a palace for the poor, and in 1751 work was started on the Reale Albergo dei Poveri. This building was originally intended to have a front of seven hundred metres, and it was to house vagabonds and orphans, the unemployed and the unemployable, where they were to be fed, educated, and, when possible, converted into useful citizens. The inspirer of this project was a Dominican of the name of Rocco, who was one of that remarkable line of priests who down the centuries have done so much for the poor of Naples. He was also a most valuable interpreter to Charles of the wishes and needs of the most lowly of his subjects. There was certainly nothing exclusive about the Bourbon regime, and the aristocracy followed the royal example. The Principe di Tarsia opened a particularly fine public library to the public, and Giovanni Caraffa, Principe de Noja, founded a museum of antiquities and coins, to quote only a couple of instances. There was a rising spirit of public service, which had been noticeable for its absence during the Austrian regime, and undoubtedly the credit for much of this must go to the King personally.

All this time the star of Fogliani was setting, chiefly owing to his inability to put the Neapolitan case adequately and convincingly in the field of international politics. In 1755 Charles dismissed him, but to soften the blow he was appointed Viceroy of Sicily. The office of Prime Minister was abolished, and the administration was divided between Tanucci, who was put in charge of Foreign Affairs as well as of Justice and the royal household, and Squillacci, who was now Secretary of Finance, War, and Marine. There was also Gaetano Brancone, who was made responsible for the curious combination of theatrical and ecclesiastical affairs. Above them all stood the King, for the royal emancipation was now complete.

Nevertheless this fact did not make for better relations with the older Bourbon dynasties. In particular there was considerable coldness between Charles and his half-brother in Madrid, and Ferdinand did not trouble to send a representative to Naples until 1753. What little interest the Spanish monarch did take in Italian affairs was centred on his uncle, Charles Emmanuel III of Sardinia, with whom he was on the best of terms, whereas in the Two Sicilies the Savoyard was regarded with the gravest suspicion. So far as Charles was concerned Louis XV was not much better, for he had married his daughter to Felipe of Parma, and was of the opinion that his son-in-law should take over the kingdom of the Two Sicilies when Charles moved to Madrid on the death of Ferdinand. Louis caused further offence by remaining unrepresented at Naples for seven years. All this occasioned Charles a great deal of anxiety, but he never wavered in his determination that he should be succeeded in Naples by his son and not by his brother—needless to say the Queen fully agreed with him.

British statesmen were by no means averse to fishing in these troubled waters, and in the last days of 1758 the British envoy, Sir James Gray, received the following letter from the Elder Pitt, then Secretary of State for the Southern Department:

The King has received a piece of intelligence of the greatest authority, concerning matters of so high a nature, and touching so personally and essentially the King of Naples, that he has commanded me to communicate the same to you for information. I will at the same time observe to you on this subject, that both the extreme delicacy of the matter, and the peculiar secrecy of the channel conveying it, are such, that the King cannot give you a greater mark of his reliance on your prudence and discretion, than by commanding me to impart to you lights of this very extraordinary nature, which it is His Majesty's pleasure you should only use, in case of a proper opening to do it with advantage, and then also to do it with the utmost circumspection and secrecy. The said intelligence is in substance as follows:

The court of France, seeing it could no longer count upon the re-establishment of the King of Spain's health, (who, besides great indispositions of the body, is in some sort disordered in mind) has renounced the designs laid during the illness of the Queen; and what had ripened since the death of that princess.[1] To these has succeeded another design, viz. it has been in agitation for three weeks or a month preceding the fourteenth of November, the date of the intelligence, to engage the King of Spain to abdicate and demit the crown in favour of Don Philip. However, this project prevents not France from employing the greatest managements towards the court of Naples, in order to put Don Carlos, as they call him, in their interest, in case he should mount the throne of Spain. In a word, the affairs of that kingdom make the chief object of the attention of the

[1] The Queen of Spain had died on 27th August 1758

court of Versailles, and there will very shortly happen a great change in Spain.

I am to add, that different advices, all concurring in something of the same nature, strongly establish the high possibility that some very dark and dangerous practices are on foot among the partisans of France, at the court of Madrid. In this state of things, it would be superfluous to enforce the King's former orders to you, to give the most watchful attention to all that is passing at the court of Naples, particularly to penetrate to what degree the actual alarms and agitation of the court may really go, in so critical and suspicious a situation; to seize also this favourable, and perhaps decisive moment of applying to their hopes and fears, and setting before their eyes, in the most striking manner, the evident utility, to their own most capital interest and immediate safety, of entering into the views of His Majesty, who has nothing more at heart, than to give the King of Naples the most essential proofs of his cordial friendship in support of his great family object.[1]

Ferdinand's mental health was, indeed, giving cause for anxiety, for he was suffering from that acute melancholia which afflicted so many members of his family, and of which Charles was in perpetual dread, but the wealth of Spain had steadily increased during Ferdinand's reign, so that the Secretary of State for the Northern Department wrote from London that she 'is now become the arbiter of all the southern courts'. The domestic revenue was increasing by five million ducats annually, and that from the Indies was nearly doubled. It was, indeed, well that the government of the country should be in such good hands, for not only were there the wounds of war to be healed, but in 1756 there were earthquakes which seriously damaged some of the most important cities of Spain. It would, too, be difficult to exaggerate the intellectual advance which was made in the reign of Ferdinand VI. The foundation of academies and other learned bodies went on apace; subsidies and annuities were granted freely to men of art, letters, and science to enable them to pursue their investigations both at home and abroad; while foreign scholars and artificers were attracted to Spain. Ferdinand had found his country struggling painfully into the light, but still in serious financial straits and with large sections of the population living in misery.

[1] cf. Coxe, W.: *The Bourbon Kings of Spain*, vol. III, pp. 229–231. London. 1813.

He was to leave her enjoying comparative prosperity, with a formidable navy, and three millions sterling in the treasury. It cannot, of course, be claimed that all this was due to the King personally, but just as a man can be judged by the company – or the women – he keeps, so can the worth of a monarch be estimated by the ministers he employs, and Ferdinand gathered together an extremely competent team which, like his father and his half-brother, he drew from all sections of the community.

The death of the Queen had an effect upon her husband which was such that to all intents and purposes he was deprived of his senses. A dispatch from the British ambassador, the Earl of Bristol, to Pitt dated 25th September 1758 well describes the condition to which Ferdinand sank at this time.

The extraordinary situation of this country from the Catholic King's indisposition is the cause that all business is at a stand. He has kept his bed for seven days, he was blooded twice within a few hours, and he has been physicked, but his aversion to business, and his reluctance to see anyone, except the two physicians, increases daily. M. Ariaga went to Villaviciosa, but was by the King's orders denied admittance. M. Eslava was refused his customary entrance. Mr. Wall has not seen His Majesty these six days. The Duke of Alba came to Madrid on the 23rd., where he now is, but the King receives no one, and for the last three days, even the Infant Don Luis has been refused access to his brother by his express commands. There is a melancholy in the King which nothing can divert, but such a settled taciturnity prevails that no direction can be given, nor any order issued. It is impossible to see what will be the result of this unsettled scene.

The Catholic King continues at Villaviciosa without any apparent change in his health. It would be difficult to describe the present situation of the Spanish ministry. Mr. Wall did not deny that the melancholy disposition of the Catholic King had now almost entirely affected his head, but added that he had not uttered a weak, extravagant, or injudicious sentiment. He will not be shaved, walks about without any covering but his shirt, which has not been changed for a surprising time, and a nightgown. He has not been in bed for ten nights, nor is he thought to have slept five hours since the second of this month, and that only by intervals of half-an-hour, sitting upon his chair. He declines lying down, because he imagines that he shall die when he does so.

Ferdinand lingered on in this melancholy condition until he

died on 10th August 1759. The news reached Naples on the 22nd, and was broken to Charles by Losada. The King must have expected his brother's death, but all the same it appears to have come as a shock to him, and for nine days he never left his apartments, which would seem to argue that he was by no means immune from the constitutional melancholy of his family.

On the other hand by the time that Ferdinand VI died his half-brother had no longer any need for anxiety with regard to the succession to the throne of the Two Sicilies. The Seven Years' War was in progress, and as Spain was neutral in that conflict neither France nor Austria, now in alliance, wished to offend her new monarch, while Charles Emmanuel, although desirous of acquiring Piacenza, was in no position to act on his own. Accordingly a compromise was reached by which the Sardinian monarch withdrew his claims in return for a cash payment, and Vienna was placated by the return of the Stato dei Presidi to Tuscany, now ruled by a Habsburg archduke since the extinction of the Medici. Needless to say no one thought of asking the opinion of the inhabitants of these various territories. There was, however, a further difficulty caused by the fact that Charles's eldest son, Philip, had from infancy been subject to epileptic fits, and by 1759 was reduced to a state of mental imbecility. In these circumstances his father took appropriate action to set him aside from the succession by having him carefully examined by specialists, and then by the Royal Council, both of whom declared that the young prince was in such a state of mental incapacity as to be wholly devoid of intellect, and without the smallest hopes of recovery.

This done, Charles convoked a gathering consisting of the ministers, the representatives of the city of Naples, the *corps diplomatique*, and a member of the Council of Castille, whom he proceeded to address in his new capacity as King of Spain and the Two Sicilies.

Among the heavy cares in which the monarchy of Spain and the Indies has involved me since the death of my brother, the Catholic King Ferdinand VI, is that derived from the notorious imbecility of my royal first-born. The spirit of the treaties concluded in this century proves that all Europe desires the separation of the Spanish power from that of Italy, at least as far as is consistent with justice. Seeing therefore myself required to provide a legitimate successor to my Italian states, now I am on the point of passing into Spain, and of choosing among the many sons whom God has given me, I am obliged to decide which of them may be deemed the second born, fit to conduct the government of my Italian states, separated from Spain and the Indies.

This conjuncture, in which the tranquillity of Europe requires that I should incur no suspicion of any desire to continue in my own person the Spanish and Italian powers, obliges me now to take my resolution. A considerable body of my counsellors of state, a member of the Council of Castille, of the chamber of St. Chiara, the lieutenant of the Sommaria of Naples, and the whole junta of Sicily, assisted by six deputies, have represented to me, that after every possible investigation, they have not been able to find in the unhappy prince the use of reason, nor any trace of reflection; and that such having been his state from infancy, he is not only incapable of religious sentiments and the use of reason at present, but no shadow of hope appears for the future. They therefore unanimously conclude that this prince cannot be disposed of as nature, duty, and paternal love would require. In this fatal crisis, seeing then by the divine will the capacity and right of second birth devolve on my third son, Don Ferdinand, still in his pupillage, it is my duty as a sovereign and a father, in the transfer of my Italian states, to adopt measures for his guardianship, which I should not be justified in exercising over a son, who is as independent a sovereign in Italy as I myself am in Spain.

Charles then proceeded to read the details of the future succession to the throne of the Two Sicilies, and then signed and sealed the instrument in which they were laid down. The last act in this ceremony now took place, and it was the delivery to the new King, Ferdinand III of Sicily and IV of Naples, of a symbolic sword with the words, 'Louis XIV, King of France, gave this sword to Philip V, your grandfather. I received it from him, and I now resign it to you, that you may use it for the defence of your religion and your subjects.'[1] Having appointed a Council of Regency, with Tanucci at its head, to administer the kingdom during his son's minority, Charles, with the whole royal family except Ferdinand and the mad Philip, on 6th October 1759 embarked for Spain, to the universal regret of his former subjects and to his own infinite sorrow.

---

[1] This sword was later presented by Ferdinand to Nelson.

VI

SPAIN AND THE INDIES

In succeeding to his brother's throne Charles also succeeded not
only to the powerful and prosperous Spain which Ferdinand had
built up, but also to his difficulties, and the most important of
these related to Spanish relations with Great Britain and France.

By a clause in the Treaty of Utrecht there had come into existence an *Asiento*, or agreement, between Britain and Spain by
which British merchants acquired the right to trade under strict
limitations with certain towns in Spanish-American waters set
apart for the purpose, and British factories in one form or another
existed in Panama, Vera Cruz, Buenos Aires, and Cartagena. From
the beginning this clause had been a fruitful source of trouble
between London and Madrid, for the days were passing when
quarrels could be confined to colonial waters. As the eighteenth
century grew older the world became a great deal smaller, and the
action and reaction of events inside and outside Europe began to
be increasingly felt. In any case the privilege of the *Asiento* lent
itself to a variety of interpretations. There can be no doubt but
that the British South Sea Company grossly abused its right to
send annually one large trading ship to the Spanish colonies, and
a widespread illicit trade sprang up, partly under cover, and
partly independently, of the Company, while smugglers went to
and fro with great frequency between Jamaica and the mainland.
Spain replied by sending out gunboats, called *guarda-costas*, whose
captains sometimes behaved with excessive severity. Recrimina-
tions and reprisals followed, and in the course of them an
English merchant captain named Jenkins was said to have had his
ear cut off by a Spanish officer. At any rate, he produced a severed
ear in a box on his return to London, and in the public mind
Jenkins' ear became the symbol of the ill-treatment to which
British subjects were liable in the Spanish dominions: in particular

the display of the ear to sympathetic legislators in the lobby of the House of Commons had much to do with rousing Parliamentary opinion against Spain.

In actual fact neither side had anything approaching clean hands. If there were Spanish privateers off the coast of Jamaica, there were English off Havana and Honduras. If Jenkins lost his ear and some other captains their goods, Spanish ship-owners had suffered in their turn. If Englishmen had been seen working in irons in the harbour of Havana, Spaniards had been publicly sold as slaves in the British colonies. Popular fancy in both countries was not slow to exaggerate what was taking place, so that in England it was believed that hundreds of sailors were rotting in Spanish dungeons, and in Spain that an English captain had compelled a Spanish nobleman to cut off and devour his own nose. Nevertheless, public opinion was definitely more bellicose in Britain than in Spain, and religious bigotry was freely invoked; indeed, had it not been for public-house Protestantism the differences between the two countries might well have been adjusted.

Spain did not want war, and made every effort to avoid it. By the Convention of the Pardo in January 1739, she agreed to pay an indemnity of £95,000 pending a peaceful settlement of the questions outstanding between the two countries, namely the right of search, and the delimitation of the frontier between Georgia and Florida. In return, Spain pressed for the payment of certain claims made by her against the South Sea Company. The negotiations continued throughout the spring and summer of 1739, and although Walpole was himself sincerely desirous of preserving peace, his administration was every day growing weaker. The Opposition stormed at him for alleged subservience to a foreign Power, while the popular agitation increased rather than diminished. Nor did the British Prime Minister get the help from Fleury which he might have expected. If, the Cardinal seems to have argued, Spanish attention can be diverted westwards, Elizabeth Farnese may cease to worry me with regard to Italian matters. Accordingly he blew hot and cold, and in due course the pot boiled over, for in October 1739 Britain declared war on Spain. This was one of the earlier examples of hostilities being forced by public opinion upon a British government contrary to its better judgement.

So Britain got its war, though whether this proved to be the war it wanted is another matter. 'They now ring the bells,' Walpole remarked bitterly, 'they will soon wring their hands', and he was right. Spain was much better prepared than was believed in London. Alberoni and Ripperdá had been succeeded in office by the much less flamboyant but extremely capable José Patiño. A Galician, he had originally been a Jesuit novice, but had forsaken the ecclesiastical profession, and had played an important part in the organization of the army during the War of the Spanish Succession. Alberoni brought him to Madrid, and on the fall of Ripperdá he was appointed Minister of Marine and the Indies, and later, Minister of Finance. His first act was to reorganize the navy, and so successful was he that in 1732 a fleet of no less than six hundred sail of all types went from Alicante, and recovered Oran from the Moors. By means of a system of bounties Patiño encouraged Spanish trade with the Americas and the Philippines, while his financial reforms carried on the work that had been initiated by Alberoni. When he died in 1736 he had restored the prestige of Spain almost to what it had been in the sixteenth century.

The Anglo-Spanish war had not long been in progress before it was seen how well Patiño had done his work. It is true that it began with a Spanish reverse, for Admiral Vernon – 'Old Grog' – sacked Puerto Rico in Panama, but the news of the disaster roused all Spain, and within a few months Spanish privateers had captured English shipping to the value of £234,000, while Gibraltar and Minorca were both threatened. The British government determined to strike its principal blow in America, and Vernon was sent to attack Cartagena with 10,000 troops. The Viceroy, Sebastian de Eslava, himself conducted the defence, and after an initial British success the invaders failed to capture the citadel in spite of their vastly superior numbers[1]: soon afterwards the climate compelled the abandonment of the attempt, and when Vernon subsequently tried to capture Santiago de Cuba a similar failure attended his efforts. By the end of 1740 the struggle between Spain and Great Britain became merged in the War of the Austrian Succession: at its termination by the Treaty of Aix-la-Chapelle the *Asiento* was renewed for four years, but, as Sir Richard Lodge well put it,

[1] Smollett served in this expedition, and his reactions are to be found in *Roderick Random*.

this 'was a mere evasion of the disputes between England and Spain which had kindled the war in 1739'.[1]

It was thus against a background of nearly half a century of ill-will where Great Britain was concerned that Ferdinand VI succeeded to the throne, and even his pacific intentions would by themselves hardly have sufficed to prevent the pot from boiling over again had there not been as British ambassador in Madrid one of the greatest diplomats of all time in the person of Benjamin Keene. The co-operation of the two men kept peace between their respective countries for a decade.

Keene was born in 1697 at King's Lynn, where his father was in business, and where he was educated at the Free Grammar School. His Norfolk birth combined with his early promise to recommend him to Walpole, while he also acquired the favour of Walpole's political heirs, the Pelham brothers. Keene first went to Madrid in 1723 in the somewhat delicate position of agent for the South Sea Company, and to that office he added in the following year the post of British Consul, while in 1727 he was promoted to be Minister Plenipotentiary. In that capacity he adjusted with the Spanish and French ministers the terms of the Treaty of Seville in 1729, though the credit for the actual signature of the treaty was assumed by William Stanhope, who returned to Spain for that express purpose after an absence of two years. As Stanhope was rewarded with the earldom of Harrington and the office of Secretary of State for the Northern Department whereas Keene got nothing, the young diplomatist was warned for the first, but not for the last, time that in eighteenth-century England it was no slight handicap to be of humble birth, more particularly if one was serving Whig masters. As a matter of fact he never seems quite to have forgiven his professed patrons, then in the plenitude of their power, for having treated him as if he had been nothing more than Stanhope's private secretary.

However, as soon as Stanhope returned to England, Keene became Minister Plenipotentiary again, and such he remained for ten years. His most memorable achievement during this decade was the conclusion of the Convention of the Pardo by which he endeavoured, in accordance with the policy of Walpole, to prevent the outbreak of war between Britain and Spain. For this Convention he was bitterly denounced in some quarters in England, and

[1] *Studies in Eighteenth-Century Diplomacy, 1740–1748*, p. 410. London. 1930.

his critics sneered at him as 'Don Benjamin' to imply that he was more of a Spaniard than an Englishman. Indeed, so strong were the feelings aroused that when it was proposed to impeach Walpole after his fall Keene was threatened with inclusion in the charge. As we have seen, the war party in England carried the day, and on the outbreak of hostilities Keene returned home.

During the war he remained in England and sat in the House of Commons, where he voted as he was instructed by his patrons, and the reward for his docility was first a place on the Board of Trade and later the office of Paymaster of Pensions. It is evident from his letters that he had neither the taste nor the aptitude for Parliamentary life, and he had no hesitation in abandoning it when in 1745 there arose a vacancy at Lisbon, to which capital he was accordingly accredited as Envoy Extraordinary and Plenipotentiary. Keene did not immediately go to Portugal, for the Jacobite rising of The Forty-Five supervened, and for a time it was uncertain whether George II or James III was the monarch to be represented in the Portuguese capital. He finally arrived in Lisbon in the early autumn of 1746, and there he remained until the conclusion of the Treaty of Aix-la-Chapelle, when he was at once transferred to Madrid as Ambassador Extraordinary and Plenipotentiary. It is thus clear that Keene had a wide knowledge and experience of Spain when he presented his credentials to Ferdinand VI in February 1749.

When Keene thus returned to Madrid he found power, under the King, mainly concentrated in the hands of two men, whose functions were inclined to overlap, and who had so little in common that they could rarely be induced to confer together. One was an aristocrat, Don José de Carvajal, who claimed descent from the House of Lancaster: he was a man of the utmost probity, and controlled the ministry of Foreign Affairs. The other was the Marqués de Ensenada, who had risen by ability from a lowly origin, and controlled the ministries of Marine, Finance, War, and the Indies. Carvajal pursued a definite policy which may be summed up as the maintenance of peace, the recovery of Spanish independence from the tutelage of Versailles, and the establishment of amicable relations with Britain, though combined with the avoidance of any open rupture with France. Ensenada professed the same principles, and for a time deceived Keene on this score, but he was in fact a good deal of an opportunist. He was more concerned with maintaining his own position than in furthering the interests of Spain, and in the end he became an avowed advocate of the French alliance. Keene found before long that he might make an agreement with Carvajal, but that Ensenada had a way of obstructing its fulfilment.

Keene's greatest difficulties, however, lay not so much in the divergent views of Ferdinand's ministers, but in the irreconcilable commercial and colonial claims of Spain and Britain. The two countries might be at peace in Europe, but they were always in a state of virtual war in the Americas, and this was to be as true during the reign of Charles III as it had been during that of his half-brother. The Treaty of Aix-la-Chapelle had done nothing to settle those maritime disputes which had occasioned the so-called 'War of Jenkins' Ear', and it is not difficult to understand why such should have been the case. Much of the trade which Britain carried across the Atlantic was in Spanish eyes illegal 'contraband', while the measures which Spain took to check this trade were termed in England 'depredations', and the Spanish *guarda-costas* were denounced as 'licensed pirates'. Spain had also a more concrete grievance. For more than half a century British ships had carried on a lucrative trade in logwood, which was cut in the swamps of Campeachy Bay,[1] but as the logwood-cutters could not live in the swamp they built huts on the not too distant Mosquito Shore, and, later, on the more convenient banks of the River Valis. The cutting and the carrying, and above all the settlement, were denounced by the Spaniards as encroachments in a part of the world which belonged to them by right of prior discovery. The dispute dated back to the time of Charles the Bewitched, when Spain had been powerless to defend her rights, and could only assert them by impotent protests, while Britain maintained that use and wont created a right. In these circumstances no formula could reconcile British enterprise with Spanish monopoly, and even if such a formula could have been devised in London or Madrid it would assuredly have failed to avert quarrels on the other side of the Atlantic.

Keene held a distinguished position in Spain, and he was rightly proud of it, but his difficulty in gaining and keeping that position can only be assessed if it is remembered that in the background of

[1] cf. Calderón Quijano, J. A.: *Belice, 1663(?)–1821*, pp. 69–331. Seville. 1944.

his major negotiations—as was to happen to his successors in the next reign too—he had to deal with an incessant stream of protests from both Britain and Spain against high-handed or illegal conduct on the part of the subjects both of Ferdinand VI and George II. Furthermore, there were powerful commercial interests, especially in England, whom peaceful relations between the two countries did not suit at all.

The chief landmarks in the history of Keene's embassy are clearly traceable. He began by concentrating upon the settlement of commercial problems, because they were the most pressing, and partly because their adjustment might pave the way to that political entente which was his ultimate object; while at the very best a commercial agreement would be a gesture of independence on the part of Spain, and would be so regarded by the government of Louis XV. There were two immediate problems, at first quite distinct, but ultimately combined together. The first concerned a treaty which George Bubb, afterwards the notorious Bubb Dodington, had managed to negotiate in December 1715, when Elizabeth Farnese and Alberoni wanted British support for their Italian schemes, and by which Spain renewed to Britain the commercial advantages she had been forced to cede in the days of her weakness under the last of the Habsburgs. When the general pacification of Aix-la-Chapelle came to be made, Sandwich,[1] the chief British delegate, either through ignorance or carelessness, failed to include Bubb's treaty among the Anglo-Spanish treaties which were renewed in the Preliminaries, and the British government attached great importance to the rectification of this omission. The second problem was a double claim on the part of the South Sea Company to the renewal of their privileges for four years under article 16 of the Aix treaty, and to the payment of pecuniary claims against Spain amounting to considerably more than a million pounds.

Carvajal soon proved adamant where Bubb's treaty was concerned. He would not admit that it was in force, because all treaties had been annulled by the recent war, and only those specially mentioned had been revalidated. In any event he refused to renew a treaty which he regarded as so disgraceful that no Spanish minister ought to have signed it. Thus the only expedient left to Keene was the negotiation of a new treaty, and to such a

[1] The 4th Earl.

course there was the obvious objection that any concessions granted by Spain would have to be shared with those states which were entitled to 'most favoured nation' treatment. Meanwhile Keene had to moot the South Sea Company's claims to Ensenada as they concerned the departments of Finance and the Indies, and his position was considerably weakened when the Spanish minister produced an agreement signed at Aix by Sandwich and the Duque de Sotomayor after the settlement of the Preliminaries. This provided that, when peace was finally made, commissioners should be appointed by both countries to consider whether some pecuniary compensation could be substituted for the renewal of the *Asiento* as laid down in the Treaty of Utrecht. Keene knew nothing of this, and there was a delay while he obtained from London the information with which he should have been supplied when he was instructed to open the negotiations. When the relevant documents did reach him they confirmed Ensenada's statement, and revealed that Sandwich had justified his signature on the ground that it was necessary to induce Spain to accede to the Preliminaries, while it would also help to drive in a wedge between Ferdinand and Louis. Keene thus found himself involved in a very complicated negotiation, and it was only after the Sandwich–Sotomayor agreement had been rejected that the South Sea Company could press for the implementation of the terms of the Treaty of Utrecht, while as for the debt which it claimed was owing, Ensenada asserted that the King of Spain also had a bill to present, and that in reality the Company were debtors rather than creditors.

Out of this welter of claims and counter-claims there gradually emerged the suggestion of a compromise which Carvajal propounded to Keene in September 1749. He said that exclusive privileges unshared by any other nation could not be *given* to Britain, but they might be justified if they were *sold* for a valuable consideration which no other Power could give. If, therefore, the British government would give up all the South Sea Company's claims, then, in return, Spain might grant to British traders the favourable conditions of the later years of the seventeenth century. Keene duly reported this proposal to London, and in reply the Duke of Bedford,[1] Secretary of State for the Southern Department, intimated approval in principle, but stated that there

[1] The 4th Duke.

Sir Benjamin Keene, by Van Loo

Marchese Tanucci

was the objection that the British government could hardly surrender the legal rights of British subjects in a public treaty. Keene was therefore instructed to persuade the Spaniards to allow the matter to be passed over in silence, but to this Carvajal would by no means agree; if, he said, London would not give way publicly then let there be a secret article pledging the King of England not to support the Company's claims.

However, the Cabinet in London felt that this would be more discreditable than a public abandonment, so to avoid a deadlock Keene was told to press for the payment of some pecuniary compensation: he was to ask for £300,000 but might come down to £200,000. Carvajal at first proved most unwilling to discuss this proposal, not least, one suspects, because it would of necessity bring Ensenada into the negotiations, but in the end he made an offer of £100,000. This placed the British government in something of a quandary, for it was difficult to ask the South Sea Company to accept so inadequate a sum in order to confer advantages, not on themselves, but on British traders in general.

By this time Ensenada had begun to make his presence felt in the discussions, and he insisted that any exclusive concessions to Britain must only be for a period of five years. This time limit, coupled with complete insecurity as to the conditions which might be imposed at its close, was unhesitatingly rejected by the British Cabinet, but in the dispatch to Keene announcing this decision Bedford told him that if Ensenada's point was dropped Carvajal's figure of £100,000 by way of compensation would be accepted. By this time the negotiations had been in progress for the best part of eighteen months, but even now that everything appeared to be in order Keene was by no means assured of success. The King and Queen were about to visit Avila and then Aranjuez, and if the treaty was not signed before their departure there might be further delay and obstruction. Nevertheless on 5th October 1750 Carvajal appended his signature just before stepping into his coach to go to Avila. All pecuniary claims on both sides were to be abandoned, the *Asiento* clause in the Treaty of Utrecht was to be abrogated, trade with the Indies was to be equally open or equally closed to all traders, and British merchants were to have the same privileges as in the reign of the last Habsburg, paying no higher taxes anywhere than those paid by Spanish subjects in the same place.

Horace Walpole's reaction to this agreement is by no means uninteresting, for in a letter to Sir Horace Mann from Arlington Street, dated 18th October, he wrote:

> But come, I must tell you news, big news! The treaty of commerce with Spain is arrived *signed*. Nobody expected it would ever come, which I believe is the reason it is reckoned so good; for *autrement* one should not make the most favourable conjectures, as they don't tell us how good it is. In general, they say, the South Sea Company is to have £100,000 in lieu of their annual ship; which, if it is not over and above the £95,000 that was allowed to be due to them, it appears to me only as if there were some halfpence remaining when the bill was paid, and the King of Spain had given them to the Company to drink his health. What does look well for the treaty is that Stocks rise to high-water mark; and what to me is as clear is that the exploded *Don Benjamin* has repaired what the *patriot* Lord Sandwich had forgot, or not known, to do at Aix-la-Chapelle.

In his work Keene had received, and freely acknowledged, valuable assistance from the Portuguese ambassador in Madrid, whose influence over the Queen was considerable.

On the other hand the treaty was bitterly resented at Versailles, where it was rightly interpreted as a sign of growing Spanish independence in foreign policy, and where it was felt that the French ambassador had proved no match for Keene, since it was several weeks before he was aware that it had been concluded. In view of the chorus of approval at home, Keene not unnaturally hoped that his reward would be the red ribbon of the Bath which was the normal award of the successful diplomatist, but all that he obtained was permission to assume publicly the character of ambassador. As he was already in receipt of an ambassador's pay and allowances he regarded the mere recognition of his status as a very inadequate reward.

As it was clear that Keene was going on from triumph to triumph, his successes, taken in conjunction with the rapid revival of Spanish power and prosperity, thoroughly alarmed the French King and ministers, who determined to make a desperate effort to regain their lost ascendancy in Madrid, and with this end in view they sent a new ambassador there in the person of the Duc de Duras. Keene and Duras were always on the most courteous terms with one another, but for the next three years there was an obvious duel between them which was followed with close interest by politicians all over Europe, for a great deal depended on its outcome. Britain and France were already engaged in a very vital negotiation as to the boundaries of Nova Scotia and the right of British settlers in North America to expand into the hinterland behind the Alleghenies. If France could retain her hold upon Spain as during the latter part of the reign of Philip V, she was likely to be the more unyielding in the New World; but if Spain took an independent line then France might be forced to compromise because in the event of war she would be deprived of the assistance of the Spanish balance which was sufficiently strong to tip the scales.

At the outset the odds seemed in favour of Duras, for during his first winter in Spain the British ambassador was laid up with the earliest of his serious attacks of fever, and although he began to recover in February 1753, he was never fully restored to health. This gave the Frenchman a good start, and he made the most of it. His principal ally was Ensenada, who he hoped would serve as a check upon the Anglophile Carvajal by inflaming Anglo-Spanish differences in the Gulf of Mexico where nearly all the officials were creatures of Ensenada, and were extremely jealous of British intrusion. Nor was this all, for there was now a new Portuguese ambassador in Madrid who had much less influence than his predecessor over the Queen.

In spite of these disadvantages Keene was determined to maintain the ground which he had gained since he took over the embassy in Madrid, and it was very rare for him to have any doubts as to his ultimate success. In the first place he relied upon the honesty of Carvajal, though he deplored the Spanish statesman's occasional irresolution and his desire, natural as it was, to avoid any irreparable breach with his colleague, Ensenada. Then there was the Duque de Huescar, who subsequently succeeded as Duque de Alba. He had been ambassador to Louis XV, but he had acquired a dislike of the French which almost amounted to antipathy, and as Lord Chamberlain he was in a position to exercise considerable influence behind the scenes, particularly in the matter of the appointment of ministers. Outside Spain the British ambassador had a valuable ally in Richard Wall, who represented Ferdinand in London, and was in origin an Irish exile from County Limerick, though he was himself born in France.[1]

Don Ricardo Wall, as he later came to be known, had originally joined the Spanish navy, and he served with it in the operations of 1718. He then transferred to the army, and was in the force under the Conde de Montemar which had placed Charles on the throne of the Two Sicilies. Feeling that his merits were going unrecognized and unrewarded, he made an opportunity to come into contact with the commander-in-chief, who asked who he was. 'I am,' came the reply, 'next to Your Excellency, the most distinguished person in the army.' 'How so?' queried the astonished general, to be told, 'You are the head, and I am the tail of the serpent.' Montemar was attracted by Wall's Irish quickness and wit, and took him under his protection. From that moment Wall never looked back, and displayed his competence and initiative in a number of posts, both civil and military, in Europe and the Indies, until in due course he attained the Spanish embassy in London.

Such being the general situation Keene decided that the most effective method of turning the tables on Duras was to secure the dismissal of Ensenada, whom he had come to consider as 'a servile, piqued dependent upon France'. With this end in view he spent the year 1753 in collecting evidence which would fatally prejudice the minister in the eyes of Ferdinand. In the course of his investigations he made three discoveries which very materially served his purpose, given the character and outlook of the King of Spain. First of all it came to light that without authority from his master or consultation with his colleagues Ensenada was encouraging the colonial governors to undertake such hostile measures against British traders and settlers that the British government would be compelled to retaliate, with the possible result of a war which would force Spain into a close alliance with France. Secondly, he was discovered to be in secret correspondence with Elizabeth Farnese at La Granja, and to be encouraging Charles in Naples in opposition to the policy of his half-brother. Lastly, Ensenada was trying to work on the King and Queen through circles in Lisbon that were hostile to Britain. These were very strong cards indeed, and Keene's chief problem was to know when to play them, for he did not wish to lay himself open

[1] cf. *The Irish Sword*, vol. II, p. 88. Dublin. 1956.

to the charge of interfering in the domestic affairs of the country to which he was accredited.

The crisis in the struggle between Keene and Duras came in 1754, for Carvajal died suddenly on 8th March, and everything turned upon the choice of his successor. Ensenada and the French ambassador had their candidate ready in one Ordeñaña, and there was an almost breathless suspense while Ferdinand made up his mind. Keene's relief can well be imagined when it was announced that Wall had been summoned from London, and that Huescar had been instructed to take charge of the foreign ministry until his arrival. Wall soon proved to have none of his predecessor's scruples in respect of Ensenada, and he had no intention of tolerating a colleague who might thwart his policy. Accordingly Keene waited no longer but gave Wall all the evidence which he had collected against Ensenada, and this Wall placed before the King. The result exceeded the wildest hopes of the British ambassador, for what specially annoyed Ferdinand was a copy of some instructions which Ensenada had sent to the Indies ordering an attack upon what he described as 'enemy settlements' at the mouth of Belize, and the seizure of all ships carrying logwood. The King took strong exception to the word 'enemy', for, as has been shown, he prided himself on not having any enemies, and he struck at once. On the night of 20th July Ensenada was roused from his bed and escorted under guard to Granada, while Ordeñaña was sent to Valladolid. That same night Wall wrote to Keene:

The thing is done, my dear Keene, by the grace of God, the King, Queen, and my Brave Duke; and wen you wil read this scrape, the mogol will be five or six leagues of going to Gronad.
This newse will not displease our friends in Ingland.

Yours, Dear Keene,
forever
Dik.

The downfall of Ensenada was in some ways the most sensational episode in Keene's career, and both in England and France it was credited to him as a personal triumph. At long last the knighthood of the Bath was conferred upon him, and Ferdinand, at the express request of George II, undertook personally to perform the ceremony of investiture, thus expressing, as it were, his gratitude to a foreign ambassador for persuading him to dismiss one of his own servants. This investiture, it may be added, took place with all due formalities on the Spanish monarch's birthday, 23rd September 1754, and Keene described it with great gusto in a long dispatch to the Secretary of State for the Southern Department, by this time Sir Thomas Robinson.

The path of Anglo-Spanish relations is rarely smooth for long, and it was soon impressed upon Keene that even if all went well in the Old World this by no means implied that the same happy state of affairs would be reflected in the Americas, and the evil that Ensenada did there survived his fall from power. Communications were slow, and some time elapsed for counter-instructions to reach the colonies, while in the interval the Spanish governors acted upon those which they had received from their former chief. So in December 1754 we find Robinson writing to Keene that Spanish troops had expelled the log-cutters, that the huts at the mouth of the Belize had been demolished, and that some ships sailing to that coast had been seized on the ground that they were lawful prize. The British ambassador was accordingly instructed to demand reparations and restitution; and to insist that the *status quo* must be restored until the dispute about legality had been settled through diplomatic channels. These instructions put Keene in a quandary. He had always realized that the recent friendship between Spain and Britain was a tender plant which required the most careful cultivation, and that the least ruffle on the other side of the Atlantic might destroy it.

Such being the case he ruefully replied that the Spanish government might possibly grant reparation on the ground that the instructions sent by Ensenada were unauthorized, but that restitution, which would be tantamount to an admission that the British settlers had a right to be there, ran counter to the whole theory of a Spanish monopoly in the New World; and he doubted whether any minister, however well disposed towards Britain, would venture on such a defiance of national sentiment. Later news made matters worse, for it transpired that the Governor of Jamaica, as soon as he heard what was happening in Honduras, had sent troops to restore the settlers to their huts, and that he had supplied them with an armed guard to resist any further attempt to evict them. As this involved the construction of a fort,

Wall pointed out very cogently that it went a good deal further than a mere return to the *status quo*.

To make matters worse, Keene was at this time by no means in the best of health, and he had in actual fact already asked for recall on that score. He was thus confronted with a very ugly situation at an unfortunate moment, and Duras seemed to have a very good chance of regaining the ground which he had lost. The international horizon, too, was rapidly becoming overcast, and the Seven Years' War was looming ahead, so that the attitude of Spain was of vital importance both to France and Great Britain. In particular Anglo-French relations in North America were every day becoming more strained, for the success of Keene's diplomacy in Madrid had encouraged the British ministers to call what they considered to be French bluff. In consequence troops under Braddock were sent to aid the British colonists, while Boscawen was placed in command of a squadron to obstruct the passage of French reinforcements. As is usual in the early stages of any war the British plans all went wrong. Boscawen in June failed to stop the transports though he did manage to capture a couple of French ships, while in the following month Braddock was routed at Monongahela. These events placed some exceedingly strong cards in the French ambassador's hands. It is true that war was not immediately declared between Britain and France, but diplomatic relations were broken off, and Duras was instructed to contend that British aggression had created the *casus foederis* under Family Compact Treaties. Above all, the incompetence of Boscawen and Braddock went a long way to lower British prestige in Madrid.

So Keene was informed that his recall was out of the question, and that he was the only man who could restore the situation. Fortunately for him it was not long before Duras began to overplay his hand, and he demanded the fulfilment of what he termed treaty obligations so imperiously as to annoy Ferdinand, who was always ready to prove that Spain was not the satellite of France. In October 1755 he demanded from Louis XV the immediate recall of Duras, and he refrained from conferring upon the retiring ambassador the Order of the Golden Fleece, which had come to be regarded as the normal perquisite of the representative of the Most Christian King. Thus the final round in the three years' duel had ended in Keene's favour.

By now the Seven Years' War had broken out, and the international situation had been profoundly altered by the Diplomatic Revolution. As the consequences of these events were to be the primary concern of Charles as soon as he succeeded his half-brother in Madrid, they demand the notice of his biographer.

As we have seen, the Treaty of Aix-la-Chapelle was a mere truce: it had satisfied nobody, which is tantamount to saying that it had dissatisfied everybody. The French felt that they had been made the catspaws of the King of Prussia, while Maria Theresa nourished a grudge against the British for compelling her to make peace when her prospects appeared so encouraging. For a few years the Powers concerned were content to lick their wounds, but in every case with the determination to renew the conflict when opportunity occurred.

One thing at any rate was clear, and it was that Frederick had by no means abandoned his designs upon his neighbours' possessions in the effort to link up his own scattered dominions in one geographical and political whole. In 1752, believing himself to be on the point of death, he had drawn up a political testament for his successor. In this document he stressed the desirability of acquiring by conquest the Electorate of Saxony, Polish West Prussia, and Swedish Pomerania, but of these he attached the greatest importance to Saxony, both on account of its wealth and of its strategic position as a bulwark of defence for Brandenberg against attack from the south. The Prussian King proposed that the Elector of Saxony should be compensated with Bohemia, which would have the added advantage of further weakening the Habsburgs. The French knew of these designs, and, with a vivid recollection of what had happened in the War of the Austrian Succession, they saw no reason why they should again pull Prussian chestnuts out of the fire. In this attitude they were encouraged by Prince Kaunitz who, after representing Maria Theresa at Versailles for three years, had in 1753 returned to Vienna to become Chancellor.

The drift to war was accelerated by the progress of events in the New World, already described. The French government did not at once declare war in consequence of the activities of Braddock and Burgoyne, but it was clear that this action would not long be delayed, and the necessity of protecting Hanover compelled Great Britain to look for assistance on the mainland of Europe. Recourse was at first had to the old ally, Austria, and Maria Theresa was found to be quite willing to help in the defence of the electorate, but only on condition that the British subsidies should be on a sufficiently large scale to enable her to take up arms against Prussia. Now this was exactly what George II and his ministers did not want, for it would have exposed Hanover to attack by the Prussians as well as by the French, and so the Anglo-Austrian discussions came to nothing.

The next British approach was to Frederick, who proved much more amenable, and in January 1756 he signed the Treaty of Westminster, by which he guaranteed the neutrality of Hanover. Thus the French, who had for many years been united with him in a defensive alliance, found themselves prevented by their Prussian ally from attacking the German possessions of George II. In these circumstances it is not surprising that Frederick's action should have roused ill-feeling in France, and Kaunitz took full advantage of French resentment. Accordingly on 1st May 1756 was concluded the Treaty of Versailles between Austria and France. Such was the famous Diplomatic Revolution which put an end to a system of alliances which had lasted for two generations.

All this meant increased responsibilities and anxieties for Keene. Britain had now no representative in France, so it devolved upon him as the nearest ambassador to collect such information as he could about the progress of events north of the Pyrenees. Another pressing problem was the difficulty of communication with London, since it was no longer possible to send couriers through France. It is true that he could try to obtain permission for Spanish couriers to carry British dispatches, but they could only do so at the risk of the Madrid government being charged by France with conduct improper in a neutral. Austrian couriers could certainly carry letters to Brussels, and forward them to Ostend, but that was slow, and in any case Austria was not to be an ally of Britain much longer. Lisbon, indeed, had a weekly packet service with Falmouth, but that also was slow and liable to be delayed by bad weather, as happened after the great earthquake when weeks passed before direct news from Portugal reached England. The only other route was by land to Corunna and then by boat to Falmouth, but this was a fortnightly service. In the end Keene solved the problem by inducing the ministry in London to institute a weekly service to Corunna, and to send a king's messenger on every boat to carry dispatches to and from the Spanish capital.

These were not, however, the sum total of Keene's worries, for he was neither the first nor the last British ambassador in Madrid whose efforts to improve Anglo-Spanish relations found one of their major obstacles in the policy of the British government. It is true that war was not declared between Britain and France until 18th May 1756, but for some months previously the attitude of the British authorities had been provocative in the extreme, and in consequence there was considerable sympathy in Spain for the French. This was bad enough, but when war did come the British government proved quite unable to conduct it successfully, for one of the earlier incidents was the capture of Minorca by the troops of Louis XV. Coming on top of the reverses in America this fresh disaster considerably increased Keene's difficulties, for every sort of pressure began to be brought to bear on Ferdinand to enter the war on what appeared to be the winning, namely the French, side. Then there was the Diplomatic Revolution, and the alliance of Great Britain with Prussia, for the representatives of Austria and France were naturally not slow to point out to Catholic Spain the dangers inherent in a junction of the two leading Protestant Powers in Europe.

Furthermore, the outbreak of maritime war raised all sorts of awkward questions as to the rights of neutral traders, and Spain clung to the doctrine that 'free ships make free goods'. To this the British government replied that no neutral could carry on trade in time of war which was not licensed in time of peace, and that in consequence Spanish ships carrying goods between France and French colonies were lawful prize because in normal times France rigidly maintained the monopoly of her colonial trade. Britain could, of course, only enforce this rule by detaining the ship and examining its cargo, while Spain resented both the rule itself and still more the method of its enforcement. In effect, the right of search, as exercised by Spain, had already given rise to one Anglo-Spanish war, and it now seemed that the same right, as exercised by Britain, was likely to give rise to another.

On the other hand Keene had the invaluable asset that he was heard with equal respect alike in London and Madrid, so in spite of another serious illness in the autumn of 1756 he set to work to

repair the damage which had been done, secure, also, in the knowledge that Ferdinand would resist all pressure upon him to enter
the war so long as this was humanly possible. Fortunately, the
situation from the British point of view was so bad that even the
most jingoistic minister in Whitehall was forced to realize the
necessity of conciliating Spain, and Keene's pacific advice was
accepted. The bellicose governor of Jamaica was removed, and a
more moderate gentleman from Virginia was appointed in his
place, and when the Spanish government contended that a treaty
of 1667 conferred special privileges upon Spanish ships the
British ministers, after disputing such an interpretation of the
treaty, gave way. Keene duly reported that these concessions gave
great pleasure in Madrid, but what he really wanted was permission to retire on health grounds. This, however, was clearly out
of the question, and a pension on the Irish establishment was no
real solution.

The year 1757 opened badly for him, and it was well that owing
to ministerial changes at home his chief in Whitehall was now no
less a figure than the Elder Pitt, for Anglo-Spanish friendship was
to be subjected to some very severe strains. In the first place the
British Admiral Sir Edward Hawke, one day to become the
famous Lord Hawke, recaptured under the guns of a Spanish fort
a brigantine which had been taken by the French, and the Spaniards declared that in the course of the operation an armed force
had been landed on Spanish soil, an allegation which Hawke for
his part denied. Wall's fury knew no bounds, and he was in no
way mollified when he heard that on his return home Hawke had
been more than graciously received by George II. Keene was
summoned, and in a stormy interview Wall threatened to enter
the war on the side of France unless Spain was accorded satisfaction. Like all really great statesmen Pitt knew when to give way
as well as when to stand firm, so he authorized Keene to declare
that Hawke's action was disowned by the British government,
and to promise the surrender of the ship in question.

Hardly had this crisis subsided than an even more serious one
arose in which Spain was the aggressor, and British public opinion
became so inflamed that no ministry would have dared to give
way. The facts were that in January 1757 a British privateer, the
Anti-Gallican, captured a French ship, called the *Duc de Penthièvre*,
off Corunna, but owing to bad weather she was compelled to put

into Cadiz with her prize. There the two ships remained un-molested for a month, but during this interval the French pro-duced – or manufactured – evidence to the effect that the capture had taken place within Spanish territorial waters. In consequence instructions were sent to the Governor of Cadiz to seize both ships, which he accordingly did, with the result that the British colony in that city sent a strongly worded protest to Pitt. Keene was then instructed to demand the restitution of the confiscated vessels, but in spite of all his efforts a specially constituted court decreed not only that the *Duc de Penthièvre* should be handed over to France, but also that the *Anti-Gallican* should meet the same fate by way of compensation.

Although only sixty Keene was now a dying man, and all through the summer of 1757 he was extremely ill. A temporary recovery, however, enabled him to take up his work again in September, and the last negotiation he undertook was in conse-quence of a dispatch from Pitt dated 23rd August. The war was going badly for Britain on every front, and Pitt was prepared to make any sacrifice to obtain assistance, as have other British statesmen in similar circumstances in more recent times. Keene was therefore commissioned to offer, in return for a Spanish alliance and for Spanish assistance in the recovery of Minorca, the exchange of Gibraltar for the recovered island and the com-plete surrender of all British claims to Honduras. The ambassador had little hope that this offer would be accepted, though a few years earlier Spain might have been tempted by a similar overture, but nothing was likely to induce her to enter the vortex of an apparently sinking ship. British naval power was discredited; the army with which Cumberland had attempted to defend Hanover was driven from one position to another, and had finally been forced to capitulate at Klosterzeven; and Frederick, Britain's one ally, had been completely defeated at Kolin by the Austrians. Ferdinand was in any case wedded to a policy of neutrality as in the best interests of Spain, and he was extremely unlikely to depart from it in favour of Britain at the very moment when France was at the head of a coalition which included Austria and Russia, and when French arms were everywhere triumphant.

All the same, for the last time, Keene rallied his failing strength to carry out his instructions, and on 26th September 1757 he wrote the last and not the least masterly of his long series of able dispatches. The gist of it was that Wall would have nothing to do with any scheme that involved hostility to France, and that he would not even communicate the proposal to his master. The dispatch ended with a pathetic appeal to be relieved of a post which he was no longer physically capable of filling, and this time the request was granted. On 29th November Keene attached a very shaky signature to a grateful reply to Pitt in which he said that he would wait to take his leave of the Queen on her birthday, and that he would then travel to Lisbon where he hoped to find a man-of-war to take him home. It was not to be, for on 15th December he died. The next day there arrived a dispatch from Pitt with a jubilant postscript to say that the tide had turned, and that Frederick had won a great victory over the French at Rossbach, but the news meant nothing to the man who had died in his country's darkest hour.

It is never easy to assess the merits or success of a diplomatist, for his work is of necessity ephemeral, and he has a very imperfect control over the material with which he has to deal. In Keene's case the material was in many ways hard and difficult to manipulate, for the commercial, maritime, and colonial quarrels between Englishmen and Spaniards rendered harmonious relations between the two countries almost impossible. In his first mission to Spain he failed to establish such relations, and his efforts to do so only exposed him to a storm of unpopularity that might have ruined the career of a less able or more timid man; but during his second embassy his services were admitted on all hands to be both invaluable and indispensable. The success he achieved – and for a time he was startlingly successful – was due to the pacific policy of Ferdinand and to his own personality. Keene belonged to that small band of diplomatists who become a real force in the country to which they are accredited. His familiarity with the Spanish language and with Spanish manners and customs, his imposing presence, his even temper, and his frank sociability made him *persona gratissima* at court, and his memory was long cherished at Madrid. No other ambassador could have ventured to intrude into the realm of domestic affairs so boldly and so efficiently as Keene did on several occasions. As is always the case in Spain, much was conceded to him because he was *simpático*.

The career of Sir Benjamin Keene has been narrated at some length not only for its own interest but for the light which it throws upon the relations of Spain with Britain and France during the years immediately preceding the accession of Charles III. It also affords an insight into the way in which diplomatic affairs were handled at that time. Charles, however, on the death of his half-brother became not only King of Spain but also of the Indies, and at this point it may not be out of place to consider the inheritance to which he succeeded in the New World.

The struggles between the Spaniards and the English in the reign of Philip II do not concern the biographer of Charles III, but with the coming of the seventeenth century fresh factors, which do concern him, made their appearance. The first was the Dutch expansion in the East, and this naturally led to conflict with Spain, which owned the Philippines. The object of the Dutch was to cut the communications between Manila and Mexico, and to embroil the Spaniards with the Javanese, in the hope of eventually securing the Philippines for themselves. However, the power of the United Provinces began to decline before this purpose could be accomplished, but to Spain this brought no real relief, for the threat from the Dutch was succeeded by the far greater danger from the buccaneers in the West Indies.

Their origin may be dated from 1625, when a band of English and French adventurers founded a settlement on St. Christopher, from which they made raids into San Domingo. In 1630 they moved to Tortuga del Mar, which lay in the main route of trading vessels. Here they were joined by kindred spirits from all parts of Europe, and for many years they were a terror to Spanish vessels and to the Spanish settlements on the mainland. The buccaneers were greatly aided by the British capture of Jamaica in the days of the Commonwealth, for they obtained considerable, if unofficial, assistance from that island, and it was in the reign of Charles the Bewitched that they did the greatest damage.

Hitherto the buccaneers had operated separately, but about this time they found in Henry Morgan a leader who possessed the necessary ability to induce them to act together. One of his earlier exploits was the sack of Puerto Bello, but in 1671 he accomplished the feat which was to make him famous. He crossed to the mainland with a fleet of thirty-nine vessels, and after marching across the isthmus, he fought a pitched battle, and then sacked Panama in circumstances of the greatest barbarity. Morgan's later career was equally notable, for he was knighted by Charles II of England,

and appointed deputy-governor of Jamaica. The success of Morgan caused him to have many imitators, and for some years no town in Spanish America was safe from attack. In 1680 John Coxon captured Santa Maria, and took several vessels in the Bay of Panama, while three years later Van Horn sacked Vera Cruz, and Davis and Swann harried the Pacific coast at will.

This, however, was the high-water mark of the buccaneers' power, for the breach between Britain and France in Europe soon prevented any co-operation between their respective nationals even in the pursuit of piracy. The other Powers, too, gradually realized that the buccaneers were a public menace, and assisted to control, rather than to stimulate, their activities. Pirates, of course, there were on the Spanish Main until well into the nineteenth century, and the governors of Charles III had always to be on their guard against them, but they never again became so formidable as they had been in the days of the last Habsburg.

In spite of wars in Europe, and of the raids of the buccaneers, the work of exploration and civilization in America had been steadily pursued throughout the seventeenth century. Sánchez Vizcaíno, in the reign of Philip III, explored the coast of California in the hope of finding a suitable harbour for ships coming from the Philippines, and one result of his activities was the foundation of the city of Monterey. Fernández de Quiros about the same time discovered the New Hebrides, as well as the coasts of New Guinea and Australia, while in 1605–1609 the northern part of Florida was opened up, and in 1617–1618 the area of Cape Horn was explored. The remainder of the century witnessed the further development of the explorations. The Spaniards gradually worked their way north through California until they came in touch with the Russians in Alaska, and up the great rivers of South America, adding vast tracts of territory to the civilized world. Other nations, too, endeavoured to obtain a footing in this part of the New World but without success, save in Guiana and at the mouth of the Mississippi, where the French established the colony of Louisiana.

It was during the seventeenth century that the administration of Spanish America attained the form which, with some modifications, was to characterize it until its final overthrow in the reign of Ferdinand VII. The basic principle was that it should approximate as closely as possible to that existing in Spain itself, and this had been clearly laid down by Philip II. The kingdoms of Castille and Aragón on the one hand, and the Indies on the other, belonged to the same monarch, and so their laws and government were to be alike in so far as their natural differences would permit. These instructions were obeyed, but, unfortunately, by the time that America had been settled on any considerable scale the machinery of government in the Peninsula itself was breaking down under the strain of supplying the needs of a world-empire, and the natural consequence was a state of confusion that was transplanted to America, where, since everything was on an infinitely bigger scale than in Europe, the results were even more disastrous.

Spain was not a unitary state after the fashion of England and France: it was rather a collection of kingdoms and duchies whose only link was the fact that they belonged to the same monarch. These different units had their own laws and customs, and the memory of past strife was still fresh. Furthermore, the system of administration which had, on the whole, worked well enough in the Middle Ages and in the sixteenth century was collapsing, and it was not until the accession of the House of Bourbon that administrative reforms were undertaken.

The fact is that at the time when she was exercising the greatest influence over her American possessions, Spain was herself beginning to decline, and it was the seeds of her own decay that were in too many instances transplanted across the Atlantic. At the same time there is no justification for the charge that the Spanish government paid no attention to the Americas. The *Recopilación de las Leyes de las India* in nine books, published in 1680, is in itself a refutation of this accusation, and the earlier ordinances display an equal care for the affairs of the New World. In effect, the intentions of the home government were excellent, but the machinery for carrying them out was defective, and was quite unable to overcome the opposition of local vested interests. It is an arguable proposition that Spain was to lose America because she interfered too much, and in the wrong way, but on the evidence it is quite impossible to maintain that her chief sin was indifference.

During the rule of the House of Austria the Spanish possessions on the mainland had been practically divided between the Viceroyalties of New Spain (Mexico) and Peru, but with the advent of the eighteenth century several important changes took place.

First of all, two more Viceroyalties were created, namely New Granada and Buenos Aires. The former, which was finally established in 1739, consisted of part of Tierra Firma and the kingdoms of Santa Fé de Bogotá and Quito, while the latter, which was to be brought into existence by Charles III himself in 1776, was composed of the provinces of del Plata, Paraguay, Tucumán, and four Peruvian districts. In 1731 Venezuela had been separated from San Domingo, and created a Captaincy-General by the name of Caracas. Chile and Puerto Rico were granted the same status, which was also that of Louisiana with Florida. There were thus at one time four Viceroyalties (New Spain, Peru, New Granada, and Buenos Aires), and eight Captaincies-General (Guatemala, San Domingo, Cuba, Chile, Puerto Rico, Venezuela, Louisiana, and the Philippines). This creation of smaller governmental units ultimately provided a great impetus towards independence, for it became possible for those who lived in them to think and act together in a way that was quite out of the question in the enormous Viceroyalties of earlier times.

The Viceroy was at the head of the whole administration, and he was usually a nobleman whose possessions in the Peninsula were such as to constitute a guarantee that he would not attempt to establish an independent kingdom in the Americas. There had been few men of outstanding ability among the Viceroys sent out by the Habsburgs, but with the accession of the Bourbons there was a decided change for the better, and the viceregal office was held by administrators of the standing of Vertiz, Ceballos, Amat, Monso, Bucareli, Gálvez, Azanza, O'Higgins, and the Marquis de Croix.

The Viceroy lived in an almost royal magnificence, and was treated with almost royal honours. In New Spain, for example, the arrival of a new Viceroy at Vera Cruz and his slow progress to Mexico City were marked by the most lavish pageantry. The different towns along the route vied with one another in spending money on banquets and bull-fights, while Indian chieftains came to kiss the hand of their new ruler and to present him with wreaths of flowers, and Indian tribesmen in long cloaks and headcrests of feathers performed their traditional dances.

Beside, rather than beneath, the Viceroy was the *Audiencia*, which was composed of lawyers, and the members of which were known as *oidores*. This body had two separate functions, for it was at once the Viceroy's privy council and a court of law, from which an appeal lay to the Supreme Court of the Indies at Seville. When it met in the former capacity the Viceroy presided, and when in the latter its own president took the chair. The *Audiencia* had certain rights with regard to the Viceroy, which severely circumscribed his authority. When his term of office expired, it could inspect and pass his accounts, and at any time it could make a report upon his conduct to the authorities in Spain, while if he died in office it carried on the administration until the arrival of his successor. Furthermore, a decree of Charles I authorized the return to the Peninsula of any Spaniard who wished to inform the King personally of abuses in the colonial administration, though, as may be supposed, those who desired to take advantage of this permission were likely to find every possible obstacle placed in their path by the Viceroy and the *Audiencia*.

In effect, the administration of the Americas was based upon a system of checks and balances calculated not so much to produce good government in the colonies as to prevent any tendency to break away from Spain. On the other hand it must be admitted that the Spanish government was by no means unmindful of the interests of the native population, though the measures which it enacted on their behalf were liable to be honoured in the breach rather than in the observance on the other side of the Atlantic.

Beneath the Viceroys, the Captains-General – for all practical purposes the powers of the two were the same – and the *Audiencias* was an elaborate municipal system, for the Spaniard, like the Roman, colonized from and through the towns. The *cabildos*, or town councils, soon became self-electing, and at the end of their year of office the *regidores*, or councillors, nominated their successors. The *alcalde*, or *corregidor*, that is to say the mayor, could not hold office again for two years, while twelve months had to elapse before the re-election of a *regidor*. In actual fact, long before the end of the seventeenth century these offices were bought and sold, and the same corruption characterized the municipalities of the Americas as marked local government everywhere at this period.[1]

---

[1] In this connection it is not without interest to note that the Corporation of Oxford, which was heavily in debt, offered to secure the election of 1766 for the sitting members in return for a loan of £4,000 free of interest.

The *cabildos* enjoyed considerable judicial and administrative power. The *alcalde* presided over a court of first instance for both civil and criminal cases, and the *cabildo* could act as a court of appeal in civil cases where the amount in dispute did not exceed a certain sum, but the jurisdiction of both *alcalde* and *cabildo* was liable to be severely circumscribed by that of the judges appointed by the *Audiencia*. In administrative matters the municipalities were theoretically autonomous, but in fact they generally took into account the wishes of the higher authorities. When any unusually important decision affecting the municipality had to be taken a kind of town's meeting, known as a *cabildo abierto*, was summoned, and it was attended by the more influential citizens.

At one time it even appeared possible that this municipal system might afford a basis for self-government in some form, for as early as 1530 Charles I had laid down regulations for convening a congress of representatives from the various *cabildos*, and during the course of the sixteenth and seventeenth centuries there were about forty such meetings. The difficulties of transport and communication, combined with the jealousy which always existed between the Viceroy, or Captain-General, and the *Audiencia* on the one hand, and the *cabildos* on the other, effectively prevented any development of this tendency, which may thus be said to have been checked by that feeling of suspicion which pervaded every part of Spanish colonial administration.

The closing decades of the eighteenth century were to witness, in addition to the fresh grouping of the Americas for administrative purposes, the introduction of *intendentes* and *subdelegados*. Even before this there had existed *visitadores*, whose duty it was to inspect the public administration, and to call attention to abuses. The power of the *intendente*, however, was greater, for he possessed a jurisdiction in matters of police, justice, finance, and war, so that he could intervene in all those departments of government that had formerly been the preserve of the Viceroys, Captains-General, and *Audiencias*, and what he was to them the *subdelegados* were to the *corregidores*. The first legislation on this matter was to be enacted in 1782, and it attained its final form in 1803.

In effect, though this is to anticipate, the centralized administrative system of France, which Philip V had introduced into

Spain, was being transplanted by his son and grandson to the colonies at the very time when the Spanish Crown, upon which in the last resort everything was to depend to an even greater extent than in the past, was itself on the eve of eclipse. To this may be attributed much of what was to follow.

VII

THE SEVEN YEARS' WAR

By the will of Ferdinand VI his step-mother, Elizabeth Farnese, had been appointed Regent pending the arrival of the new King, and on 17th August 1759 she arrived in Madrid. She would appear to have had an enthusiastic reception from the *madrileños*, but from the beginning it was clear that her position was distinctly equivocal in view of the doubt concerning her relations with her son, and above all with her daughter-in-law, for they were both extremely temperamental ladies. At first all promised well, and Amalia wrote to say how much she hoped that her mother-in-law would live with the King and herself at the Buen Retiro, which prompted Lord Bristol,[1] who had succeeded Keene as British representative at Madrid, to write to Pitt on 8th October that 'sooner or later some great *éclat* will break out between the two queens, and then the mother will move out of the palace with a bad grace, a step which she might now take with a good and natural one, for it is scarcely possible for a royal family to be worse lodged than in the Buen Retiro'.

Charles had a perfect crossing from Naples, and he arrived at Barcelona on 17th October. From the beginning he made a good impression in the Catalan capital, which was enhanced when he restored many of the liberties and privileges of which it had been deprived by his father for its opposition to him in the closing stages of the War of the Spanish Succession. From Barcelona he proceeded to Zaragoza, where he spent a month, partly to take

---

[1] The 2nd Earl, British ambassador to Spain, 1758–1761. He was later, 1766–1767, Lord Lieutenant of Ireland. He resigned that office without having set foot in the country, but he nevertheless pocketed without scruple not merely the annual salary of £16,000, but also the allowance of £3,000 for the Lord Lieutenant's 'equipage'. Lord Bristol died in 1775 of 'palsy from repelled gout'.

stock of the general political situation and partly because his son, the future Charles IV, developed measles. In these circumstances it was the beginning of December before he reached Madrid, and met the mother he had not seen for so many years. Both he and the Queen showed Elizabeth all filial duty and respect, but it soon became clear that she was to have no share in politics. In the family circle Lord Bristol's prophecy was not long in becoming fulfilled, and Elizabeth again retired to San Ildefonso. From time to time there were rumours that she was about to play a leading part in affairs of state again, but nothing came of them, and at San Ildefonso she died on 20th July 1766.

Elizabeth Farnese was not alone in finding that the change of monarch was of no benefit to her personally, for Ensenada and Ordeñaña were equally disappointed. They had hoped for a return to office on the death of Ferdinand VI, but all they received was a pardon, and consequent permission to return to court. In fact Charles made very few changes, and he retained most of his brother's ministers, though he substituted Squillacci for Valparaiso as minister of finance. Losada was appointed esquire of the body, and the resignation of the Duke of Alba was accepted. These arrangements were not hurried, so it was not until July 1760 that the King made his public entry into Madrid, took the usual oaths, and received the homage of his subjects. Once more the incapacity of his eldest son was announced, and his second son, Charles, was acknowledged Prince of Asturias and heir to the Spanish throne.

This ceremony had hardly been completed when on 27th September the Queen died. Her health had deteriorated ever since her arrival in Spain, which in any case she contrasted unfavourably with Naples, and matters were not improved by a nasty fall from a horse. She was only thirty-six at the time of her death, and her husband was inconsolable. He never married again in spite of the pressure which was brought to bear on him in various quarters to do so, and he remained faithful to Maria Amalia for the rest of his life. No scandal ever attached itself to him, and his austerity became proverbial.

In due course Lord Bristol gave his views upon the new regime to Pitt under date of 31st August 1761.

In order to give you a thorough light into the Spanish system, I lay hold of this opportunity to acquaint you, not only with the characters of the personages who compose this court, but also with their connections or friendships: by this you will be able to judge of the situation of affairs.

I begin with the very responsible one of the Catholic King, who has good talents, a happy memory, and an uncommon command of himself on all occasions. His having been often deceived, renders him suspicious. He ever prefers carrying a point by gentle means, and has the patience to repeat exhortations, rather than exert his authority even in trifles. Yet, with the greatest air of gentleness, he keeps his ministers and attendants in the utmost awe.

As a branch of the House of Bourbon, the Catholic King has an affection for France; but as a Spaniard, and as a powerful prince upon a distinct throne he wishes not to have it thought that his kingdom, during his reign, is directed by French counsels, as it was in the time of Philip V. What he takes most to heart, is, to secure his son, the King of Naples, upon that throne where he has placed him. Every view, and each negotiation, to procure tranquillity to Spain, is with the prospect of being entirely at liberty to assist the young Sicilian monarch, in case any Power should attempt to disturb him in the quiet possession of his dominions.

The Queen Mother's capacity is not equal to what it was once reputed to be. Her Majesty, one may infer from many little artifices, has not yet discovered, what every other person is convinced of, that she neither has nor will obtain any influence in affairs. She notoriously slights the three principal persons here, General Wall, Marquis Squilaci, and the Duke of Losada; and I have myself been present when she has ridiculed some of them in a manner which was not to be expected from one in Her Majesty's station.

The Marquis Squilaci is not bright. He is fond of business, and never complains of having too much, notwithstanding the variety of departments that center on him. He would be averse to any war; and as the Royal coffers are far from being full, and the measures he has already taken to replenish them have occasioned a great clamour against him, he thinks he could never stand his ground if the exigency of the State drove him to invent new methods of raising additional taxes. I believe His Excellency is incapable of taking any bribes, but I would not be equally responsible for his wife, the marchioness's indifference with regard to presents. She is suspected to receive considerable remittances from France, but this being difficult to prove, I relate it as the general opinion. However, the Marquis d'Ossun's[1] behaviour gives ground to these suspicions.

[1] The French ambassador, who had followed the King from Naples to

The Duke of Losada has a moderate genius, but an incomparable character for worth and honesty. The strongest encomium of him is the King of Spain's having so invariably distinguished him for upwards of thirty years. For had there been anything amiss in this nobleman, the discernment of his Sovereign would have detected it, and that would have occasioned His Catholic Majesty's withdrawing his friendship from the confidant. The Duke does not interfere with the political affairs of Europe; and, therefore, my mentioning him here is chiefly because he bears so principal a part in the palace.

As several other persons have opportunities of talking to the King of Spain, who are from their offices immediately about the Royal person, and for that reason can now and then drop words or hints about affairs, without presuming to offer advice, I will continue to give the characters of some whose names perhaps have never reached England.

The Marquis of Montealegre, *mayor domo mayor*, is a thorough Spaniard, who concerns himself only in the discharge of his office, and who will ever be inclined to peace; yet, from bigotted principles, would choose to have a war with heretics, rather than with those of his own communion.

I have, upon a former occasion, sent word, that the Duke of Medina Celi was an illustrious cypher, whose great name procured him the post of Master of the Horse, in which employment he attends upon the Catholic King every day at his hunting. But this great nobleman's capacity does not reach far enough to govern the Royal stables, or even those which are dependent upon himself, with propriety. I believe, if he was asked where England lay on the map, he would be at a loss where to point at the spot; yet he is so good a courtier, that he would clamour for any war, the instant he thought his Sovereign was inclined for it.

Don Pedro Stuart, grandson of the late Marshal Berwick,[1] waits upon His Catholic Majesty as regularly, in the office of Master of the Horse, and officiates in the absence of the Duke of Medina Celi. He is a Lieutenant-General in the Marine, and reckoned the best sea officer in the Spanish service. He has great vivacity in his imagination,

Madrid by special request, since Charles disliked new faces even among the diplomatists accredited to him.

[1] The hereditary interest of this branch of the House of Stuart in naval matters had its origin with its founder, James II. Another member, Don Jacobo Stuart, was taken prisoner by Nelson, something of a Jacobite himself, in a sea-battle in 1796, cf. Oman, Carola: *Nelson*, p. 196. London. 1947.

with good parts, though uncultivated. He is very well looked upon by the King, and has been very explicit in his sentiments, how prejudicial a war with England, at all times, must be to Spain.

Prince Masserano, and the Duke of Bournonville and Baños, three captains of the Body Guards, have all frequent occasions of being in conversation with their Sovereign. The first, by descent an Italian, is most servilely attached to the French interest. The Duke of Bournonville, with excellent talents, but the most corrupted morals, is by birth a Fleming, and though he wishes well to France, there is no cause he would either adopt or relinquish to serve any private purpose. The Catholic King likes neither of them; but distinguishes the Duke of Baños, a Spaniard of the antient House of Ponce de Leon, who thinks of nothing but the business of his profession, and with a moderate capacity, has conduct enough to behave unexceptionally to all parties.

M. Ariaga, the Secretary of State for the Marine, is a quiet man; but too easily led by the Jesuits. He is convinced that the Spanish Navy neither is, nor can be, in a situation to cope with that of Great Britain. He would be against a war, and from principle as well as experience, is satisfied that Spain could not be a gainer by interrupting the present peace it enjoys.

I cannot omit Don Joseph Augustin de Llano, nephew of Don Sebastian de la Quadra, formerly Secretary of State for Foreign Affairs. He is the first secretary to Mr. Wall, and does almost the whole business in His Excellency's department; and to his opinion Mr. Wall pays the greatest deference. Although he is young, he has been for a great number of years in that office, and is as able a man as any in this country. I wish, for that reason, he was more inclined for England than I fear he is. As General Wall is not the most correct writer, M. de Llano pens all the dispatches and memorials of consequence: I have discovered that the celebrated peevish one from this court, delivered to me at the beginning of the present year, was of this gentleman's composition.

The Marquis de la Ensenada must not be forgot. He is vain and presumptuous, has some experience, but never had any application. The three First Secretaries of the different departments he once possessed did the whole business of those offices. They prepared notes for him, which were to be carried to the *despacho*; and he received his lessons from them, because he neither had the capacity requisite for business of such importance, nor would give himself the trouble necessary to examine into affairs. Yet this man flatters himself with the prospect of being employed. He has dedicated all his attention to the Duke of Losada, whom he has gained, and is very assiduous in the palace, where he makes his appearance both in the town and country seats.

His views are to succeed the Marquis Squilaci, some time or other, which the marquis knows, and from apprehension of his driving that point too fast, has grown shy of him. He has never been even upon speaking terms with General Wall; as the order for his arrest passed through that minister's hands. General Wall and the Duke of Losada are apparently well together; yet there is no connection between them, because of that nobleman's unaccountable partiality to M. de la Ensenada. The Duke of Losada and the Marquis Squilaci are upon the same terms, and for the same reason. Mr. Wall, Don Julian Ariaga, and the Marquis Squilaci, without being particularly united, sincerely wish each other to continue in their several employments, for none of them attempt to encroach upon what is out of his peculiar province. Of course, they go on with harmony, and are ready to serve each other upon all occasions. So that notwithstanding the Duke of Losada's favour towards the Marquis de la Ensenada, that strong triumvirate serves as a barrier to Ensenada's ambition, a passion that would guide him to devote himself either to the English or French interest, whichever would best answer his purpose to get into power; although he would, when he was rivetted, shew himself to be what he was before stigmatised with the character of, a pliant tool to any French ministry.

It is surprising that amidst the great number of foreign ministers at this court, there is not one, except the Marquis de Silva, who is not blindly attached to our enemies' interests. That worthy minister is cordially inclined to England; but M. Wassenaar, the Dutch embassador, and the Count de la Tour, who has the same character from the court of Turin, are, though not so avowedly as the ministers from Naples, Vienna, Poland, Sweden, Denmark, Venice, and Genoa, yet zealous partisans of France.

I have now to the best of my capacity related what I have long made it my study to examine into. You may draw the natural and just inferences from what I have laid down, and by being acquainted with the ground I have to tread upon, you will perceive the difficulties that are to be encountered with. I hope to meet with indulgence for my want of success in the execution of His Majesty's commands, as I can safely assert that my zeal for the King's service alone enables me to struggle with the variety of impediments I so frequently experience in the discharge of my duty.[1]

This dispatch has been quoted at length because it gives an inside

[1] Add. MS. 32, 927, ff. 285–287.

story of the balance of forces among Charles's advisers at the beginning of his reign. Admittedly Bristol was biased, but although an unattractive character he was shrewd and experienced, and his observations are worth attention.

A few months later he sent another dispatch to the Earl of Egremont, who had by then succeeded Pitt as Secretary of State for the Southern Department, dealing with the Spanish Armed Forces, which is also of interest. He was not very flattering in respect of either the navy or the army, but whether in adopting this attitude he was stating his real beliefs or merely saying what the British ministers wanted to hear is not easy to decide. He estimated the navy at 58 ships-of-the-line, 27 frigates, and 16 chebecques, but for various reasons he did not consider that more than 49 of the ships-of-the-line and 21 frigates were serviceable. The seamen theoretically amounted to 50,000 but the number to be depended upon were not more than 26,000. Such was Bristol's view: in actual fact the Spanish men-of-war were better found than the British, but no British ambassador could be expected to recognize the fact.

After many vicissitudes since it had originally been modernized by Gonsalvo de Córdoba at the beginning of the sixteenth century,[1] the Spanish army was now modelled on the French. The Household Troops were composed of two regiments of Foot Guards – Spanish and Walloon – each consisting of six battalions, and three troops of Horse Guards – Spanish, Italian, and Flemish – each troop consisting of three squadrons, amounting in all, horse and foot, to between nine and ten thousand men according to the ambassador's reckoning. Of cavalry and dragoons there were sixty-two squadrons with a total of eight thousand sabres. The infantry of the line consisted of eighty-eight battalions of Spanish and foreign infantry, and among them was the Irish Brigade whom we have already seen in action at Velletri.[2]

There had been Irish units in the Spanish service for many years, but the acceptance of the throne by the Duke of Anjou led to the arrival in the Peninsula of several of the old Jacobite regiments, and among the first of them was O'Mahoney's

[1] cf. Petrie, Sir Charles: *Don John of Austria*, pp. 72–74. London. 1967.
[2] *vide supra*, p. 52

Dragoons,[1] which, together with the Berwick Regiment in the French service, were present at the battle of Almansa in 1707. Three of the infantry regiments actually remained in existence until 1818, and distinguished themselves in the Peninsular War. Irlanda[2] was originally the Queen's Regiment of Foot in the Jacobite army, where it had seen service with James II in Ireland, and it was transferred from the French to the Spanish establishment in 1715, with seniority from 1698. Hibernia was of composite formation, and first took the field in 1710. Waterford, created in 1709, was disbanded in 1734, and its effectives were distributed among the other three Irish regiments, while Limerick passed into the Neapolitan service, and was dissolved at the end of the eighteenth century. In view of the widespread opinion that green is a peculiarly Irish colour, it is not without interest to note that the uniform of the Jacobite army was red, and in later days the facings of Ultonia and Irlanda were blue, while those of the other Irish regiments were green. In 1802 the uniform was changed to blue, as for all the foreign units in the Spanish service. The officers remained Irish or of Irish descent, to the very end, but from the middle of the eighteenth century onwards the rank-and-file were heavily diluted with men of other nationalities.

Bristol estimated that the total Spanish establishment on paper amounted to 109,600, but that as many units were not up to strength he would not put it any higher than 80,000 of all arms.

By this time Charles was on the verge of committing one of the few real mistakes of his career, namely the involvement of Spain in war with Great Britain: not that there was, as English historians are always inclined to assume, anything fundamentally evil in taking the opposite side to Great Britain in an international conflict, but rather that at this particular moment to clash with her was palpably to embrace the losing side. The Prussian victory at Rossbach, news of which had arrived too late to cheer Keene's last moments, had been the prelude to a long series of disasters suffered by France and her Austrian ally: she had been swept out of India and Canada; her West Indian possessions were being snatched from her one by one; in Germany, although the fortunes

---

[1] cf. MacSwiney of Mashonaglass, Marquis: *Notes on the Formation of the First Two Irish Regiments in the Service of Spain in the Eighteenth Century. Journal of the Royal Society of Antiquaries of Ireland*, Series Six, XVII. Dublin.

[2] In 1718 all Spanish regiments received local appellations.

of war fluctuated, on the whole they were distinctly unfavourable to the French, and Rossbach had been followed by Minden; while, unkindest cut of all, the island of Belle Ile, off the very coast of France itself, was captured by the British.

Why, in these unpropitious circumstances, so shrewd a statesman as Charles should have decided to come to the aid of Louis XV is one of the mysteries of history, more particularly since a policy of neutrality had paid Spain so well during the reign of Ferdinand VI. One possible reason is that the King had neither forgiven nor forgotten the way he had been treated by Commodore Martin. Then, again, there has to be taken into account the fact that family relationships meant much to the King, and he was always inclined to be sympathetic towards his French cousins: Choiseul was fully aware of this, and exploited it to the uttermost. Also, Charles may well have overrated the capabilities of his own subjects, and, fearful that the French defeat would prove too complete, imagined that Spanish intervention would restore the balance. That many of his immediate advisers were Francophile is proved by Bristol's dispatch to Pitt, quoted above, and the strongest influence in the opposite direction, namely that of the Queen, had been removed with her death. Whatever the reason, Charles had not been long upon the throne before he decided to take the plunge, a decision to which, needless to say, he was egged on by the Duc de Choiseul, the minister of Louis XV.

This is not to say that Spain was without definite grievances against Great Britain quite apart from the prejudices of her King. She complained that her ships had wrongfully been made prizes of war in a conflict in which she was neutral, that she was shut out of the Newfoundland fishery, and that fresh British settlements had been made in the Bay of Honduras.[1] As early as September 1760, the Conde de Fuentes, the Spanish ambassador in London, presented Pitt with a memorial on the Newfoundland fishery, in which it was stated that a copy had been communicated to the French government. This roused the wrath of Pitt who saw a threat in the reference to France, and who bluntly replied that the matter had nothing to do with her.[2] A month later Dutens, the secretary to the British embassy at Turin, told him that he did not believe that Charles would much longer remain a passive spec-

[1] cf. Calderón Quijano, J. A.: *Belice, 1663(?)–1821*, p. 179. Seville. 1944.
[2] cf. *Chatham Correspondence*, vol. II, p. 69n.

tator of the war.[1] By now Pitt's suspicions that France and Spain were working together were fully aroused, and he had the correspondence between Fuentes and the Spanish ambassador in Paris, the Marchese Grimaldi, regularly intercepted. From this he learnt that the two diplomatists were the protagonists of Franco-Spanish co-operation, for on 10th March 1761 Fuentes was found writing that 'if this is done, at the end of the year we shall have a peace to our liking and France's', while England will by 'force or fear' be compelled to do justice to Spain.

In this mistaken belief that Pitt could be frightened by the prospect of the two Bourbon Powers acting together the Comte de Bussy, whom Choiseul had sent to London to see if there was any hope of terminating hostilities, proceeded to present a memorandum to the effect that the British government should adjust its differences with Spain, for his master 'cannot disguise the danger he apprehends, and of which he must necessarily partake, if these objects which seem nearly to concern His Catholic Majesty shall be the occasion of a war'. Pitt told the Frenchman, again quite bluntly, that Spanish grievances in no way concerned him, and refused to accept the memorandum. At the same time Bristol was instructed to remonstrate with Wall on the subject of Bussy's action. He was to say that as regards the prizes there were courts whose business it was to decide such matters, that Britain would not allow Spain any share in the Newfoundland fishery, but she was willing to discuss Spanish grievances in respect of Honduras provided that they were not sent through France. Furthermore, the ambassador was to demand an explanation of the naval preparations which Spain was making. Bristol did what he was told, but his protests got him nowhere. Wall declared that the King concurred in Bussy's memorandum, and though he said that no offence was intended he maintained that Spain and France had every right to concern themselves with each other's affairs 'for mutual assistance'. In forwarding this information to Pitt the ambassador added that in his opinion a declaration of war by Spain could not long be postponed.

The autumn of 1761 was marked by a steady deterioration in Anglo-Spanish relations. Pitt, who had secret information that France and Spain were every day coming closer together, wished to recall Bristol, and declare war immediately, but to this not only

[1] cf. Dutens, Rev. L.: *Mémoires d'un Voyageur*, vol. I, pp. 178–179.

were his ministerial colleagues opposed but also the young George III. They felt that there was no *casus belli* against Spain, and one could not be founded on secret information. The result was a political crisis in Britain, and the resignation of Pitt on 5th October, which left the King and most of the Cabinet quite unmoved. During September and October the peace party in London was strengthened by the conciliatory attitude of Wall, who did not wish Britain to take any drastic action until the treasure-ships from America had arrived at Seville. By 2nd November they were safely home, and after that there was a perceptible change in Wall's approach, while at Christmas the Third Family Compact, to which Naples and Parma also adhered, was published.

It had actually been concluded, as Pitt had suspected, in the previous August, and after stipulating for the mutual aid to be afforded, the four Powers promised not to treat for peace 'save by mutual and common agreement and consent'. By a secret convention Spain undertook to declare war on 1st May 1762 if peace between Britain and France had not been concluded by that date, and Portugal was to be compelled, if necessary by force, to embrace the cause of the Bourbon Powers. Further, any 'Power which shall become the enemy of one or other of the two Crowns was declared the enemy of both'—a clause which was clearly aimed at Great Britain.

Not the least interesting aspect of the Third Family Compact was the commercial. In the first place, Spaniards and Neapolitans were no longer to be classed as aliens in France, while the French were to enjoy the same advantages in Spain and the Two Sicilies. Further arrangements included freedom of import and export for subjects of each crown in the dominions of the others; equal treatment in the matter of trade, taxes, and navigation; and a united attitude on the part of the representatives of the Bourbon Powers in their relations with foreign states. The growing importance of economic considerations is thus strongly emphasized in this otherwise largely dynastic agreement, and it may be observed that the prospect of freer trade between the Bourbon states – the creation of a 'Common Market' as a later generation would have described it – did little to recommend the Third Family Compact in British commercial circles.

Matters had now come to a head: on 2nd January 1762

Britain declared war on Spain, and one of the most disastrous years in Spanish history began. Then was seen the falsity of Choiseul's calculations, for France, with the unhappy connivance of Charles, merely involved her ally in her own downfall.

The Seven Years' War, in which Spain had now been plunged largely by the action of her monarch, had more claim to be regarded as global than the so-called First World War in the twentieth century, and there was as much fighting in the New World as in the Old. In one respect it ran true to type, in that Britain made a poor showing at the start, but gathered strength as the conflict progressed. This was particularly unfortunate for Spain, for by the time that she came into contact with the British the latter had got into their stride. It is true that Pitt himself was no longer in office, but the impetus which he had given to his fellow-countrymen's war-effort was still carrying them forward to the great detriment of the Bourbon Powers.

As soon as hostilities began Charles and his ministers applied pressure to Portugal to terminate her old alliance with Britain, close her ports to British shipping, and throw in her lot with France and Spain. The King of Portugal was the weak but well-meaning Joseph I, while his chief minister was the redoubtable Pombal. The Lisbon earthquake in 1755 had prevented the latter so far from carrying out the reforms upon which he had set his heart, and the country was ill-prepared to face any aggression. Its trade was mostly in British hands, and although it is true that Pombal by no means liked this state of affairs, he was equally not at all enamoured of the mixture of cajolery and threats which Madrid used to persuade him to put an end to it. Until very recent times Spanish statesmen have never been at their best in their dealings with the Portuguese, and those of Charles III, prior to the arrival in power of Floridablanca, were no exception. They clearly could not understand why their neighbours would not co-operate with them, and they forgot the centuries of hostility which separated the two nations. Charles was later to be more understanding, but not until Pombal had disappeared from the political scene.

The Spanish campaign against Portugal may be described briefly. The Spaniards invaded the country in two columns, of which the northern one overran Traz-os-Montes, and for a time threatened Oporto, while the southern one, south of the Douro, advanced as far as Almeida, and captured it. There their progress ceased, for their method of wooing had not recommended itself to the Portuguese, and Pombal was by no means averse to welcoming a British counterweight; so eight thousand British soldiers were landed at Lisbon under the command of the Graf von Lippe-Bückeburg, ably seconded by General Burgoyne, later of Saratoga fame, and the invaders were forced back to their own side of the frontier, where they still were when the war came to an end in the following year.

Spanish arms in the New World were no more fortunate. The original plan of campaign in that theatre had been for a joint attack on Jamaica by a combined Bourbon force, and a French squadron of seven sail actually broke blockade at Brest with that end in view late in 1761, but they arrived to find Martinique in British hands. This was a very serious reverse, for the island was the seat of French government in the West Indies, as well as being a place of the first commercial importance. Its fall was followed by that of Grenada, St. Lucia, and St. Vincent, with the result that Britain became mistress of all the Windward Islands. Thus within six months of entering the war Spain, far from being in a position to co-operate with France in an attack upon the British possessions in the Americas, found herself faced with a British offensive with which she would have to deal alone. It was also clear that the blow would fall soon, for the hurricane season was not far off, and such proved to be the case. It fell on Havana, the capital of Cuba, in the late spring. Pitt was no longer in office, and his successors were small and unimaginative men, but all they had to do was to take his plans out of a pigeon-hole, and this is what they proceeded to do. The force allocated for the purpose consisted of a fleet of 140 transports, and troops to the number of 14,000. In a masterly piece of seamanship Admiral Pocock felt his way with astonishing skill and audacity along the uncharted channel between the Bahamas and the northern shore of Cuba, which no man-of-war had previously navigated, and thus completely surprised Havana by his appearance. The next step should have been to storm the city, but this was far too adventurous a course for the British commander-in-chief, the 3rd Earl of Albemarle, who had been A.D.C. to the 'Butcher' Duke of Cumberland at Culloden, and had been jobbed into his present post by his erstwhile master. This worthy proceeded to open trenches in the classical manner, but in the wrong place, and under a July sun. The fort which came under immediate attack was The Moro, and the defence was conducted by Don Luis Velasco, who comported himself in a manner worthy of the greatest days of his nation. Albemarle gave him plenty of time to strengthen his position, but the total strength of the Spaniards in Havana only amounted to 4,600 regulars and 13,000 hastily raised militia.

The siege of The Moro lasted forty-five days, and at first, largely owing to the incompetence of Albemarle, it seemed as if the Spaniards must be victorious in spite of their inferiority in numbers. The British men-of-war were driven off with great loss, and the besieging batteries answered with a superior fire. An accidental conflagration destroyed one of the principal British works. Sickness and thirst made the most frightful ravages among troops unaccustomed to a tropical climate, and the besieged were already anticipating relief from the same causes as had frustrated the ill-fated enterprise against Cartagena in the previous war. It was not, however, to be, for superior numbers began to tell, and the arrival of fresh troops in the shape of 4,000 Americans from New York finally turned the scale. A practicable breach was effected, and duly stormed with heavy losses on both sides, while Velasco was killed in the fighting. Even so, another fourteen days elapsed before Havana itself surrendered.

The terms granted by the victors were not ungenerous. The survivors of the Spanish garrison, reduced to a mere 900, were to be returned to their own country; the established government and religion were to be maintained; and officials belonging to other parts of the Spanish dominions were to be conveyed home in a manner suitable to their rank. The British material gains were enormous, for after a struggle of little more than two months they had not only obtained possession of Havana and a district 180 miles west, but also of a booty amounting to three million pounds in public property, an immense quantity of naval and military stores, and the remainder of the Spanish fleet in Cuban waters consisting of nine ships-of-the-line and three frigates.

At the other end of the world the Spaniards experienced an equal disaster when in the following September the British captured the Philippines, though only after an equally spirited resistance. A force of 2,300 men under the command of a General

Draper sailed from Madras, appeared before Manila unheralded, and speedily occupied the suburbs of the city. Authority there was temporarily being exercised by the Archbishop, who soon proved himself to be a worthy representative of the Church Militant. He had a mere 800 regulars at his disposal, but he raised a force of *filipinos*, and with them he managed to hold out for twelve days. When he was forced to capitulate generous terms were given to him, too, for though a large amount of government property became the spoil of the victors, the owners of private property were allowed to ransom it on payment of four million *duros*. Half of this sum was accepted in bills on the Spanish Treasury in Madrid, which, not unnaturally in the circumstances, refused to honour them.

The only compensation for these disasters was the acquisition of the fortified post of Colonia del Sacramento, opposite to Buenos Aires across the estuary of the River Plate, which the Portuguese had established in 1678 when pushing south from Brazil. The capture of this place was extremely profitable, for with it the Spaniards became possessed of twenty-six British merchant ships, besides merchandise and military stores to the value of four million pounds. It also enabled them to ward off an enemy blow aimed at Buenos Aires itself, for after the fall of Havana and Manila a privateering expedition, half British and half Portuguese, consisting of three frigates, a 'snow',[1] and five transports carrying a thousand soldiers arrived, only however to find that Colonia, which was to have been their base, was already in Spanish hands. All the same they tried to recapture the place, but the British flagship caught fire, and blew up with great loss of life. Eighty Englishmen swam ashore naked from the burning wreck; were clothed by the Spaniards; treated 'more as sons than as captives'; and became merged in the population.[2] The rest of the expedition with much difficulty reached Rio de Janeiro.

After these disasters overseas Spain had some reason to fear a British assault upon her own coasts, but as so often in her history threats of this nature rallied her people round their ruler, and the Aragonese, with the dependent countries of Murcia, Granada,

[1] A square-rigged ship that differs from a brig in having a trysail mast close abaft the mainmast.

[2] cf. Kirkpatrick, F. A.: *A History of the Argentine Republic*, p. 35. Cambridge. 1931.

Valencia, and Catalonia, who were most seriously menaced, presented a common address to the King:

The nobility of your kingdoms attached to the Crown of Aragón supplicate Your Majesty to entrust to their zeal the defence of their coasts. It cannot be considered as too great a presumption to challenge the English power, which by public, injurious, and offensive writings has outraged the courageous inhabitants of Spain. If a long peace, or some short and feeble war, has prevented the Spanish nobles from displaying that valour, which is sufficiently known in the Old and New World, and sufficiently fatal to the English, who now insult us, the present contest has shown that their martial fire is not extinct, that they are still animated by the same sentiments. He is not a gentleman who has not acquired his title by illustrious deeds in defence of his country.

All burn with unfeigned ardour to seek this defence in martial glory. We therefore pray Your Majesty to accept the half of our forces to carry the war into hostile countries, instead of waiting for the enemy in our own; the other half will suffice to keep them far distant from our shores, should they have the temerity to approach us. We have little concern in regard to the quality of the posts which Your Majesty may assign us, less for the climate whither we may be sent, and none for pay. Those who seek only to establish an incontestable title to the rank of gentleman need no reward but an open field to display their valour and affection to their country. Your enemies, Sire, shall know that Spain is a vessel sustained by two anchors in the tempest; that is by its religion and by its customs. In imitation of the Romans, who once received peace from our ancestors, we exhort Your Majesty never to grant it but with victory in your hands.

Now, Sire, is the time to exalt, under your glorious auspices, the fame of the nation by humbling England, which madly aspires only to the ruin of all Europe. As she has nothing in view but commerce, that is a sordid gain, she reluctantly wages war against a warlike nation, which knows no baseness, and feels only affection for its King and country. Money may be wanting at London as at Carthage; but virtue, constancy, and strength will never fail among us more than in ancient Rome. Your enemies, Sire, will destroy themselves by the violent efforts which they must make to defend themselves against us.

There was to be no call for the implementation of these noble resolves since the war was coming to an end. There was nothing to encourage France and Spain to continue it; Austria and Prussia were far from satisfied with their respective allies; and only Great Britain was on the flood-tide of success. Peace was by no means desired by the British people, but George III and Bute realized that nothing was to be gained by a continuance of hostilities, and in any case George wished to concentrate not so much on defeating Louis XV and Charles III as on overthrowing the Whig oligarchy which had been all-powerful in British political circles ever since his great-grandfather had come over from Hanover. In these circumstances the real difficulty lay not so much in settling the terms of peace as between London, Madrid, and Paris, as in securing a majority for them in the House of Commons, and more than a little bribery took place before this was assured. In one day £25,000 was paid out of the Treasury, and it is said that even so small a sum as £200 was not refused.[1]

The preliminaries for peace were signed on 3rd November 1763, and the definitive treaty on 10th February of the succeeding year at Paris: five days later Austria and Prussia made peace at Hubertsburg. In spite of her reverses Spain came far better out of the final settlement than might have been expected – certainly better than she would have done had Pitt still been at the helm in London. Cuba and the Philippines were restored to her, but she had to cede Florida to Great Britain. She also gave up her claim to participate in the Newfoundland Fishery, she agreed that the dispute concerning prizes should be settled by the courts, and she acknowledged the British right to cut logwood in the Bay of Honduras. This last point was covered by Article 17 of the Treaty of Paris, but it was not long before its exact interpretation became a matter of dispute between Madrid and London.[2] Finally, France handed over Louisiana to Spain as compensation for the loss of Florida, and Portugal was restored to her pre-war frontiers.

---

[1] cf. Hunt, W.: *The Political History of England*, vol. X, p. 40. London. 1905.
[2] cf. Calderón Quijano, José Antonio: *Belice 1663(?)–1821*, pp. 183–192. Seville. 1944.

VIII

THE EXPULSION OF THE JESUITS

THE Treaty of Paris had not long been concluded before the Spanish political scene was changed by the resignation of Wall. The Family Compact and the resulting participation in the Seven Years' War were not to his liking. In spite of his Irish background he was not basically Anglophobe, and he had been happier when he was working with Keene in the previous reign. During the recent conflict he had loyally supported the policy of the new King, but now that it was over he felt that he had had enough, and that as he was already in his eightieth year he was entitled to end his days in peace. This, however, was easier said than done, for not only had Charles the highest opinion of his services, which he certainly did not wish to lose, but, as we have seen, he had a strong aversion to a fresh face among those around him. In these circumstances Wall had to resort to a subterfuge to secure his release. He began to complain of giddiness and bad sight, and to give colour to this pretence before he appeared in the King's presence he rubbed his eyes with an ointment which produced a temporary inflammation, while he never showed himself in public without a shade. In due course this subterfuge worked, and Charles reluctantly accepted the minister's resignation. Wall retired to his property near Granada, where he lived until 1778, universally respected by his adopted fellow-countrymen.

He was succeeded in the foreign department by a very different man with a very different point of view, namely the Marchese Grimaldi, who had recently been representing Spain at the court of France. As his name implies he came of a noble Genoese family, and was in fact originally destined for a clerical career. He went to Rome for that purpose, but for some reason he abandoned the idea, and was sent by the Republic of Saint George on a political mission to Madrid towards the end of the reign of

Philip V. In the Spanish capital, then the Mecca of the foreign
adventurer, he was a great success, being at once good-looking,
a brilliant conversationalist, and the possessor of a most insinuating
manner. Such being the case he had no great difficulty in trans-
ferring from the Genoese to the Spanish service, where from the
first he embraced the rôle of a pronounced Francophile, which
secured him the favourable notice of Ensenada. Grimaldi served
on various missions to Vienna, Hanover, The Hague, and
Stockholm, but it was not until after the death of Ferdinand that
the plum of the Spanish embassy in Paris fell into his lap. He
soon became *persona grata* to Choiseul, who may well have
recommended him to Charles as a successor to Wall.

The resumption of diplomatic relations with Great Britain
consequent on the conclusion of the Treaty of Paris had been
marked by the arrival in Madrid in December 1763 of a British
ambassador in the person of William Henry Nassau de Zuylestein,
4th Earl of Rochford.[1] He had already had considerable experience of diplomacy, so his views on the Spanish scene are not
without interest if somewhat prejudiced. They are contained in a
dispatch to the Earl of Halifax, Secretary of State for the Southern
Department, under date of 13th January 1764.

He strongly refuted the theory that Charles was weak, but was
of the opinion that he devoted too much time to sport, for if he
would pay more attention to affairs of state the ambassador was
convinced that he would 'manage them more wisely and better
than any of his present ministers'. Somewhat surprisingly Rochford went on to say that he did not believe that the King had
wanted war with Britain, but that his hand had been forced by
Choiseul. How far he later realized that he had been duped must
be a matter of opinion, but 'his suspicions have been strong
enough to awaken his attention, and some reflections upon them
often escape from him'. As illustrative of this the ambassador told
a story that when Charles was examining a new building in the
course of construction Grimaldi began to criticize the style of the
architecture, whereupon the King remarked to Losada, 'They

---

[1] His family had come over from Holland with William of Orange in
1688, and had done very well out of the events of that year. His personal
extravagance was considerable, and it was said that before his creditors
would allow him to leave Madrid he had to pawn his plate and jewels for
£6,000.

wish me to do everything in the French manner, but I am determined to do it in my own.' Summing up, the ambassador wrote, 'It is clear to me that His Catholic Majesty is not personally inclined to the French, and whoever is disposed to lead him that way must be very cautious', for Charles was 'extremely discerning'.

His general knowledge of the state of Europe, and the political interest of Spain, is good and just, and it would be impossible to put any gross imposition upon him; for his steadiness, I may even venture to say obstinacy, to the principles he has once laid down will deter his ministers from making any attempt contrary to those which their master has adopted. . . . He knows his country is greatly exhausted, and he will soon find out that they have no resources. His private expenses for the chace, buildings, making roads etc. drive Squilaci, the minister of the finances, to the greatest difficulties to find supplies. Great encouragement, therefore, is given to the introduction of foreign manufactures, as the duties upon them raise an immediate fund, whilst the greatest discouragement is given to the manufactures established here, which are daily going to decay, because there is no fund to employ or support them.

The King, his ministers, and the whole nation are sensible and conscious of their weakness, from the experience of the last war, as well as from their present situation. It is, therefore, very obvious that besides their professions to me, which are very strong, they will be obliged to abide by the terms and conditions of the last definitive treaty.

Of Grimaldi the ambassador was profoundly suspicious, and he described the minister as 'plausible'. When he succeeded Wall he was 'insolent beyond measure, particularly to the foreign ministers', but they subsequently 'reduced him to a proper size'. He had always been friendly with Rochford, who nevertheless did not trust him, for his views were definitely Francophile, and he carried on a private correspondence with Choiseul behind the back of d'Ossun. In Rochford's opinion Grimaldi was 'entirely unacquainted with commercial affairs', though he himself was convinced to the contrary. Among his party was the Conde de Aranda, a man of great ambition, whose immediate objective was the war ministry, then held by Squillacci in conjunction with that of finance. The earlier career of Squillacci in Naples has been traced on an earlier page. The British ambassador found him 'indefatigable in business and rather likes it'. He was generally unpopular in the country, but ignored the fact. He had the support of Losada, whose character and position Rochford summed up when he wrote, 'although the duke's genius is but moderate, he is a thorough honest man, is more esteemed by the King of Spain than any person here, and has had his master's confidence for a number of years past without the least variation'. Such was the team which controlled the destinies of Spain in the years following the conclusion of the Treaty of Paris.

The first step of Charles was a wise one, for it was to use the Family Compact, of which Spain had hitherto only experienced the disadvantages, to strengthen her international position by permanently repairing the breach with the Habsburgs which had, at intervals, existed since his father defeated them in the contest for the Spanish throne. The Diplomatic Revolution had made Austria the ally of France, and as Spain was also now closely associated with the latter Power, nothing would appear to have been easier than to communicate with Vienna through Paris, but in actual fact this soon proved not to be the case. A close Franco-Austrian understanding might be the policy of Choiseul, but it was not that of Louis XV. The French King was as distrustful of Vienna as he was of St. Petersburg and Berlin, and he subsequently resisted any extension of Austrian influence in Poland or Turkey. It can hardly be denied that in the long run Louis proved to be right, for the Austria of the later eighteenth century was far from being the 'satisfied' Power which she had been on the morrow of the Treaty of Utrecht when Louis XIV was considering a settlement with her. Under the growing influence of the King of the Romans, after 1765 the Emperor Joseph II, her foreign policy became distinctly adventurous, and had Choiseul had his way France might have been involved in schemes which accorded ill with her true interests. In the meantime, however, the opposition between the official diplomacy of the country and the secret agents of the King caused the greatest confusion in all the courts of Europe, notably in the Spanish owing to the close connection existing between Choiseul and Grimaldi.

The situation was further complicated by the desire of Vienna to be included in the Family Compact, which might have suited Choiseul but which was by no means to the liking of his master. Grimaldi's observations on this to Rochford were a masterpiece of disingenuity in view of the situation in which he and Charles were placed. 'Nothing could embarrass us', he said, 'so much as the court of Vienna's desire to accede to the Family Compact. For on one hand we wish, on many accounts, to be well with that court, who alone can support His Majesty's son and brother in Italy, but the Family Compact is an *affaire de cœur* and not an *affaire politique*. The moment any other Power that is not of the family accedes to it, it becomes a political affair, and may alarm Europe, which is the furthest from our thoughts, for I would have the peace last if possible these twenty years. You may depend upon it, neither the court of France, nor His Catholic Majesty, will admit the court of Vienna's accession to that Compact.'[1]

A series of marriages then took place between the Houses of Habsburg and Bourbon, of which the most important was that of Charles's daughter, the Infanta Maria Luisa, to the Archduke Leopold of Tuscany. Though few realized it at the time, the day of dynastic alliances was coming to an end, but Charles's policy in this respect may be said to have been successful, for in the following century the thrones of the Bourbon rulers in Naples and Parma were being upheld by Austrian bayonets.

It was, however, to be domestic, rather than foreign, affairs which were principally to occupy Charles's attention during the next few years. Peace, retrenchment, and reform were the bases of his policy, but although his subjects welcomed peace and were not averse to retrenchment – at any rate in theory, and so long as it did not affect them adversely as individuals – they had no use for reform, especially in Madrid where it was most needed. The capital was one of the most backward and filthy in Europe. The people even of the lower class still swaggered about armed to the teeth; and in defiance of pragmatics, the big slouch hats of the men were pulled over their eyes, and the corner of their long cloaks thrown over the lower part of the face until they looked, as Squillacci put it, more like conspirators than the subjects of an enlightened monarch.

The decline of Madrid may be said to date from the reign of Philip IV, when the value of money was steadily falling, and uncontrolled inflation, with its attendant calamities, was the order of the day. Contemporary statesmen were woefully ignorant of economics, and although Olivares was an abler man than he is

[1] Lord Rochford to the Earl of Halifax, 25th June 1764.

often depicted he did not possess the talents necessary to rescue his country from the slough into which she was sinking. Edicts against luxury were indeed issued, and the King set an example by a reduction in the expenses of his court; but all this was to no purpose, for prices were steadily rising, while the whole financial and economic system was antiquated. The cost of collecting the taxes was not infrequently in excess of the amount obtained, and every monopoly, of which there were many, had its own officials. Owing to the *alcabalas* or taxes on sales, tolls, inland customs dues, and *octrois* to which goods in transit were subject, it was quite out of the question for them to compete with those of foreign origin, except at first hand in the place where they were produced.

If the Spain of the last Habsburg was in a state of decadence the fact left her inhabitants profoundly indifferent. If the national finances were in disorder; if poverty was increasing with the rise in the cost of living; and if the population was declining, as so often happens after a period of great prosperity, it would not appear that the Spanish people were particularly unhappy in the reign of Philip IV. In Madrid, at any rate, leisure was general. As was still to be the case a century later, with sword and dagger at their sides, the members of the lower orders jostled those of the upper classes in the streets, and by their swagger maintained their pretension to be treated on the same footing as the aristocracy. It is true that there was no longer any industry worth the name, but one went very elegantly dressed in cloth and linen that came from Holland and Flanders. Most professions were in the hands of foreigners, and the few ships which plied between the Spanish ports were Dutch. There were already forty thousand French in the capital, which proves that there was still money to be made there, or they would not have come. As in Britain in not dissimilar circumstances three hundred years later, moralists might groan about the public depravity, the frivolity of all classes, and the increasing looseness of the women, but it made little difference for the pleasure-resorts were always full.

The situation certainly did not improve as the seventeenth century drew to its close, and in the surrounding villages people were often on the verge of starvation, with the result that the food supply of Madrid was seriously menaced. In fact so threatening did the situation become that in 1664 a military force was sent to compel the farmers to send their produce into the city. In 1680 there was so much destitution and suffering that the people rose and formed bands for the purpose of pillage. At all times beggars swarmed in the capital, and gangs of desperate robbers prowled in the surrounding country.

There was some improvement under Philip V and Ferdinand VI, but it was Charles who really tackled the problem of Madrid seriously. He was determined to make his capital a bright, clean European city of the modern type. Streets were to be paved and swept; pipes and gutters were to carry off the drainage; and the warning cry of '*Agua va*' was to be heard no more. Within twelve years he had achieved his aim, and Henry Swinburne, an intelligent traveller who visited the city in 1776, wrote, 'The appearance of Madrid is grand and lively; noble streets, good houses, and excellent pavement, as clean as it was once dirty.' The people of Madrid have, indeed, every reason to be grateful to Charles, for to his initiative they owe the fine Customs House, the Prado Gallery, the General Hospital, the Alcalá Gateway, the Observatory, the Botanical Gardens, and the Natural History Library. It was not, however, until after a notable struggle that the King had achieved his objective.

Charles had proved in Naples and was proving in Madrid that he was a cosmopolitan. He had ruled in Italy through Spaniards, and he saw no reason why he should not rule in Spain through Italians, but although nationality clearly meant very little to him it meant a great deal to his subjects. Squillacci was extremely unpopular, and when to the dislike of him was added a violent antagonism to his measures, the danger-point had been reached. In March 1766 a strict pragmatic was issued forbidding the wearing of cloaks beyond a certain length, and wide-brimmed hats, on pain of imprisonment, while public officers were posted with shears to clip any offending garments to the required dimensions. It is always dangerous to interfere with the habits of costume of the man in the street in this way, and in the present century the Greek dictator, General Pangalos, was generally considered to have exceeded even the limits of dictatorial power when he attempted to prescribe the length of women's skirts, and compelled the police to equip themselves with tape-measures to see that his commands were obeyed. Even the all-powerful administration of Sir Winston Churchill in the Second World War failed to persuade the male population of Great Britain to wear their trousers without a turn-up. On 23rd March, Palm Sunday, the storm broke, and from the beginning there was every evidence that, far from being spontaneous, it had been carefully organized. On that day some men ostentatiously paraded in the Plaza of Anton Martin in the proscribed garb. They were at once challenged and resisted arrest, whereupon an infuriated mob collected, and the police were overpowered. From that moment law and order were at a discount, and the crowds filled the streets shouting '*Viva el Rey*', '*Viva España*', and '*Muera Esquilache*'. The minister himself escaped, but his house was sacked.

From that moment events took a course which has been so distressingly familiar in Spain and elsewhere on many a subsequent occasion. Those who had raised the storm proved unable to stay it, and for the next two days slaughter and pillage reigned supreme. Unfortunately a picket of Walloon Guards fired on the rioters, and as the Walloons were foreigners too, that merely accentuated the fury of the mob. From that moment there was no controlling the crowd, and every Walloon who was found was murdered. The corpses were dragged through the streets, while their heads, crowned with broad-brimmed hats, were carried on the tops of poles. As usual on such occasions the demands of the rioters grew with their successes, and what had started as a protest against the sumptuary regulations of Squillacci soon developed into a demand that no one but a Spaniard should be in the government; that the Walloon Guards should be abolished; that the price of bread should be lowered; and that the King should personally promise compliance with these demands.

Charles was obviously taken by surprise by these events, and equally mystified by the behaviour of the rioters, for they injured no one except the unfortunate Walloons provided their hats were right, and in particular no attempt was made to interfere with the foreign ambassadors, the British representative being greeted with shouts of '*Viva Inglaterra*' and '*Abajo Francia*'. The King's first move was to send the Duques de Medina Celi and Arcos to address the mob, but this proved to have no effect, for nothing would satisfy it but the head of Squillacci. All this time the alarm in the palace was increasing, and courtiers were running hither and thither in a state of consternation. Finally Charles felt that he had no option but to give way, so he appeared on the balcony of the palace, and promised to dismiss Squillacci, appointing a Spaniard in his place; to repeal the offending sumptuary edict; to reduce the price of bread, oil, soap, and bacon; to suppress the monopoly for supplying the city with provisions; and to pardon the insurgents. The royal capitulation, for it was nothing less, was made in the most solemn manner, for a friar with an uplifted crucifix read the articles distinctly, and at the conclusion of each Charles signified his approval. That evening a general amnesty was proclaimed, and the crowds dispersed with acclamations of loyalty to the throne.

The King now took a step for which he has been censured by generations of historians, whose personal experience of facing angry mobs is possibly extremely limited[1] – that is to say that at midnight he went to Aranjuez with the whole of the royal family, yet it is surely impossible to resist the conclusion that to leave the capital was the best thing he could have done in the circumstances. Had Louis XVI taken the same line at the crisis of his fate the French Revolution might have assumed a very different form – that is to say even if it had ever taken place at all. At Aranjuez he was free from mob pleasure, and was able to act as he thought best, not under duress.

The *madrileños*, or their leaders, were not slow in realizing that with the departure of the King their potential hostage had escaped them, and that their position was in consequence considerably weakened. Accordingly the mob came, or was brought, out into the streets to demonstrate once more; the troops were disarmed, whether with their consent or not seems doubtful; the gates were shut; and no one was allowed out of the city. As the Walloons had either been massacred or had accompanied Charles to Aranjuez, and the Spanish troops were clearly unwilling to act against the insurgents, for forty-eight hours Madrid was in the hands of the populace. All the same no damage was done to life or property, and the only excesses perpetrated were on the mangled bodies of the murdered Walloons which were dragged through the streets, their eyes and tongues torn out, and finally burnt.

If the insurgents soon realized that the withdrawal of the King

---

[1] For instance, in defiance of all the evidence Mr. Christopher Hollis has referred to Charles as 'a man of little courage'. *A History of the Jesuits*, p. 148. London. 1968.

meant that their bargaining-power had diminished, Charles fully appreciated that his had increased, so when his rebellious subjects sent a coach-maker to Aranjuez with a message demanding an immediate return to Madrid, the King returned an exceedingly diplomatic answer which proved that he had studied statecraft in Italy to considerable purpose. His reply was addressed not to the leaders of the insurgents but to the Council of Castille,[1] and it began by saying that recent events had so affected his health that an immediate return to the capital was out of the question. At the same time he announced that Squillacci had been dismissed, and that Don Michael Musquiz had been appointed to the department of finance in his place. Charles further called on the people of Madrid to stop demonstrating, to deliver up the arms they had seized, and to return to their normal occupations: until these conditions had been fulfilled he would not again be seen in his capital. The message was received with tumultuous enthusiasm, and the *madrileños* hastened to comply with the royal conditions, though that there was still an undercurrent of discontent is attested by the appearance of a number of placards bearing the words *'Si entraran los Vallones, no reyneran los Borbones'*.[2]

Meanwhile Charles had been much occupied in ensuring that the fallen minister got out of the country with his life. Fortunately Squillacci had been absent from Madrid on business on the day that the insurrection broke out. He got as far as the Puerta de Alcalá before he realized what was afoot, and he then made a rapid circuit of the city, arriving safely at the palace, whence he went to Aranjuez with the King. His wife and daughter had equal good fortune, for they, too, had been in the country, but on their way back they met the Dutch ambassador, who sheltered them in his embassy until they were able to join Squillacci. On the morning of 25th March Charles sent them to the coast under the escort of a troop of light horse, and if they were molested on the way he gave the officers instructions to say that they were conducting a state prisoner. As it was they reached Cartagena in safety, and

---

[1] At this time it consisted of thirty magistrates who made and promulgated the laws, appointed to offices, supervised the administration, and exercised justice in the last resort. All petitions to the King had to pass through its hands, and its participation was necessary before any royal decree could be put into execution.

[2] 'If the Walloons enter, the Bourbons shall cease to reign.'

from there went to Italy. Squillacci never again set foot in Spain, but for a time he represented Charles in Venice, and he died in 1785.

There can be no doubt that these Squillacci riots made more impression upon the King than any other event in his life, and that for a variety of reasons. In the first place they had taken him completely by surprise, for he had been out of Spain so long that he had never envisaged the probable effect of his sumptuary legislation upon the ordinary Spaniard. Secondly, they had been directed against a minister in whom he had every confidence. These in themselves were sufficient grounds for annoyance, but what was most disturbing of all was the gnawing doubt whether they were spontaneous. Were the sumptuary regulations, or even the cost of living, the real reasons that brought the *madrileños* out into the streets, or merely the excuse? The rioters seemed to be acting to order, but who was giving them the orders? The calmness of so many of the high aristocracy at a time when they might reasonably have expected to be massacred was difficult to account for, and distinctly disquieting. As Charles was pondering over these considerations at Aranjuez news came in of repercussions in the provinces of the happenings in Madrid, particularly in Cuenca, Andalucia, Navarre, and Guipúzcoa, but especially in Zaragoza and Barcelona where there was bloodshed.

The first step was clearly to appoint a minister to restore normality, and for this purpose the King's choice fell on the Conde de Aranda, who had had considerable experience of public life as ambassador to Poland and as Minister for War, and who was now Captain-General of Valencia. A homely and affable man, but notable for vigour and decision of character, and highly popular, he was appointed President of the Council and Captain-General of New Castille, while at the same time to reinforce his authority a body of ten thousand picked troops was moved towards Madrid, to which city, however, the King himself displayed no desire to return: indeed, he was only dissuaded by Grimaldi from moving the capital to Seville.

During that autumn of 1766 the King continued to ponder over the cause of the riots. For some time he was inclined to suspect the French, but the Gallophobe attitude of the mob seemed to rule them out as the instigators of the trouble. The behaviour of the aristocracy and of some politicians no longer in office had

The Cutting of Cloaks and Hats, 1766

The Expulsion of the Jesuits from Spain, 1767

certainly been highly suspicious, so as a measure of precaution Ensenada was exiled from the capital, and took up his residence at Medina del Campo, where he died at an advanced age. Finally, Charles came to the conclusion that the real culprits were the Jesuits, who wished to replace him on the throne by his brother, Luis, and having made up his mind to act on this assumption Charles returned to the capital at the end of the year. His attitude towards religion and the Church while still in Italy has been discussed earlier, but his motives in ordering the expulsion of the Jesuits from his dominions were far from being personal, rather were they determined by the position and activities of the Order at the time.

In the eighteenth century the Jesuits were still very powerful, and, as in earlier days, their influence was largely to be attributed to the fact that they were still the confessors of princes and nobles, while the education of youth was to a very considerable extent in their hands. Their activities, both religious and commercial, still included the whole Catholic world, though their proselytizing zeal was no longer pursued with the energy of yore. They now adhered without deviation to the doctrine of ecclesiastical orthodoxy and subordination: whatever was in any manner opposed to these – whether it was positive unbelief, Jansenist tenets, or theories of reform – all were included by the Jesuits in one common sentence of condemnation and anathema.

The first attack on the Order came in the domain of opinion and literature, and in Spain the protagonist was Padre Jerónimo Feijoo who, in his *Teatro Crítico*, exposed all the fanaticism and narrowness of judgement of the masses, and of those who refused to follow the new and fashionable scientific currents. In these circumstances it is remarkable that the Jesuits made no effort to defend themselves against these attacks, and neither they, nor any of those who thought with them, produced one single original and effective book in their defence, while the works of their opponents were deluging the world and forming public opinion.[1] Such being the case it was not long before it became clear that they had lost the battle on the intellectual front, which was the more important to them since it was now transferred to the political field, where, unfortunately for the Order, the helm of state was largely held by reforming ministers such as Choiseul

[1] cf. Ranke, L.: *History of the Popes*, Book IX, ch. 3.

in France, Squillacci in Spain, Tanucci in Naples, and Pombal in Portugal.

At first the intention was not to abolish the Order, but to bring about what would today be termed its disestablishment and disendowment, nor was it anticipated that the attitude of the Holy See would present any very serious obstacle, for Benedict XIV was no friend to the Jesuits, whose conduct he had often condemned, particularly in respect of their missions. In 1741 he had even gone so far as to issue a Bull in which he disowned them as 'disobedient, contumacious, captious, and reprobate persons'. Pombal attacked them in the first instance on the score of their commercial activities, and in this he secured the support of the Pope. A visitation of the Order in Portugal with Papal backing produced a damning report, of which the minister was not slow to take advantage. In the meantime the Jesuits had been attacked in France on the same score, for the bankruptcy of a mercantile house in Martinique, in which a Père Lavallette, s.j., had been concerned, had involved a large number of business men in its fall. Now the Frenchman is peculiarly vulnerable where his pocket is concerned, and the affair created a stir which certainly did the Order no good. Charles was always liable to be affected by the progress of events in France, and it would be unreasonable to suppose that the repercussions of this affair formed an exception.

By this time, that is to say the summer of 1758, it was clear that nothing less than a drastic reform would suit the Catholic Powers, but there was reason to suppose that the Pope was thinking along the same lines, and in this way abolition might have been avoided. Unhappily, just at this critical moment Benedict XIV died, and his successor, Clement XIII, was a man of very different character and views. A contemporary wrote of him, '*La diffidenza che ha di se medesimo e la severchia umiliazione che lo deprimo lo fa differire ai sentimenti altrui che sono per lo più o sciocchi o interessati o maligni.*'[1] Ranke described Clement as 'pure in soul and upright of purpose; he prayed much and fervently; his highest ambition was to obtain the glory of canonization'.[2] In effect, he was a weak man, but like

---

[1] 'The distrust that he feels of himself, and the excess of humility by which he is depressed, makes him defer to the opinions of others, who are, for the most part, either incapable, interested, or ill-intentioned.' *Carattere di Clemente XIII e di varj altri personaggi di Roma*, MS. in British Museum, 8430.

[2] *History of the Popes*, Bk. IX, ch. 3.

so many weak men he was an obstinate one, and he was certainly not a man of the world, which the Chair of St. Peter required as its occupant in existing circumstances. Not unnaturally he held the conviction that all the claims of the Papacy were sacred and inviolable, and he lamented that any of them had ever been relinquished. What he failed to appreciate was that the times were not propitious for their assertion. Holding these views, it is not surprising that he should have regarded the Jesuits as the most faithful defenders of the Papacy and the Catholic faith. He approved of them as they were, and he saw no need for their reform.

In these opinions Clement was supported by his immediate circle, and above all by Cardinal Torregiani, who was Cardinal Secretary of State. Spiritual considerations would not appear to have made the same appeal to him as they undoubtedly did to the Pope himself, and he had the reputation of taking a personal interest in the farming of the Papal revenues, while power for its own sake in this world seemed to him more desirable than approval in the next. Reform of any sort thus ran counter to his interests, and when the Jesuits complained that they were everywhere misunderstood by the secular authorities Torregiani adopted their cause as his own.

If neither the Pope nor the Cardinal were men likely to favour a compromise, still less was the General of the Jesuits, Lorenzo Ricci. Louis XV had no desire to destroy the Order, but it was the age of the benevolent despotism, and the Jesuits must acknowledge the fact: so he appointed a commission which unanimously decided that the obedience which the General, resident in Rome, was empowered to demand by the statutes of the Order was incompatible with the laws of the kingdom, and with the general duties of a subject towards his sovereign. In the light of this report Louis proposed to Ricci that a Vicar should be appointed for France, that he should reside there, and be pledged to render obedience to its laws. It does not seem to have occurred to Ricci that the opponents of his Order were divided into moderates and extremists, and that his policy should be to play upon the differences between them by coming if at all possible to terms with the former; so the reply he made to the French monarch's proposal was that so essential a change in the constitution was not within the limits of his power. Application was then made to the Pope, and his answer was quite uncompromising: the constitution had been distinctly approved by the Council of Trent, and confirmed by so many solemn edicts of his predecessors that he could not venture to change it.[1] Every kind of modification was rejected, and Ricci summed up the attitude of Clement, Torregiani, and himself in the words, *'Sint ut sunt, aut non sint.'*

The fat was now well and truly in the fire. On 6th August 1762 the Parlement declared that the institution of the Jesuits was opposed to all authority, spiritual and temporal, ecclesiastical and civil, and was designed with a view, first, to render them independent of such authority by any means, secret or open, direct or indirect; and secondly even to favour their usurpation of the government. It therefore decreed that the Order should be excluded from the kingdom irrevocably and for ever. In this attitude it was widely supported by the Church in France.

Charles was too sensitive to the progress of events north of the Pyrenees not to be impressed by these happenings, but nearer home, in Portugal, he had cause to regard the Jesuits with considerable suspicion. Opinions differ with regard to Pombal. The late Arthur Hassall held that throughout his public career he 'showed remarkable courage, activity, and energy' and 'his period of office may be regarded as the golden age of Portuguese industry in every branch of commerce',[2] while more recently another Oxford historian has written of 'his reign of terror', has stated that he 'must almost certainly have been mad', and has declared that 'it must remain an indictment of the Portuguese nation that they tolerated him even for a period'.[3] Whichever of these opinions is correct there can be no doubt that Pombal was the spearhead of the campaign against the Jesuits in the middle of the eighteenth century, and he used an argument very likely to appeal to Charles and his fellow-monarchs, for he accused the Order of regicidal principles and practices. In September 1758 King Joseph of Portugal was attacked and wounded, and after an enquiry of three months all members of the families of Tavaro and Aviero were seized. It was then asserted that their papers proved the complicity of the Jesuits in a plot to assassinate the Portuguese monarch.

[1] cf. Wolf: *Geschichte der Jesuiten*, vol. III, p. 365.
[2] *The Balance of Power*, p. 292. London. 1908.
[3] Hollis, Christopher: *A History of the Jesuits*, pp. 139–140. London. 1968.

What truth there was in the charge it is impossible at this distance of time to say. In the sentence pronounced on 12th January 1759 the point principally insisted upon would have been certain 'legitimate suspicions' against 'the perverse regular clergy of the Society of Jesus'. Of these the most important were their ambitious purpose of making themselves masters of the reins of government; their arrogance previous to the criminal attempt upon the King combined with their despondency after its failure; and their intimate connection with the chief defendant, Mascarenhas, with whom they had formerly been at variance. A Father Costa was even reported to have declared that any man who should murder the King 'would not be guilty of even a venial sin'. The value of these statements, however, is diminished by the fact that the confessions on which they were based were obtained under torture, and the whole judicial investigation into Joseph's attempted murder was irregular in the extreme. Admittedly Charles was in Naples when these events took place, but it is only natural that the memory of them should have been in his mind when the Squillacci disturbances occurred. The Jesuits had undoubtedly been moving freely among the *madrileños* at that time, and their influence over the mob was clearly considerable, which in itself provided ample food for thought. In particular it would seem to be certain that the King's hostility towards them only dated from the riots.

There was another reason, peculiar to Spain, which accounted for Charles's suspicion of the Jesuits, and that was their increasing co-operation with the Inquisition against what may be termed the Enlightenment, of which the King was the patron. This co-operation was new, for the only Jesuit to become Inquisitor-General had been Everard Nithard in the reign of Charles II, who was in any event a German, and had accepted the office against the wishes of the Order. In the eighteenth century the Jesuits found new enemies and therefore new allies, among the latter being the Holy Office. Charles had certainly no liking for the Inquisition, but it seemed to him to be moribund. All the same he kept a close watch upon its activities, and in 1761 he exiled the Inquisitor-General, Quintano, from Madrid for having published in Spain without his approval a Papal Bull condemning the *Exposition de la Doctrine Chrétienne* of the anti-Jesuit French priest *Mésenguy*, while from this time it was laid down that the Inquisition was not to publish any Papal decrees without the King's permission. The close connection which had grown up between the Holy Office and the Jesuits was not likely to do either of them much good in Charles's eyes.

Ossun reported an interesting conversation which he had with the King at this time:

He swore that he had no personal feeling against the Jesuits, and until the most recent plot, had declined on several occasions to adopt counsels adverse to their own interests. He had in this way disregarded the warnings of faithful servants, who had told him how since 1759 these Religious had not ceased to revile his government, to defame his character, and even to question the sincerity of his religious faith; and had replied (to these faithful servants) that he believed them to be prejudiced and misinformed.

The insurrection of 1766, had, however, opened his eyes, for he was certain that the Jesuits had fomented it, and had proofs that it was so, since several members of the Society had been arrested while distributing money to groups (of rioters). They had been corrupting the *bourgeoisie* by calumnious insinuations against his government, and had only been waiting for a signal. The first opportunity had sufficed them, and they were content to concoct a pretext out of the most puerile trifles, the form of a hat here and a cloak there, the malversations of some superintendent, the knaveries of some *corregidor*. Their enterprise had failed because the tumult broke out on Palm Sunday.

It was on Holy Thursday during the Stations that he was to have been surprised and surrounded at the foot of the Cross. The rebels pretended no doubt that they were only resorting to violence that they might exact conditions. Continuing his narrative, the King protested twice over that his words were true, and cited the testimony of the most upright judges and incorruptible magistrates of his kingdom, and added that, if he had anything to reproach himself for, it was that he had been too lenient with this dangerous body. Then heaving a deep sigh, he said, 'I have learnt too much.'[1]

It has also been stated, though the evidence is not conclusive, that the King was influenced by a much more personal motive as the result of a trick which had been concocted by Aranda. According to this theory a letter purporting to be from Ricci to

[1] cf. Smith, Rev. Sydney F.: The Suppression of the Society of Jesus, *The Month*, Summer Numbers, 1902.

the Jesuit Rector of the Imperial College in Madrid was forged in which was the statement that Charles was not the son of Philip V but of an adulterous connection between Elizabeth Farnese and Alberoni. This missive was deliberately delivered to the Rector while he and his community were at their devotions, and he gave instructions for it to be placed, with some other documents which had arrived at the same time, on his desk. Shortly afterwards, and before he had had time to go through the waiting correspondence, the police arrived with a search warrant, found the incriminating paper, which in due course was laid before Charles, and as a result the scales were tipped against the Jesuits.[1]

Having made up his mind to act, the King lost no time in acting, and the only person he took into his complete confidence was Aranda. Between them they drew up the necessary instructions to the local authorities which were to be opened at a particular hour. It is often said that Madrid is the most difficult city in Europe in which to keep a political secret, but that was certainly not the case on the present occasion. At midnight on 31st March 1767 the six Jesuit colleges in Madrid were surrounded by troops and police, and entrance having been obtained the bells were secured so that they could not be rung to assemble a crowd, while a sentinel was placed at the door of each cell. These precautions having been taken, the rector was instructed to assemble the community in the refectory where the decree of expulsion was read to them. Each member was then permitted to take with him his breviary, linen, chocolate, snuff, and a few other personal possessions together with his money on specifying the amount in writing. After a brief interval to collect their goods and chattels the fathers were led in companies of ten to the place where carriages had been collected for their conveyance to the coast, each carriage being escorted by two dragoons. On arrival at the port of embarkation the unhappy men were bundled aboard transports, and taken to Civitá Vecchia. The same procedure was adopted in the provinces and in the Spanish possessions overseas, but nowhere was there any resistance.

For the deported Jesuits their arrival at Civitá Vecchia was not the end of their misfortunes. The Papal governor applied to Rome

[1] cf. Marr, C.: *Journal zur Kunstgeschichte und zur Allgemeinen Literatur*, vol. IX, p. 213. Nuremberg, 1775–1789; also, March, J. M.: *Beato José Pignatelli y Su Tiempo*, vol. I, pp. 105 et seq. Barcelona. 1935.

for instructions, but Clement replied that they were not to be allowed to land, on the pretext that if all the Catholic sovereigns of Europe should expel the members of the Society of Jesus into the States of the Church these would soon prove too small, and their resources too inadequate, to accommodate them. While the governor was communicating with Rome the Jesuits remained crowded like convicts on board the transports, and many of the older and more infirm died. Eventually they were allowed to land in Corsica, nominally a Genoese possession, but where Paoli was heading a rebellion. There they remained until they were permitted to settle in the States of the Church, and to receive the scanty pittance of the equivalent of a shilling a day allowed by the Spanish government.

The Spanish people, even in Madrid, knew nothing of what was happening until 2nd April. On that day the decree of expulsion was promulgated by the public crier at the gates of the palace, facing the principal balcony, and at the Puerto de Guadalajara, where merchants and tradesmen carried on their business, in the presence of court and municipal officials, and to the accompaniment of trumpets and kettledrums. This form of promulgation, which would appear alien to the customs of Western Europe, seems to have been a survival from Moorish times, for in the East public acts were wont to be proclaimed in this way. Whatever the immediate effect upon the average *madrileño* when the Spanish bishops were asked their opinion of the decree, forty-six out of the sixty of them approved of it, such was the alienation of the Jesuits from the great forces in Church and State.[1]

Charles has been much criticized for the expulsion of the Jesuits, but the most recent authority, Mr. Nicholas Henderson, takes a favourable view of his action. 'Charles's behaviour', he says, 'throughout was typical of him. Pious though he was, he had no doubt that the things of Caesar had to be rendered unto Caesar, if necessary by force, and certainly without regard to individual feelings.' He clearly convinced himself that in acting as he did he had done nothing that did not become a good Catholic, for to the Prior of the Escorial he defended his action with the words, 'I may often be wrong, but I can assure you, as if I was at the bar of Heaven, that I have never done anything unless I believed it was most fair and useful.' That was all very well, but it is impossible

[1] cf. Kamen, H.: *The Spanish Inquisition*, p. 253. London. 1965.

to resist the conclusion that the manner of the expulsion of the Jesuits is a blot – if the only one – on the King's escutcheon, and it was more worthy of the Second Republic than of a Catholic sovereign.[1]

Admittedly the part played by his younger brother, Luis, is not clear. This prince was originally in Holy Orders, and became Cardinal Archbishop of Toledo, but he resumed the lay habit, though both Ferdinand and Charles refused him permission to marry. His political importance lay in the fact that he had been born in Spain, whereas Charles's sons had been born in Naples, and Philip V had limited the succession to members of the royal family born in Spain. If Charles were illegitimate then the rightful King was Luis. Monarchs are not unnaturally always susceptible to dynastic considerations of this nature.

Charles wrote to the Pope on 31st March 1767:

The principal obligation of a King is to watch over the maintenance and tranquillity of his states, the honour of his crown, and the domestic peace of his subjects. To fulfil this duty, I am under the urgent necessity of expelling the Jesuits from my kingdoms, and transporting them to the ecclesiastical territories, that they may remain under the wise and immediate direction of His Holiness, the common father of the faithful. Not intending, however, to charge the apostolic chamber with their maintenance, I have taken proper measures for paying to each during life a pension more than sufficient for his support. I request Your Holiness not to regard this resolution otherwise than as an indispensable civil precaution, which I have not adopted till after mature examination and profound reflection. I hope, therefore, that Your Holiness and the Court of Rome will render me the justice which such a resolution deserves, and from which will result the greatest glory to God. I intreat your holy and apostolic benediction.

Clement was not in the least mollified, though it was not until 16th May that he replied. He began with a eulogy of the Jesuits, and then proceeded with a forecast of the grave dangers to the Catholic Faith which would be likely to ensue from their expulsion. Next came what may perhaps be described as an *argumentum ad hominem*.

[1] *History To-Day*, vol. XVIII, no. 10, p. 682.

We present not the prayers of your Royal spouse, who from the height of Heaven perhaps recalls to memory your affection for the company of Jesus; but the prayers of the spouse of Christ, the Holy Church, which cannot without tears behold the total ruin of so useful an institution. We add our own particular requests to those of the Roman Church. She rejoices in the attachment of Your Majesty, and of your glorious predecessors, to the see of St. Peter; she boasts of always having given to the person of Your Majesty and the Spanish monarchy the greatest proofs of peculiar love. We adjure Your Majesty then by the sweet name of Jesus, which is the glorious device of the sons of St. Ignatius; by the name of the Blessed Virgin, whose immaculate conception they have always defended; we adjure you by our old age to yield, and condescend to revoke or suspend the execution of your order.

Let the motives be reasonably discussed; give room to justice and truth to dissipate the cloud of prejudices and suspicions; listen to the counsels of the first born of Israel, the prelates and religious, in an affair which affects the State, the love of the Church, the salvation of souls, and your own conscience. We are convinced that Your Majesty will perceive the ruin of the whole body to be unjust, and not proportioned to the guilt, if there be any, of a few individuals. Convinced of Your Majesty's rare piety and known equity, we are full of confidence that you will hear our tender exhortation, embrace our pastoral and paternal advice, and comply with our prayers, no less reasonable than just. With hopes so well founded we give Your Majesty and your Royal Family our apostolic benediction.

Charles remained unshaken, and replied on 2nd June:

My heart is filled with grief and anguish at receiving the letter of Your Holiness in answer to the information announcing the expulsion of the Jesuits from my dominions. What son would not be melted when he saw a respected and beloved father overwhelmed with affliction, and bathed in tears? I love the person of Your Holiness, in whom I observe the most exemplary virtues ever united in the Vicar of Jesus Christ. Your Holiness may judge what share I take in your concern. The reasons and convictions which have led to this resolution, Most Holy Father, are too strong and indubitable to induce me to expel only a small number of the Jesuits from my dominions, instead of the whole body. This, again, I assure Your Holiness, because the truth of my explanation may redound to your consolation. I pray God that Your Holiness may be perfectly convinced of it. Moreover the divine goodness has permitted that in this affair I should keep in view the account which I am one day strictly to render of the government of my people, of whom I am not only obliged to defend the temporal property but the spiritual welfare.

Directed therefore by such a principle, and to such an end, I have taken exact precautions that no aid due to men devoted to the Church should be wanting for the expelled Jesuits, even in the most distant regions. Your Holiness may be tranquil on this subject, since it appears to be that which gives you the greatest cause of complaint; and deign to encourage me with your paternal affection and apostolic benediction.

This was not, however, by any means the end of the business. The Jesuits had already been expelled from France, but with more humanity than in Portugal and Spain, for those who wished to remain in the country were permitted to do so. Austria and Sardinia did not join in their expulsion, but the Bourbon princes of Italy followed the example of Paris and Madrid. Tanucci, who now ruled Naples in the name of the young King Ferdinand, pushed the Jesuits across the frontier with scant ceremony, and Ferdinand of Parma, who had recently succeeded Charles's brother, the Infante Don Felipe, acted in the same manner. Clement XIII, who would appear to have been badly informed about international affairs, thought that he could coerce so petty a princeling as the Duke of Parma, so all the thunders of the Church were launched against him, he was threatened with excommunication, and with a renewal of the Papal claim to suzerainty over his duchies. The result was what might have been expected by anyone better informed than Clement. The Bourbon rulers were at once up in arms to defend the weakest member of the family: France occupied Avignon while Neapolitan troops not only seized Pontecorvo and Benevento but also crossed the frontier into the States of the Church. On this the Pope took alarm and offered to negotiate, but found that the Bourbon Powers would now be content with nothing less than the complete suppression of the Society of Jesus, and that they intended to hold his property in pawn until he had met their requirements. At this stage in the controversy, on 2nd February 1769, Clement XIII died.

It was clear from the beginning that the ensuing Conclave would be marked by no inconsiderable acrimony. The Curia was divided between the Zelanti, who wished to maintain all the ancient privileges of the Holy See in their integrity, and the Regalisti, who realized that some concessions to the civil power were essential. In those days, and for well over a century afterwards, the Kings of France, Portugal, and Spain had a veto on the election of a Pope, and this was naturally an asset to the Regalisti since it could be used to frighten their opponents. The struggle in conclave lasted for some time, and it was not until the beginning of May that Cardinal Ganganelli emerged victorious, when he took the name of Clement XIV.

Mr. Christopher Hollis has recently described Clement as 'probably the worst but by no means the wickedest of all the Popes', and he has charged him with being 'possessed of an insufficient faith in God',[1] an opinion which was not that of contemporaries, at any rate outside the ranks of the Jesuits. It must be remembered that in his philosophical views he was a Platonist, and in religion he was a Franciscan, nor was he altogether free from Jansenist opinions. The Jesuits alleged that in the Conclave he had given a definite promise to suppress their Society, and that his election was the price of this pledge—a very serious charge which was tantamount to an accusation of simony, but it is much more likely, given his nature, that his moderation proceeded from his kindliness of heart.

The new Pope moved cautiously, though from the beginning he gave every evidence of a desire to effect a compromise. One of his first acts was to revoke the brief against the Duke of Parma, and another was to receive an ambassador from Portugal, a step which his predecessor had refused to take. Concerning the Jesuits, however, he said that he required time to examine the question, but that was just what the Bourbon Powers had no intention of giving him: Charles was especially clamorous for immediate action. In taking this line he was almost certainly influenced by a sudden realization of the fact that the expulsion of the Society had not solved his problems, and that only its suppression would serve his purpose, for a year after its members had been expelled an event took place which showed that in Madrid at any rate they were by no means forgotten. At the festival of Saint Charles the King, as was the custom, appeared to the citizens of the capital on the balcony of the palace, where he was greeted with

[1] *A History of the Jesuits*, p. 152. London. 1968.

an uproarious demand for the return of the Jesuits. Whether this demonstration was spontaneous or organized it is impossible to say, but Charles took the view that one of the instigators was the Cardinal Archbishop of Toledo, the Primate of Spain, who was in consequence banished.

Renewed pressure was now put on the unhappy Pope, who in consequence gave way, and on 21st July 1773 he abolished the Society of Jesus by a Bull in which he ascribed his consent to respect for the representations of the King of Spain, who had insisted on the measure as necessary to the tranquillity of Christendom and the peace of his own dominions.

Whether in adopting this policy Charles was really acting in the best interests of the Spanish monarchy is another matter. For centuries the throne had been invested with a religious sanction, and in consequence Church and State had become almost indistinguishable. Charles undoubtedly increased the power of the crown, but he placed the monarch in a position of dangerous, if splendid, isolation. The Cortes had become nothing but a name, the Inquisition was powerless, and the very foundations of the Church were undermined, so that when the storm came the monarchy had no outside support upon which it could rely.

IX

REFORM IN THE AMERICAS

If Charles's preoccupation in the years that immediately followed the Treaty of Paris had been the Squillacci riots and the expulsion of the Jesuits, his attention had also been required by the progress of events in the Americas, for beyond the odd cession or retrocession of territory the peace had settled nothing in the New World as between France and Spain on the one hand and Great Britain on the other. There were the same old rivalries to which were now added disputes over various clauses in the treaty, and there was a determination on the part both of Grimaldi and Choiseul to turn the tables on London at the earliest possible moment. Nor did it seem likely that this would be long postponed, for in 1765 the Stamp Act was passed by Parliament, and it speedily aroused violent hostility in the British colonies in North America. To this internal dissension was added the usual British haste to disarm after a victorious war, so that the Spanish and French ministers had every justification for believing that time was on their side.

All the same, Choiseul was disposed to accelerate matters, which he proposed to do in conjunction with Grimaldi. The method proposed was to burn the docks and naval arsenals at Plymouth and Portsmouth, which would constitute a telling blow at British maritime resources. Knowledge of what was intended seems first to have reached Whitehall in a 'most secret' dispatch from Rochford to Halifax, date 17th September 1764.

I have learnt that about three weeks since Grimaldi received a letter from Choiseul telling him that everything was ready; and in his answer, which was sent by the last Spanish messenger who went to London, Grimaldi, after approving the scheme, added the sooner it is put in execution the better.

The scheme is this: two French engineers were sent to England in June last; they went to Portsmouth and Plymouth; staid some time; and returned to France. They are since returned to England; and are now there. They reported to M. de Choiseul that they had gained by bribery the necessary people to assist them, some of whom are English. In short, that in the dark nights, between 1st and 15th November, the shipping and dockyards at Portsmouth and Plymouth would infallibly be destroyed, and that they had invented a new kind of fire for that purpose. I would not willingly give credit to so diabolical a desire, but I can see no reason to doubt my friend's intelligence. He heard Grimaldi relate the whole to his intimate and bosom friend, Masones, who was formerly ambassador at Paris; and has further told me that it has since been confirmed to him.

On 25th February of the following year the ambassador is found writing again:

An Englishman, whose name is Milton, was the first projector of this scheme, and upon its miscarrying, he is returned to France, and was three days at Prince Masserano's,[1] who, I am also informed, is sending, or has sent, away from Portsmouth some of the others who were engaged in it. But what gives most light into this business is the names of two persons, one at Portsmouth and the other at Plymouth, who have houses and live constantly there, and where I am assured may be found enough to convince anyone of what had been carrying on. Their names, as far as I can trust to French spelling, are Worley and Leynit. But my friend had not time or opportunity to learn which lived at Portsmouth and which at Plymouth, and wrote down their names only from hearing them pronounced.

There was apparently no suggestion or suspicion that either Charles or his cousin at Versailles had any knowledge of what was afoot, but the fact that such dangerous schemes were in the wind cannot but have influenced the attitude of the British government in its negotiations with their ministers over the complications which arose in one connection or another.

Not the least important concerned the archipelago which the Spaniards called Las Islas Malvinas, the French Les Isles Malouines, and the British the Falkland Islands. In 1764 the French navigator Bougainville established a French settlement there, and the Spanish government at once protested against this

[1] The Spanish ambassador in London.

encroachment on its American possessions, with the result that France recognized the justice of this claim, and ceded the settlement to Spain, whereupon a Spanish governor was appointed. Meanwhile the British had also encroached upon Spanish territory, for they had established a small naval post at Port Egmont in another part of the group. For four years the two settlements, Spanish and English, seem to have been ignorant of the other's presence, but in 1769 they came into contact when a British naval officer, Captain Hunt, warned off a Spanish schooner which he met on a cruise. On this the governor of the Spanish settlement protested, but only to be told by Hunt that he must depart since 'the islands belong to His Britannic Majesty'. The Spaniard returned the compliment, and also notified his superiors of what had happened. The immediate upshot was that the Captain-General of Buenos Aires, Francisco Bucareli, in obedience to orders from Madrid, proceeded to eject the British by force, though it must be admitted that they only put up a token resistance for the sake of form.

When the news of these events reached Europe an outbreak of hostilities appeared to be by no means unlikely, and there was a good deal of bellicose talk both in Madrid and London. In consequence of his private understanding with Choiseul it was assumed by Grimaldi that Spain could rely upon French aid in the event of war with Britain, but he was soon undeceived, for in December 1770 Louis XV, realizing the direction in which the minister's policy was leading the country, dismissed Choiseul, and announced the fact to Charles in a note written in his own hand which said, 'My minister would have war, but I will not'. Whether the Spanish monarch had previously appreciated how close to the edge of the precipice he was must be a matter of speculation, but from now onwards he was a fervent partizan of a peaceful accommodation, and when Mr. Harris[1] arrived at the Spanish court to negotiate this, the King greeted him with the words, 'I have always seen you with pleasure, but never with so much pleasure as at the present moment.'

In January 1771 a settlement was reached by which the Spanish government gave satisfaction by expressing displeasure at Bucareli's action, and by undertaking that 'things shall be restored . . . at Port Egmont precisely to the state in which they

[1] Subsequently the 1st Earl of Malmesbury.

Palace of La Granja

Palace of La Granja

were before June 10th 1770.' This, it may be added, was immediately done, and Port Egmont was formally handed over to a British naval party in September 1771. The Spanish declaration, however, stipulated that 'the engagement . . . to restore . . . the possession of the port and fort called Egmont cannot nor ought in any wise to affect the question of the prior right of sovereignty of the Malvine Islands, otherwise called Falkland Islands.'

As in the case of Gibraltar at a slightly later date there seem to have been divided counsels as to the importance of this bleak and windswept archipelago. Lord North, then Prime Minister, speaking 'unofficially' he was careful to explain, told the French chargé d'affaires in London in November 1770 that if satisfaction for Bucareli's affront were given, the British would evacuate the islands which they did not value. However this may be, in May 1774 the British withdrew their settlement, leaving a leaden plate bearing an inscription which claimed the islands for Great Britain. On the other hand the Spanish settlement of La Soledad was maintained, and Spanish governors of Las Islas Malvinas, subordinate to the government of Buenos Aires, were regularly appointed down to 1811, which would seem to argue that Spain maintained effective possession, while this was not the case with Great Britain.[1]

The affairs of the River Plate began at this time to play a larger part in the calculations of Madrid than ever before, and there reform was very definitely in the air. From 1767 a ship carrying mails and merchandise sailed from Corunna to Buenos Aires every three months, and later every two months. In 1776 trade with the other American dependencies of Spain was permitted, but not overland trade with Peru, since Colonia del Sacramento was once more in Portuguese hands. However, largely due to the aggressive policy of Pombal, in that same year hostilities with Portugal began again, and Pedro de Ceballos, who had taken Colonia thirteen years earlier, was sent with a force of nine thousand men and a large naval squadron to pursue hostilities with the maximum energy: he was also given a commission as Viceroy so long as the expedition should last. He took Colonia a second time, and having thus removed the main obstacle to in-

---

[1] cf. Kirkpatrick, F. A.: *A History of the Argentine Republic*, pp. 35-36. Cambridge. 1931; Ferrer del Rio, Antonio: *Historia del Reinado de Carlos III en España*, vol. III, pp. 59-95. Madrid. 1856.

ternal trade he decreed on his own authority freedom of trade with Peru. He also took this opportunity to urge upon Charles that the Viceroyalty should be permanent. His advice was taken, and in 1778 Buenos Aires, now the Viceregal capital of a vast territory, was opened to trade with all parts of Spain and the Spanish Empire.

In the meantime the war against Portugal had come to an end. In February 1777 Joseph I died, and one of the first acts of his daughter, Maria I, was to dismiss Pombal, who had been scheming to keep her from the throne by abrogating the decree which had established the female succession. She was the niece of Charles, who had assured her of his support in the event of Pombal's attempting to carry out his designs against her, and her gratitude to her uncle on this score, combined with the fall of the minister, favourably prepared the ground for peace between their respective countries.[1] On 1st October 1777, therefore, the Treaty of San Ildefonso was concluded between Spain and Portugal. By this Portugal ceded Colonia, and with it the navigation of the River Plate, also of the Rivers Paraguay and Parana as far as the conflux of the Peperiguazu with the Uruguay. The frontier between Brazil and Paraguay was delimited by the relinquishment by Spain of a portion of territory on the Laguna Grande and Mairin to which she had hitherto laid claim, while as compensation for Colonia the Spanish government ceded an immense territory on the Amazon.

The setting-up of a Viceregal Court marked a definite step in the history of the River Plate, and particularly in that of Buenos Aires itself, which soon became a centre of cultural and economic activity. With the free ingress of all ships flying the Spanish flag there were to be seen strings of Negro slaves disembarking to march far into the interior, with caravans of bullock-carts carrying European goods to Upper Peru or coming back with silver and *vicuña* wool for shipment to Spain. Notable, too, was the rapid growth of population through the movement of trade and the arrival of Europeans. All this resulted from release from economic dependence upon Peru.

At the same time the population was very mixed, yet notwithstanding the earlier restrictions upon trade, and in comparison

[1] British embarrassment in North America had also made it hopeless for Lisbon to look to London for help.

with their fellows in Lima and Mexico, the lack of most of the refinements of life, the people of the River Plate had from the beginning enjoyed a rude pastoral abundance, which, however, alternated with scarcity in time of drought, when the crops failed and the unfenced cattle wandered off into the Indian country in search of water and pasture. The garrison in Buenos Aires and the crews of the ships which put in there lost many deserters, who were attracted by the easy conditions existing up-country, and by a life of half-savage plenty with a minimum of work. Hunting wild cattle was in particular at once a business and a sport. Groups of horsemen, armed with a sharp-edged steel crescent fixed in a wooden shaft, galloped in among the wild herds, hamstringing the bulls, and sometimes, in spite of official prohibition, the cows too. When enough animals lay helpless, the riders feasted on freshly-killed beef roasted in the hide—what was called a *barbacoa*, and then proceeded to despatch and skin the rest of the prostrate animals. A few tongues would be cut out as a delicacy, and the carcasses were then left to the vultures and wild dogs.

Cattle played an important part in life. In 1719 the *cabildo* of Buenos Aires called for the loan of 1,600 horses for a great cattle-hunt in the Banda Oriental, and the response is illustrative of the wealth of the citizens in horse-flesh. One of them offered 1,000 horses, another 500, and a third 200, all ready in the Banda Oriental. The following year there were complaints that the Santafecinos had driven off 400,000 cattle, and killed many more. Then it is reported that vagabonds aided by Indians were selling cattle to the Portuguese in Colonia; that these outlaws lived without justice, obedience, or fear, and some served the Portuguese there; that Spaniards, with Indian wives, were living among the Indians; and that there were gangs of criminals and runaway husbands. In effect, both the *gaucho* and the *malo gaucho* of the nineteenth century already abounded in its predecessor.

Defence against the Indians was also a common concern, and every city was on its guard against this peril either singly or in concert with its neighbours. Relations with the Indians differed: in Buenos Aires the problem was to protect the outlying cattle-farms from their sudden raids, for they were experts both as horsemen and as cattle-thieves. The townships of the north-west and also the up-river cities of Santa Fé and Corrientes had as

neighbours numerous Indian tribes, some of whom were nominally allies, but most of them were inveterate enemies. In these
places the white colonists were *encomenderos*, that is to say, lords
of the Indian vassals, but these latter were diminishing in number,
largely owing to smallpox, measles, and drink. There was no particular reason why these *Indios encomendados* should be loyal to their
Spanish masters, nor were they, and they were generally ready to
welcome the incursions of their savage kinsmen from the forests.
As a result some towns were swept out of existence, and they
were all continually on the watch to maintain themselves, while
every able-bodied citizen was enrolled as a militiaman.

Hostilities were frequent. In 1627 a wanton affront to an Indian
chief provoked a revolt which resulted in a ten years' war in
Tucumán. In 1666 an attempt was made to gather the Indians
into *reducciones*, or reservations, and two hundred families of
Quilmes Indians were taken from Tucumán to Buenos Aires,
where they were settled in the village of Quilmes. There they
became what were called *mitayos*, or forced labourers, and worked
in the capital. This proved to be no solution of the Indian problem, and Santa Fé had to be moved to a safer site. Expeditions
against the enemy were from time to time organized by the
Buenos Aires government, but owing to the mobility of the
Indians these had little lasting effect. In the eighteenth century the
enemy became even more daring, for they raided the *estancias*
near the city for domesticated cattle, and in the course of these
incursions men were killed and women carried off. There were
faults on both sides, and the white men were liable to ignore
treaties, making little difference between friendly and hostile
Indians. An Englishman of the name of Falkner wrote an account,
which was published in Hereford in 1774, of the type of frontier
warfare which took place when he said, 'The Indians fell upon
the village of Lujan, killed many Spaniards, took some captives,
and drove away some thousands of cattle.' Next they attacked
'the district of Magdalen, four leagues from Buenos Aires . . . and
scoured and dispeopled in one day and a night the most populous
and plentiful country in those parts: the inhabitants of Buenos
Aires were in the most terrible consternation.'

The situation was not improved by the expulsion of the Jesuits,
and it is at least doubtful whether Charles had given any consideration to the effects of the measure in the Americas. From its

arrival in the New World in the reign of Philip II the Society of
Jesus had as its objects, both in the colleges in the cities and in its
missions in the wilds, the instruction and the civilization of the
Indians. Their reports to the crown had two results—namely the
Ordinances of Alfaro, and the foundation of the Jesuit missions
of La Guaira. In 1609 Alfaro, a magistrate of Charcas, was sent
to investigate the treatment of the Indians by the colonists, and
to make suggestions for any necessary reforms. These suggestions
were embodied in his Ordinances which aimed at checking the
excesses of the *encomenderos*, limiting and regulating forced labour,
and forbidding the removal of Indians from their homes. Naturally these reforms made no appeal to the colonists, who were
doing very well out of the existing abuses, and they declared that
Alfaro was putting dangerous ideas into the heads of the Indians,
so his proposed rules were null and void.

This failure, however, must not be allowed to obscure the fact
that although Spanish administration in the Americas was des-
potic, it was also idealistic. Though successive kings of Spain
were eager to extract revenue from their colonies, they intended
also to impress Spanish culture upon the New World, as well as
to protect and educate the native races. Their hope was that the
Indians might be exempted from all obligation to work for the
creoles, that they might eventually be incorporated into Spanish
civilization, and given the same rights and duties as their white
fellow-subjects. They were certainly conscious that free Indians
could be made to pay tribute, whereas enslaved Indians would
chiefly benefit their owners; but their piety was not only
hypocritical. Though they identified their religion with the greatness of their country and the power of the monarchy, and believed
that the enemies of God and Spain might justifiably be put to the
sword, they also believed that the conquest of America was
legitimate only if it proved beneficial to the races which had
been conquered. No imperialist government in history has shown
a more genuine concern for the welfare of a conquered
people.

In that same year, 1609, some Italian Jesuits undertook with
royal authority the pacification of the savage country on both
banks of the Upper Parana. This became an isolated Indian
reservation consisting of a number of villages each ruled by a
Jesuit priest with one or two assistants. It was closed to coloniza-

tion and to the entry of white men. In 1730 the Indian inhabitants numbered 141,000, but the figure varied as they were very susceptible to epidemics.

As may be supposed, there was much tension between the Jesuit missionaries and the colonists, and the latter heartily welcomed the expulsion of the Order. The motives for that measure have been considered on an earlier page, but among them were distorted accusations of independent aims in these missions. With the same needless violence and brutal suddenness as in Spain itself, the Jesuit fathers were taken both from their colleges and *estancias* in or near the cities, and from their missions in the wilds. Some attempts were then made to administer these latter either through civil magistrates or through other religious Orders, but the region soon became depopulated and sank back into barbarism. Ruins of solid and richly adorned churches, overgrown by forest, attest the tragic past of a region which has only been opened up again in our own time.

Pedro de Cebellos was Viceroy for only two years, and he was succeeded by Juan José de Vertiz y Salcedo, who, although he had been born in Mexico, had long served in the River Plate, first as a soldier, then as a Colonial Governor, and next as subordinate to Cebellos. One of his first acts was to tackle the Indian problem, which he did by establishing forts on the frontier, but also by conciliatory methods of approach which achieved some success; though none of this prevented him from becoming involved in the great Indian revolt of 1780–1783, as will be shown in due course. For the rest Vertiz proved himself a worthy disciple of his royal master. He strove to make his capital more worthy of its new dignity by cleansing, lighting, and partly paving the main streets. He founded the College of San Carlos for higher education, and this was the germ of the later university. He introduced a printing-press which had lain idle at Córdoba since the expulsion of its Jesuit owners, and he opened a theatre in spite of episcopal and other clerical protests. He also set up a medical school, a hospital, an orphanage, and a foundling asylum. In a different field Vertiz did much for the exploration of Patagonia, though some of the settlements made in the bleak south were later abandoned, though Paragones, at the mouth of the Rio Negro, endured.

In the Spanish dominions in North America the reforming

zeal of the King was as prominent as on the River Plate, and the Viceroyalty of New Spain was no exception. Early in his reign Charles sent José de Gálvez to Mexico as a *visitador*, and his prolonged and searching investigation uncovered abuses which had grown up during the two preceding centuries. Gálvez was a remarkable man, and but for his premature death he might have gone down to history as the equal of Aranda, Campomanes, and Floridablanca. He was born in the province of Malaga, and his family was gentle, if obscure, but little seems to be known of his earlier years, and the greater part of his life was spent in America. He subsequently became Minister for the Indies, and thus gained power to enforce the reforms which he had found advisable. The system of *corregidores* and *alcaldes mayores* was swept away, and they were replaced by twelve *intendentes* who were more carefully chosen, as well as being more honest and efficient. The Indians were, in consequence, freed from much illegal oppression. In economic matters the trade regulations were relaxed in the same way as in the River Plate: Mexico was allowed to trade with all Spanish ports, tariffs were almost abolished, and the annual fleets were abandoned. The monopoly of the wealthy *gachupines*,[1] who bought up the goods brought by the fleets, was broken, and the smaller merchants were enabled to trade with Spain. Gálvez died in 1787, having been made Marqués de Sonora, and the King paid a special tribute to him when he spoke of the 'understanding, experience, and zeal of the present Minister of the Indies, with whom I am extremely satisfied'.[2] The result was a rapid increase in Mexico's foreign trade and in the royal revenues, as well as an improvement in the whole economic position of the country. Science and the arts were encouraged, and new institutions, notably the School of Mines and the Academy of San Carlos, established. Furthermore, the quality of the Viceroys improved, and the best of Charles's appointments were equal to the great administrators of the sixteenth century. Such were Antonio de Bucareli, whose period of office from 1771 to 1779 was long remembered as one of unexampled peace and prosperity, and the Conde de Revilla Gigedo, who was appointed after Charles's

---

[1] i.e. a wearer of spurs, but according to another interpretation the word meant a greenhorn or tenderfoot.

[2] cf. Casado, Vicente Rodriguez: *La Politica y Los Politicos en el Reinado de Carlos III*, pp. 247–249. Madrid. 1962.

death but while his ministers were still in power, was a man whose zeal for justice and for public improvements was unsurpassed by any official ever sent by a European Power to the New World.

Some idea of life in New Spain at that time is afforded by the experiences there of the Ultonia Regiment which was in Mexico from 1768 to 1771. It arrived at Vera Cruz on 18th June of the former year, and the voyage from Cadiz had taken eighty days. Nine companies made up the battalion; one a grenadier company of sixty-one officers and men, the others being all line companies, one of sixty-two officers and men, one of sixty-three, and two more of sixty-four each. The total strength, including the staff, was thus five hundred and eighty-five officers and men, but the names suggest that by that time only a small percentage of the rank and file was of Irish birth or lineage, and that the regiment was fundamentally Irish only in its name, its traditions, and the persons of most of its officers.[1]

Ultonia soon completed the two-hundred-mile march to Mexico City, where it relieved the Regimiento de America, which returned to Spain. The state of affairs which it found there may be gathered from the instructions which the Viceroy de Croix left in 1771 for his successor Bucareli. 'The populace, composed of diverse races, is vicious, drunken, debauched, thieving; it carries knives called *belduques* and likes to use them; it is hostile to our troops and is given to outbreaks. At the time of my arrival corpses were found in the streets every morning; in a single month twenty-nine of them were removed. I sent out patrols night and day. On one occasion these patrols were greeted with a hail of stones. The soldiers fired upon the rioters, killed two of them and arrested five, who were led through the streets with stones around their necks, and sentenced to five years of imprisonment and two hundred lashes. That treatment greatly pacified such rioters.'[2]

On the other hand, if the relations between the soldiers and the civil population often left a great deal to be desired, so did those between the soldiers themselves. We hear, for example, of a complaint by the Armourer of the Regimiento de Saboya against the Armourers of Ultonia and Flandes over the alleged illegal occu-

[1] W. S. Murphy in *The Irish Sword*, vol. II, p. 258. Dublin. 1956.
[2] *Correspondence du Marquis de Croix, Vice-Roi du Mexique*, p. 262. Nantes. 1891.

pancy by the two latter of a house in Mexico City. Then there was a dispute involving an ensign of the name of Fitzgerald concerning a woman variously described as a washerwoman, a woman of vicious habits leading an irregular life, or simply a young prostitute, for which Fitzgerald ended up in prison. Deserters, too, could be a nuisance, and in April 1771 one from Ultonia named Pedro Dubison was charged with having robbed two civilians of money and clothing. Dubison pleaded guilty to the theft of clothing but denied taking the money. These incidents go a long way to support the theory that the morale and discipline of all the Spanish regiments quickly deteriorated when they were stationed in Mexico, and Ultonia would not appear to have been an exception.

On the other hand not all Charles's reforms were wise, or appreciated by the Mexicans, and the expulsion of the Jesuits proved as grave a mistake in North America as it had on the River Plate. The utmost pressure was put by Madrid on the local authorities, and it is even said that the Viceroy was threatened with death if he allowed a single Jesuit to remain in the country.[1] So before dawn on 2nd June 1767 royal officials entered the Jesuit convents, seized the six hundred and seventy-eight members of the Order, and sent them to Vera Cruz. When the news of what had happened became known, large crowds gathered to watch the departing carriages, and the troops were forced to use the butt-ends of their muskets to make a passage for them. Indeed so unpopular was the operation that there were risings in several towns, for which some ninety people were executed. The Jesuits had controlled one hundred and three Indian missions and twenty-three colleges in the Viceroyalty of New Spain, and their activities as educationalists soon proved to be irreplaceable.

The reign of Charles III was also a period of territorial expansion, caused as much by external dangers as by internal need. In order to meet a possible threat from the French in Louisiana, the friars had as early as 1716 moved into Texas, and built missions with a view to establishing Spanish influence over the Indians there. On the Pacific coast José de Gálvez, to guard against Russian encroachments from Alaska, organized the most ambitious Spanish colonial enterprise since the sixteenth century. A

[1] Parkes, H. B.: *A History of Mexico*, p. 116. London. 1962.

body of friars, led by Junipero Serra, penetrated into Upper California, and in 1776 Anza led a party of colonists on a thousand-and-mile trek from Sonora, through the deserts of Arizona and the territories of the savage Apaches, to the Bay of San Francisco. When Charles died, the Spanish dominions in the New World had reached their widest bounds. Eastward the scattered settlements stretched to Puerto Rico, westward to the present State of California, northward to what is now the State of Missouri, and southward to Chile. In the West Indies, out of the four large islands, only Jamaica had been lost to Britain and western Hispaniola to France. On the mainland, what are now Florida, southern Alabama, and Mississippi; all of the area of the United States to the west of the Mississippi River; and Mexico, Central America, and all South America with the exception of the Guianas and Brazil, acknowledged the sway of Spain: to this must be added the Philippine Islands in the Far East.

The Spanish annexation of Louisiana, however, in consequence of the Treaty of Paris, had met with a good deal of resistance on the part of the inhabitants. Charles's excellent assessment of character was never better displayed than when he sent Antonio de Ulloa, a distinguished naval officer and a scholar, to New Orleans in 1766 to take possession of the colony in his name. All the same, his arrival was bitterly resented by the colonists, who refused to receive him. As he had arrived without any military backing Ulloa was compelled to assume a position which was at once ambiguous, anomalous, and undignified, and for some time without daring publicly to exhibit his powers he ruled the colony through the last French governor, Philippe Aubry. This, however, was not good enough for the colonists, who protested to Paris. When they discovered that no comfort was to be found there, they sought the armed support of the British at Pensacola; this, too, was denied them, and some of the more active creoles seem to have toyed with the idea of independence. In the meantime, in November 1768, they compelled Ulloa to leave the colony.

If they thought that this insult would be ignored in Madrid they were soon to be convinced of their mistake, for in the summer of the following year Alejandro O'Reilly arrived in New Orleans with two thousand one hundred troops. As the whole white population of the city was only between five and six thousand, the new governor was from the beginning in a much stronger position than the luckless Ulloa. For many years O'Reilly had much less than justice done him by historians for his actions in Louisiana, but recently the balance has been restored,[1] in a study in which full use has been made of the latest evidence. He came with *carte blanche* powers to punish the leaders of the revolt against Ulloa, and he certainly did not allow the grass to grow under his feet. He took formal possession of New Orleans on 18th August, and within a week he had investigated the causes of the insurrection as well as having arrested the ringleaders. Of the latter five were shot, and six were imprisoned for various terms. O'Reilly has been accused of irregularity in matters of procedure in connection with these trials, but they were in fact eminently fair and conducted in accordance with the existing Spanish legal customs. The men were rebels judged by the standard of any age, and in their behaviour to Ulloa they had insulted the Spanish Crown. Furthermore, O'Reilly combined the mailed fist with the velvet glove, for only the leading insurgents were punished, while the lesser were pardoned. It has been stated,[2] however, that he exceeded his original instructions and that Charles did not wish any death sentences; but the records show that in 1772 the Council of the Indies approved of all the actions taken by O'Reilly in Louisiana, and the King added his seal of approval to that of the Council—he could hardly have done otherwise.

Having thus established his authority and that of his master O'Reilly turned to the defences of the colony. His objects were two-fold, namely to obviate as far as possible the need for a large garrison of regular troops by the organization of an effective militia, and to enlist a number of French ex-officers in these units in order to strengthen their loyalty to the Spanish Crown. He was also favourable to the recruitment of coloured soldiers, and the coloured militia was commanded by a free mulatto of the name of Pedro Simón. No significant changes were made in the conditions of Negro slavery, but O'Reilly ordered the immediate freedom of all Indian slaves without compensation to their owners. His policy in other matters, too, was decidedly liberal for the age in

[1] By Jack D. L. Holmes in *The Irish Sword*, vol. VI, pp. 234–247. Dublin. 1964.
[2] Notably by Henry P. Dart in the *Louisiana Historical Quarterly*, vol. IV, p. 274. New Orleans. 1921.

which he lived, for he issued an ordinance by which immigrants could be granted plots of two hundred and forty acres and upwards. In fine, O'Reilly was typical of the able men whom Charles chose to serve him.

X

SPAIN AND HER NEIGHBOURS

IT has already been shown how the disturbances of 1766 resulted in the rise to power of the Conde de Aranda, and he remained Charles's principal adviser for the next seven years. He was an Aragonese, and displayed many of the characteristics of that kingdom. Independence and pertinacity were his outstanding characteristics, but they were rarely combined with tact, as one anecdote well illustrates. One day at a meeting of the Cabinet the minister was urging his point of view with his usual perseverance, when the King exclaimed, 'Conde de Aranda, you are more obstinate than an Aragonese mule.' 'Please, Your Majesty,' replied the Conde, 'I know one more obstinate.' 'Who?' demanded the monarch, to which the answer came, 'His Sacred Majesty, Don Carlos the Third, King of Spain and the Indies.' Charles laughed at the sally, and for some time afterwards the story was one of his favourites.

Aranda was descended from one of the oldest families in Aragon, and to a distinguished ancestry he added considerable wealth. He was possessed of great intelligence, but of greater vanity, while he was a zealous, but not too prudent, reformer. Like his master, he was cosmopolitan in his outlook, and had travelled widely. He was particularly interested in military matters, and he had studied the Prussian army, then the admiration of Europe, on the spot. A residence in Paris had opened his mind to the views of the Encyclopaedists, and rendered him sceptical of the claims of the Church. As Charles was affected in the same way it is not surprising that for some years the King and Aranda should have formed an ideal combination, while he was fortunate in having for a master one in whose character gratitude was a prominent feature.

One of the earlier innovations of Charles and his minister was the institution of a census,[1] for before this the population had been the subject of calculation and conjecture, and the most exaggerated figures had been quoted. That the Roman provinces of Lusitania, Tarraconensis, Gallaecia, Carthaginiensis, and Baetica should in the heyday of the Empire have had thirty million inhabitants, as is sometimes stated even today, seems impossible in a non-industrial age; and, incidentally, the figure of twenty million given for Spain in the reign of Philip II is scarcely more credible for the same reason. Aranda's officials arrived at an estimate of nine million, and the minister did not hesitate to ascribe this relatively low figure to past misgovernment. However this may be, the census provided a useful basis on which to work for his reforms.[2]

Neither Aranda nor the King was slow in realizing that the expulsion of the Jesuits had left a vacuum in the world of education which must be filled, and a system was arranged by which the instruction of youth was entrusted to a body of secular priests, while seminaries were instituted on a new and enlarged plan either under the patronage or the protection of the monarch. In another field, in 1772, a drastic reformation was made in the currency, which had become shamefully debased: the old coins were called in, and replaced by new money of good quality and superior execution. Indeed there was no sphere in which Aranda's reforming zeal was not most marked. The import and export of grain were permitted under certain restrictions with regard to price levels in the home market. Raw material was allowed to enter the country free, but a prohibitive tariff was put upon such manufactured articles as were likely to compete with Spanish products. A government registry for titles and mortgages was created to render the transfer of land both easy and cheap.

In these activities Charles set an example which was followed by many members of the aristocracy, who were as active in this direction as they had been in the reign of his father. Foremost among them was the ninth Marqués de Santa Cruz, a descendant of the old sea-dog who had played so important a part in the victory of Lepanto, and who, had he lived, might well have made a success of the Armada. He was not only a close friend of

---

[1] It was not until 1801 that a census was taken in Great Britain.

[2] The population of Spain rose by 1,500,000 during the reign of Charles III.

Charles, whose will he witnessed, but he was his Mayordomo Mayor. His interests lay in philosophy, science, mathematics, and chemistry, and he was Director of the Royal Spanish Academy. He seems, too, to have been a man of great charm, for his contemporaries all pay tribute to his *'modestia y humilidad'*. Equally remarkable was his second wife who was a painter of no small merit, for she was a member of the Academy of San Fernando as well as of the Italian academies of San Luca in Rome and Bellas Artes in Florence.

Not the least important achievement of this period of the reign was the development of the Sierra Morena, hitherto the lurking-place of brigands and outlaws,[1] who were the terror of travellers. Some six thousand Bavarian immigrants were settled there in thirteen new villages, and in spite of its unfavourable situation the colony made satisfactory progress. This scheme owed a great deal to one of the outstanding figures of the reign, namely Pablo de Olivade. He had been born in Peru, and came to Spain in 1752, but he spent his most formative years in France, whose thought and culture he adopted to the exclusion of all else. Indeed so much was this the case that his reading was virtually only in French, and when in 1776 the officers of the Inquisition searched his lodgings in Madrid they found only two Spanish books in a collection of about thirty. He obtained a government post after the Squillacci riots, and that proved the beginning of a successful career in the public service, until in 1767 he became Intendant of Seville and Andalusia. In this position he not only inaugurated the scheme for the colonization of the Sierra Morena, but he put forward a scheme for educational reform which was adopted by Charles and Aranda.

At this point Olivade's luck turned, for in 1775 one of the German colonists of the Sierra Morena, a Capuchin, denounced him as 'the most dangerous intellectual in Spain'.[2] This in due course led to his recall to Madrid, and to his arrest by the Inquisition in November 1776, on a charge of heresy and atheism. As was usual in such cases Olavide now disappeared for a couple of years, and his friends neither knew where he was nor whether he was

[1] There were still one or two to be found there even in the opening years of the present century.

[2] cf. Defourneaux, M.: *Pablo de Olavide ou L'Afrancesado (1725–1803)*, p. 327. Paris. 1959.

dead or alive. On 24th November 1778 he was produced at an *auto-de-fé* behind locked doors in the presence of about forty witnesses. When, during the reading of the sentence, he heard himself pronounced a 'formal heretic' Olavide cried out, 'No, not that', and fainted. The sentence passed on him was banishment, and confinement for eight years in a monastery; but it caused such an uproar in high places that the Holy Office dropped the matter. The importance of the Olavide case is that it very definitely marked the waning of the Inquisition.

As may be imagined, neither Charles nor Aranda viewed the institution with any great liking. The King, on being asked why he did not abolish the tribunal, is reported to have said, 'The Spaniards want it, and it does not bother me.' As for Aranda, during his residence in Paris he made no secret of the fact that should he ever be called to power he would endeavour to obtain the abolition of the Inquisition, and when he did obtain office d'Alembert announced this intention in the Encyclopaedia. On reading the article Aranda exclaimed, 'This imprudent disclosure will raise such a ferment against me that my plans will be foiled', and he proved not to be far from right.

The last victim of the Inquisition to be burnt alive was an old woman in Seville in 1780 accused of sorcery.[1] By then the one powerful weapon remaining to the tribunal was that of censorship, but under Charles even this had been slipping from under its control into that of the Council of Castille. In 1768 the King issued an ordinance which affirmed the Council's control, and at the same time laid down liberal rules by which authors were to be given a hearing, circulation was to be unimpeded until judgement was passed, and all prohibitions were to be approved by the government. Finally, in 1773, bishops were deprived of the right to issue an *imprimatur*, which was reserved to the government alone, so that henceforth the whole apparatus of literary control was in the hands of laymen, usually informed intellectuals, who sat on the Council of Castille.[2]

By this time Aranda himself was tottering to his fall, and this was caused not so much by his policy as by his personality. He was liable to lose his temper when thwarted, and even when this

---

[1] Six years later Phoebe Harris was burnt in front of Newgate, cf.Radzinowicz, L.: *History of the English Criminal Law*, vol. I, p. 211. London. 1948.

[2] cf. Kamen, H.: *The Spanish Inquisition*, p. 259. London. 1965.

did not happen he took refuge in fits of sullenness. In particular he was involved in incessant bickerings with Grimaldi, whom he derided and despised, and he once went so far as to call him, in the King's presence, the most weak, indolent, sycophantic, and time-serving minister with whom Spain had ever been cursed. Charles was extremely tolerant where the eccentricities of his ministers were concerned, but over the years Aranda began to go too far. He was an enthusiastic Aragonese, and he manifested a strong desire to revive the customs and privileges of his native kingdom. This could hardly fail to revive in the King's mind memories of Philip II and Antonio Perez,[1] and thus heightened any suspicions of the minister which he might previously have entertained. Like so many politicians with an exaggerated idea of their own indispensability, Aranda had acquired the habit of threatening to resign if he encountered opposition, and he played this card very successfully on more than one occasion. Finally, however, he took this line once too often, for to his surprise in 1773 Charles accepted his resignation, and as a mark of his gratitude and consideration appointed him to be his ambassador to Louis XV.

Aranda was succeeded by Grimaldi, who lost no time in justifying the strictures which his predecessor had passed upon him. He was anxious to distinguish his administration by some exploit which would appeal to Spanish patriotism, but which was not likely to provoke the hostility of France and Great Britain; so he recommended an expedition against Algiers. There was something in the policy he advocated, for it is not too much to say that the history of the foreign relations of the Barbary States is one long indictment, not of one, but of all the maritime Powers of Europe, on a charge of cowardice and dishonour. There had in earlier days been some excuse for hesitation when faced by the powerful armaments and skilled seamanship of Barbarossa or the fateful ferocity of Dragut; but that all the maritime Powers should have cowered and cringed before the miserable braggarts who succeeded the heroic age of the Corsairs, and should have suffered their trade to be harassed, their lives menaced, and their honour stained by a collection of insolent savages with negligible armaments, seems absolutely incredible, but it is literally true.

Spain was not the only sufferer, for in 1740 the Bey of Tunis

[1] cf. Petrie, Sir Charles: *Philip II of Spain*, pp. 291–295. London. 1963.

ordered the French consul to kiss his hand. When that official refused he was threatened with instant death, so he hastened to comply with the demand. When on the accession of George III a British ambassador came to Tunis in a man-of-war to announce the fact the Bey issued the same order, but on this occasion a compromise was reached by which some of the officers kissed the beylical hand instead of their chief. These Pashas, Deys, and Beys were almost without exception merely sullen and ignorant common soldiers whose tenure of supreme power was usually brief, while their foreign policy was made up of lawless piracy and the levying of blackmail from most of the European Powers, accompanied by acts of insufferable insolence towards the foreign representatives. This state of affairs was accepted submissively by the Western governments, who communicated with these brigands on equal terms, and William III of England even went so far as to sign a letter to one of the most notorious Deys of Algiers 'Your loving friend'.

Indeed the history of the Barbary States may be described as one of piracy without and anarchy within, and Tunis, Tripoli, and Algiers showed very similar symptoms. At Tunis thirty Deys, appointed by the Ottoman Sultan, succeeded one another between 1590 and 1705, which gives an average reign of less than four years. Most of them were deposed, many murdered, and one is related on credible evidence to have been torn to pieces and devoured by the enraged population. In 1705 the soldiery elected their own governor, and gave him the title of Bey – an action in which the Sultan had no alternative but to acquiesce. Eleven Beys then followed one another until the establishment of the French protectorate in 1881.

The same picture is afforded by the contemporary annals of Algiers. Hasan Chāwush was deposed in 1700, and was succeeded by the Aga of the Spahis, Mustafa, whose nickname was *Bigotillos*. He was something of a coward but he engaged in two successful campaigns against Tunis and one against Morocco, until he had the misfortune to find the bow-string round his throat in 1706. Uzeyn Khōja followed, but he only reigned for one year, after which he was banished to the mountains, where he died. The next Dey, Bektāsh Khōja, was murdered on his judgement seat in the third year of his reign, while his successor Ibrahīm Deli, known to his subjects as 'The Fool', made himself so hated for his unconscionable licentiousness that within a few months he was assassinated, and his mutilated body was exposed in the street. To him succeeded Ali in 1710, and he is chiefly known for the murder of some three thousand Turks. Whether because of or in spite of this he continued to reign for eight years, and he died in his bed.[1]

As regards the policy to be adopted towards the Barbary States at this time, government circles in Madrid seem to have been divided between 'hawks' and 'doves', and there was an influential body of opinion which favoured the evacuation of all the Spanish footholds on the Barbary coast except Oran and Ceuta. Then came a Moorish attack on Melilla and Peñon de Velez which roused Spanish resentment against them, and the 'hawks', with Grimaldi at their head, carried the day.[2] The decision was taken to make an example of Algiers, which was not only the central point of the Barbary States, but was also considered the most vulnerable. Accordingly an expeditionary force was organized at Cartagena consisting of 46 warships and 22,000 men, and placed under the command of O'Reilly, who had returned from America and was now Captain-General of Madrid. Apart from his exploits in Louisiana he had been one of the few Spanish generals to distinguish himself in the Portuguese campaign. He was a close friend of Grimaldi, and he was highly thought of by the King. Unfortunately for him the Moors knew what was afoot long before the expedition sailed.

This event took place at the end of June 1775, and set at rest the rumours which were circulating throughout Europe regarding its destination. Some of them had been very wide of the mark. When the Duke of Gloucester, brother of George III, met the Conte de Pignatelli, the Neapolitan minister, one night at Vauxhall, he said, 'O'Reilly is going to take the Spanish fleet to his native land—I mean Ireland', to which Pignatelli replied, 'His Catholic Majesty would never think of taking advantage of the difficult situation in which the Cabinet of St. James's finds itself', referring to the trouble with the American colonies. 'So much the worse for his policy,' was Gloucester's answer, 'for I can assure you that if Spain was in the position in which we are, we should

[1] cf. Playfair, Sir R. Lambert: *Scourge of Christendom, passim.* London. 1884.
[2] cf. Casado, Vicente Rodríguez: *Política Marroquí de Carlos III,* p. 237. Madrid. 1946.

not hesitate to invade Cuba or one of her other colonies.'[1]

The expedition anchored in the bay of Algiers on 1st July, and all on board had the highest hopes of success, but everything proceeded to go wrong from the start, for it was not long before it was proved that the King's confidence in O'Reilly was in some respects misplaced. His gravest error was in the matter of supplies and ammunition, for from the beginning there was a shortage of provisions, while the infantry were sent into action with a mere eighty rounds per man. His military intelligence was almost non-existent, with the result that he had only the vaguest information concerning the strength and disposition of the enemy, while the Algerines were extremely knowledgeable regarding the Spanish movements through, it is said, their spies in Marseilles. Furthermore, to stimulate his subjects' enthusiasm, the Dey offered a golden doubloon for every Christian head that was brought to his palace.

Divided counsels also soon made themselves felt on the Spanish side. The naval commander was Don Pedro González de Castejón, a competent but not an inspired sailor, whose relations with O'Reilly were far from cordial. As a result, probably, of a difference of opinion between them, there were several days' delay in the disembarkation of the troops, and this was not only bad for Spanish morale, but it gave warning to the Algerines of the danger which threatened them, and gave them time to complete their preparations to resist it. Whether the fault was that of O'Reilly or of González de Castejón, the responsibility was the former's as commander-in-chief, and he proved that though he might have been all right in command of a brigade against the Portuguese, or as a colonial governor, he was out of his depth when it came to conducting combined operations. He made all the mistakes which were later to mark the conduct of the Anglo-French operations at Gallipoli in the First World War.

The rest of the story is soon told. The Spaniards, mostly raw troops for some obscure reason, were landed in two divisions. The first of these made a rapid advance on the city of Algiers, deceived by a feigned retreat of the enemy, but soon became entangled in the difficult terrain. The Algerines counter-attacked, the Spaniards retreated, and before long the retreat became a rout. By this time the second division had landed, but it was thrown

[1] cf. Tapia Ozcariz, Enrique de: *Carlos III y Su Epoca*, p. 316. Madrid. 1962.

into disorder by the flight of the first. The whole army would have been cut to pieces had it not been for the discipline and courage of the regiment of Hibernia, whose gallantry at Velletri we have already noticed, which covered its retreat, thus performing the same service as the picquets of the Irish regiments in the French service had done for the Highlanders at Culloden.

Entrenchments were thrown up, but these afforded only a very temporary respite, for they were soon enfiladed by the fire of the Algerine guns. Furthermore, provisions ran out, and the effect of the drink, which O'Reilly ordered to be issued in the hope of restoring morale, upon the empty stomachs of the soldiers can be imagined. Discipline broke down, and there was nothing for it but to re-embark. This led to scenes of further disorder, and by the time the expedition finally got to sea again it had lost sixteen guns, several chests of ammunition, its tents, and 1,500 killed, while it took away some 3,000 wounded. There was one further humiliation, for when O'Reilly proposed to bombard Algiers it was found that there were only enough rations left to last over an immediate return to Spain.

The arrival of this ill-fated expedition at Alicante bearing the first news of its failure created consternation throughout the country, and there was an immediate demand for a scapegoat, O'Reilly himself narrowly escaping the fury of the populace. By now, however, Charles had considerable experience of riding out storms of this nature, and his skill did not fail him on the present occasion. He was the last man to throw his servants to the wolves, so that although O'Reilly was told to absent himself from Court he was given a command elsewhere out of the public eye. Among the subscribers to Sylvester O'Halloran's *General History of Ireland* in 1778 he appears as Captain-General of Andalusia and Inspector-General of Spanish Infantry.

Charles's relations with O'Reilly are described in the *Hibernian Journal* of 15th January 1787:

The report published in the foreign prints, and from thence copied into those of Great Britain and Ireland, about General Count O'Reilly's having murdered one of his coachmen, and that he was tried for the same, is entirely a falsehood, for it was fabricated and published at Avignon, and thence circulated through the rest of Europe, for which the printer of the *Avignon Gazette* has since been taken up and committed to prison. As this gentleman is a native of this kingdom, and as brave an officer as any in Europe, we are the better pleased to have authority for contradicting the report.

Though political necessity obliged the Spanish monarch to suspend Count O'Reilly from his military employments, yet there is no person in his dominions enjoys more of his Sovereign's esteem. Count O'Reilly was Captain of the Household Guard when the insurrection happened at Madrid some years since, about the order for changing the Spanish dress to that of the French. When the conspirators broke into the palace, and endangered the life of the Monarch, O'Reilly bravely rushed into the middle of them, sword in hand, and was principally instrumental in suppressing the riot. This so endeared him to the King that he appointed him Governor of Cadiz and Commander in Chief of the forces; nay he went so far as to furnish the following singular proof of his regard: – Having caused a fine road to be made from the palace of the Escurial to St. Ildefonso, it was carried on in a straight line till the workmen were interrupted by an old stunted oak, which they were going to remove, but the King gave orders that it should be suffered to stand and the road turned round part of it in the segment of a circle. Being done accordingly, he commanded the straight line to be resumed. 'This tree', said His Majesty, 'I shall call O'Reilly, for if I was gone to-morrow, this venerable tree and poor O'Reilly's existence would fall sacrifices to my subjects.'

When the War of American Independence broke out O'Reilly is said to have told Charles that with 30,000 men he could make a complete conquest of Ireland.[1]

The actual fall of Grimaldi was delayed for several weeks, but the failure of the expedition to Algiers had rendered it inevitable. Quite apart from the fact that Aranda was intriguing against him from Paris, he had not a friend in the government, while he had before his eyes the fate of Alberoni, Ripperdá, and Squillacci, all like himself foreigners called to rule over a high-spirited nation. None of the existing ministers could be called his friends, and it was at this time that there were fresh arrivals in the persons of Don Pedro González Castejón, with whom O'Reilly had had differences at Algiers, at Marine, and Don José de Gálvez, at the Indies, both of whom were his opponents. In the hope of restoring the balance Grimaldi extracted the reluctant consent of the King to the admission of the Prince of Asturias to the Cabinet,

[1] *Dublin Mercury*, 30th November 1776.

but the future Charles IV soon proved to be the mere mouthpiece of Aranda. Such was the situation until November, with Grimaldi desirous of resigning and the King refusing to accept his resignation; but in due course Charles realized that this state of affairs could not continue indefinitely, and on 7th November 1776 Grimaldi ceased to hold office.

This event, however, brought little comfort to Aranda and his supporters, for the King asked Grimaldi to recommend a successor. Indeed it may even be that Charles was annoyed at the attempt to dictate to him, particularly when he found his son, of whose abilities he had no high opinion, one of the most vociferous for the recall of the ex-minister. Grimaldi's choice fell upon Don José de Moñino, a man of forty-eight, who had recently been created Conde de Floridablanca, the Spanish ambassador to the Holy See, and it was at once accepted by Charles, who promptly appointed Grimaldi to fill the vacant embassy. The retiring minister continued to carry on his duties until Floridablanca arrived in Madrid, and the parting between him and his master reflected the greatest credit upon both of them. Charles assured Grimaldi of the continuance of his esteem, and announced his intention of consulting him on all important occasions. He also conferred a dukedom upon him and made him a grandee. After a brief holiday the former minister took up his post in Rome.

Floridablanca is one of the great names of Spanish history. He was born in the village of Hellin, in Murcia, the son of a notary, and his background was that of a *golilla*.[1] By temperament and training he was solemn, precise, and methodical, and he was a firm believer in authoritarianism. In later years he came to be known to his contemporaries as 'the old fox'. After graduating in public life as one of the fiscals of the Council of Castille, he early obtained by his merits the embassy at Rome, where he carried out to the King's satisfaction the negotiations relating to the suppression of the Jesuits. Floridablanca was of a conciliatory character and pleasant manner. He was hardly known to Charles personally when he succeeded Grimaldi, but he soon gained the King's confidence, and never afterwards lost it.

If his predecessor's ministry was marked by failure in Africa, his own was characterized by success in the Iberian Peninsula itself.

---

[1] Literally a 'ruff', as worn by magistrates, a description similar to that of *rond de cuir* in France.

The situation in the British North American colonies was rapidly deteriorating, and no one could tell what the future might bring. If it brought renewed war with Great Britain it was of the utmost importance that Portugal should not, as so often in the past, be an ally of the enemy. As we have seen, the accession of Maria I and the consequent dismissal of Pombal made the task of the King and Floridablanca comparatively easy, and Charles even persuaded his niece to come to Madrid to make the final arrangements for an *entente* between the two countries. This was finally concluded by the Treaty of the Prado, on 24th March 1778, which may be described as a postscript to that of San Ildefonso in the autumn of the previous year. Briefly, it was agreed that neither Power should engage in a war, conclude an alliance, or take any step to the prejudice of the other, while they mutually guaranteed their respective territories in the New World and in the Old, as laid down in the Treaty of San Ildefonso. If either Power should be involved in a war the other was to observe the strictest neutrality. Commercially the subjects of both countries were to enjoy 'most favoured nation' rights with regard to the other. Finally, Portugal ceded to Spain the islands of Annobon and Fernando Po on the coast of Africa. By this treaty the Spanish position in respect of Portugal was assured in the event of war with Britain, and Floridablanca was fully justified in regarding it as one of the most important and solid achievements of his ministry.

Charles was more fortunate in his dealings with his niece in Lisbon than with his son in The Two Sicilies. About this time the king's messengers from the Spanish and Neapolitan courts respectively are said to have met in Zaragoza, when the Spaniard said to the Italian, 'I have a mighty piece of news in my bag, brother.' 'What news is that?' asked the Neapolitan. 'The resignation of Grimaldi.' 'You must take me for a lame duck,' retorted the other, 'I have Tanucci's resignation in mine.' Both, we are told, were equally amazed, and, after embracing each other and thanking God that they were messengers, departed on their respective ways.

When the Neapolitan reached Madrid he found a very angry King, for Charles had not been consulted in the retirement of the man whom he had appointed to supervise the administration of The Two Sicilies when he himself had left Italy. Had he realized that his son was completely under the influence of his wife, Maria Carolina, a daughter of Maria Theresa, he would have been less surprised, for the Empress's daughters had inherited all their mother's love of intrigue without her ability in its conduct, and the minister's dismissal was very definitely the Queen's doing. Tanucci received the same courteous treatment that Grimaldi had done, and it must have been some satisfaction to him to receive a letter from the King of Spain in which Charles wrote, 'Believe me, nobody sympathizes with your misfortune more than I do. Let us help each other to bear all the disgusts and trials which God wished to send us in our old age. . . . You may be sure that I shall not cease writing to you, unless God sends me some infirmity which prevents me, for I know how you have always served me, and I esteem and love you.'

It only remains to add that Tanucci, unlike Grimaldi, was not given a post abroad, but from time to time he attended meetings of the State Council. Ferdinand, too, had by no means forgotten his past services, and on one occasion he went so far as to declare that 'Tanucci knows more than the lot of us put together'. When Sambuca, Tanucci's successor, tried to interrupt him, the King shouted, '*Zittati tu. Isso è lo maestro; noi siamo li ciucci.*'[1] If Charles was in any doubt where power now lay in the Naples he had left, he must have been undeceived not only by the fall of Tanucci, but also by a letter which he received from Ferdinand shortly after that event:

Regarding my wife, instigated by her country she has plucked up courage with this change, and makes every effort to enter the government. . . . I shall try to prevent her from succeeding though she may threaten me in every street, declaring that she will show me who she is and who her parents are, and that it has been a great favour and fortune to receive her in our family. In Your Majesty's reply please do not show that you are acquainted with this, or, if you wish to warn or command me, do so in a separate letter, for if she came to hear of this I should be troubled as long as I live, as she preaches nothing else but the closest confidence between husband and wife, and wishes to see and know all my affairs, and read all my letters. But when I speak of wishing to see some letter she writes home, or know what she is writing, there is a fight: and if I insist she loads me with abuse, so I keep silent for the sake of peace.

[1] 'Be silent! He's the master, and we are the donkeys.'

In September of the following year further bad news came from Naples to Madrid, and it was to the effect that Don Felipe, Charles's eldest son who had been barred from the succession owing to his imbecility, had developed smallpox. 'Our learned doctors could not decide whether it was smallpox or a malignant fever causing skin eruptions,' wrote the Abbe Galiani, 'so that the King and Queen fled to Caserta in dismay.' According to Sir William Hamilton,[1] as recorded by Wraxall, the unfortunate prince 'was treated with certain distinctions, having chamberlains placed about him in constant attendance; who watched him with unremitting attention; as otherwise he would have committed a thousand excesses. Care was particularly taken to keep him from having any connection with the other sex, for which he manifested the strongest propensity; but it became at last impossible to prevent him altogether from attempting to emancipate himself in this respect. He has many times eluded the vigilance of his keepers, and on seeing ladies pass through the apartments of the palace, would attack them with the same impetuosity as Pan or the Satyrs are described by Ovid when pursuing the Nymphs; and with the same intentions. More than one lady of the Court has been critically rescued from his embraces. On particular days of the year, he was allowed to hold a sort of Court or Levée, when the foreign ministers repaired to his apartments to pay their compliments to him: but his greatest amusement consisted in having his hand held up by his attendants, while gloves were put upon it, one larger than another to the number of fifteen or sixteen.'[2] Don Felipe died on 19th September 1777, but his father refused to allow any mourning.

Of Charles himself we have an account at this time by the English traveller, Henry Swinburne:[3]

His dress seldom varies from a long hat, grey Segovian frock, a buff waistcoat, a small dagger, black breeches, and worsted stockings; his pockets are always stuffed with knives, gloves and shooting tackle. On gala days, a fine suit is hung upon his shoulders, but as he has an eye to his afternoon sport, and is a great economist of his time, the black breeches are worn to all coats. I believe there are but

[1] Husband of Nelson's Emma.

[2] Acton, Harold: *The Bourbons of Naples (1732–1825)*, pp. 178–179. London. 1956.

[3] cf. *Travels through Spain in 1775 and 1776*. London. 1787.

three days in the whole year that he spends without going out a-shooting, and those are noted with the blackest mark in the calendar. Were they to occur often his health would be in danger, and an accident that was to confine him to the house would infallibly bring on a fit of illness. No storm, heat, or cold can keep him at home; and when he hears of a wolf, distance is counted for nothing; he would drive over half the kingdom rather than miss an opportunity of firing upon that favourite game. Besides a numerous retinue of persons belonging to the hunting establishment, several times a year all the idle fellows in and around Madrid are hired to beat the country, and drive the wild boars, deer, and hares into a ring, where they pass before the Royal Family.

The King made no secret of his devotion to the chase, and not long before his death he told a foreign ambassador that he personally had killed, according to his game-book, 539 wolves and 5,323 foxes, adding with a smile, 'You see my diversion is not useless to my country.'

XI

THE KING'S DILEMMA

WHILE Charles was vainly endeavouring to bring the Algerines to heel, and was successfully negotiating an agreement with Portugal, the differences between Great Britain and her American colonies had come to a head. In April 1775 the first blood had been shed at Lexington, and on 4th July of the following year there was issued the Declaration of Independence. There can be little doubt that the European courts, not excluding the Spanish, were extremely surprised at the subsequent course of events, and with reason. The Treaty of Paris had put Great Britain in a very strong position indeed, and no one could have anticipated the sudden reversal of fortune which overtook her during the succeeding years.

It was due to two main factors, namely the isolation of Britain after 1763, and the repercussions of the Treaty of Paris in the New World. The Diplomatic Revolution had put an end to the old Austro-British alliance, which had existed for two generations, and the anger of Frederick the Great at the treatment he received in 1762 prevented any further understanding between London and Berlin from taking its place.[1] With France or Spain there could be no real friendship, while Russia was too far away to constitute at that time an important factor in British policy. So long, however, as Britain was not in difficulties in other parts of the world her overwhelming naval supremacy rendered the attitude of the Continental Powers a matter of comparative indifference to her, and George III, unlike his two immediate predecessors, took no interest in the fate of Hanover. It was when trouble came elsewhere that the lack of friends on the mainland of Europe was so severely felt, and isolation in the War of American Independence

[1] There was, indeed, much to be said against Britain's cynical disregard of her ally in that year, but not by one with the record of the King of Prussia.

proved to be far from splendid; as, indeed, was again to be the case when not dissimilar conditions obtained at the end of the following century and Britain was at war with the Boer Republics.

What had caused this situation to arise was, curiously enough, the Paris settlement of 1763. Canada may have been won on the battle-fields of Germany, but the American colonies were lost in the French capital. No longer threatened on three sides by the Bourbon Powers, they soon began to feel strong enough to stand alone, and it is no mere coincidence that only thirteen years after the conclusion of the Treaty of Paris the Declaration of Independence was signed. Rarely has there been so rapid a reversal of fortune in international affairs as that which Great Britain experienced between 1763 and 1776.

If the courts of Europe were surprised at the outbreak of the struggle between Britain and her American colonists they were equally so at the British conduct of the war, which was no less unfortunate than the policy which had made the conflict inevitable. There was in the colonies an important body of opinion actively favourable to the maintenance of the British connection, while an even greater number of colonists were indifferent or uncertain. To conciliate these friendly or wavering colonial minds, to respect the property of every friendly American, and wherever possible to enlist the help of American loyalists in the tasks of civil government should have been a prime object of British policy, but nothing of the kind was done. While the Indians, whose support had most unhappily been invoked by the British, alienated every frontiersman with their excesses, the army of Lord Howe, largely composed of Hessians and Hanoverians, pillaged indifferently the houses of friend and foe. It is a sufficient commentary upon the British conduct that during the whole course of the war no more than two thousand five hundred loyalist volunteers were enlisted in the British ranks.

The outbreak of the War of American Independence placed Charles in a dilemma from which it was not easy for him to extricate himself. As at his arrival in Spain from Naples at the height of the Seven Years' War he came under great pressure from both sides. The British government endeavoured to alarm him with fears for the tranquillity of his own colonies if he came to the aid of insurgents just across the frontier, and his experience in Louisiana had been such as to give point to this argument. At any rate at the beginning of the contest Floridablanca inclined in the same direction, and he assured the British ambassador, by this time Lord Grantham,[1] that he considered the independence of the American colonies as no less detrimental to Spain than to Great Britain herself.

On the other hand there was the argument, strongly urged by Aranda from the Paris embassy, that Britain's extremity was Spain's opportunity. Charles was pressed to seize such a favourable moment of crushing a rival enfeebled by internal divisions and the colonial rebellion, and so robbed of that influence which she had formerly exercised among the nations of Europe. That world opinion was hostile to Britain is undoubtedly true and, although a prejudiced witness, Benjamin Franklin did not exaggerate when he said, 'Every nation in Europe wishes to see Britain humbled, having all in their turn been offended by her insolence, which in prosperity she is apt to discover on all occasions.' Even so, Charles might have decided to adopt that same policy of neutrality which his brother had followed in the previous conflict, had not Britain proved incompetent as well as insolent, for the capitulation of Burgoyne at Saratoga in October 1777 went a long way to convince him that Britain's days of greatness were at an end.

From that moment the fugleman of the colonists' supporters in Europe was France, though this did not necessarily render them or their cause the more acceptable to the King of Spain, who had bitter memories of his earlier co-operation with his northern neighbour. Since then, however, there had been changes in that country. Louis XV had been succeeded by his grandson, who, if he had possessed an atom of firmness, and a more sensible wife, would have made one of the best monarchs whom France had ever known, and Choiseul had been replaced by Vergennes, as Minister of Foreign Affairs. The last-named had been born at Dijon in 1719, and came of an old Burgundian family. He had served a long apprenticeship to diplomacy, and was possessed of a considerable knowledge of European politics, though he re-

---

[1] Ambassador to Madrid, 1771–1779. His rapacity in securing a pension of £2,000 per annum when the Shelburne ministry went out in 1783, though he was already in receipt of another pension of £3,000 p.a. for life, and had married a rich wife, was unfavourably noted by contemporaries.

mained an experienced diplomatist rather than a statesman to the day of his death.

As early as July 1776, even before Silas Deane, the representative of the American Congress, had reached Paris to enlist French support, Vergennes submitted a memorial to Louis XVI on American affairs. In it he clearly demonstrated the importance of maintaining a close alliance between the different branches of the House of Bourbon, and of opposing on all occasions the interests of Great Britain, while especial stress was laid upon the necessity of aiding the Americans in their struggle for independence. The defeat and submission of the colonists would, Vergennes insisted, be followed by disastrous consequences for the French and Spanish possessions in the West Indies. If, however, the Americans won by their own exertions, they would themselves be disposed to conquer the French and Spanish West Indies so as to provide markets for their products. Hence it was of supreme importance that France should at once lay the colonists under a debt of gratitude, and at the same time avenge upon England 'the evils which since the commencement of the century she had inflicted upon her neighbours and rivals'. Vergennes ended by urging that the intentions of the French government should be kept secret, and that while the Americans should be prevented from making peace by 'secret favours and vague hopes', the English ministry should be dexterously tranquillized 'as to the intentions of France and Spain'.

To this policy Turgot, the Comptroller-General of the Finances, was opposed, not through any lack of sympathy with men fighting in defence of their liberty, but from fear that a war against Britain, inevitably a long one, would ruin France. He remembered the blows dealt to French credit by the Seven Years' War, and was of the opinion that, without discouraging the Americans, there should be indefinite temporizing. Turgot stressed the point that if Britain persisted in subjugating her colonies by force she could only succeed at the cost of exhausting herself, while France in the meantime would have been able to restore her finances and increase her navy; so that if the struggle with Britain had to come it could be started with superior forces. On the other hand, if Britain was defeated and forced to grant the Americans their independence, the results would have been secured without dealing a blow or costing any money.

The views of Vergennes were supported by the majority of his fellow-countrymen, including Louis XVI himself, for they were inspired either by resentment for former defeats at British hands, or, like the *philosophes*, by feelings of sympathy for religious or political liberty. Still, it was not until after the capitulation at Saratoga that any definite step was taken by the French government, but in February 1778 treaties with the Americans were signed in Paris to the effect that neither of the contracting parties would make peace without the consent of the other, or until the independence of the United States was acknowledged by London. War between Great Britain and France accordingly began in the summer.

Charles followed the trend of French opinion very closely, but he was not subject to the same pressures as his cousin Louis, and when hostilities broke out between Britain and France he adopted a policy of neutrality. A new ambassador was sent to London in the person of the Marqués de Almodóvar, and Charles offered to mediate. How optimistic he really was regarding his efforts it is impossible to say, just as the sincerity of the British government in negotiating with him is open to question, for on 13th October 1778 George III wrote to Lord North, 'I have no doubt next spring Spain will join France, but if we can keep her quiet till then I trust the British Navy will be in a state to cope with both nations.'[1]

In Europe the main bone of contention between the two countries was Gibraltar. Britain had long cast her eyes on the place before she finally acquired it, and Oliver Cromwell had meditated its conquest. The statesmen of the restored Stuarts were equally interested, more particularly after the British abandonment of Tangier in 1684, and in that year Samuel Pepys, then Secretary of the Admiralty, discussed with the engineer, Major Martin Beckmann, the possibility of replacing the African port by the Spanish one, where his own brother-in-law had for some time past been in charge of British naval stores. Beckmann said that more than any other place it dominated the Straits, and that it could be captured without the loss of a single life, while it could afterwards be fortified for a mere trifle against all the fleets and armies of the world. Pepys and Beckmann agreed to keep the

[1] *The Correspondence of King George the Third from 1760 to December, 1783,* vol. IV, p. 208. London. 1928.

project to themselves in case it should leak out and Britain should be anticipated by some other Power. So secretive did they think it advisable to be that they did not even inform their master, Charles II, of what they had in mind.[1]

With these ideas in his head it is not surprising that Pepys should have pursued a steady process of infiltration, and two years later by his instructions Jonathan Gouden, the Mediterranean victualler, was empowered 'to make presents to the Governor and officers of Gibraltar as there shall be found occasion for the procuring their assistance in the better carrying on His Majesty's service'. In 1687 a British squadron entered the Mediterranean for the purpose of bringing pressure to bear on the Dey of Algiers, and it is significant to note that it was strategically based on Gibraltar. During the years which followed, Britain and Spain were both members of the League of Augsburg against Louis XIV, and the British Navy used Gibraltar without let or hindrance in the reign of William III as it had done in that of James II. With the accession of Philip V, however, and the passing of Spain into the Bourbon camp, a new situation confronted Whitehall, for it was clear that the Rock was no longer going to play the part in British Mediterranean strategy that it had done ever since the abandonment of Tangier. The position as London saw it was that either a substitute must be found, or Gibraltar must become a British possession.

There can be little doubt but that these considerations were uppermost in the mind of Sir George Rooke when he executed his *coup de main* on 4th August 1704. Prior to his arrival at the head of an Anglo-Dutch force the city had in 1700 given its allegiance to Philip V in preference to the Archduke Charles, whose claim was, of course, being supported by Great Britain and the United Provinces. It had a small garrison, which was quite inadequate to resist the invaders, so the commandant surrendered to the enemy who were, or so he believed, acting in the name of the Archduke. The Corporation was not prepared to acknowledge the Archduke, so it transferred itself to La Roque, whence it presumed that it would be able to return to Gibraltar on the termination of hostilities. As soon as the Corporation and the garrison had departed Rooke formally took possession of the town, not in the

[1] cf. Bryant, Sir A.: *Samuel Pepys, The Saviour of the Navy*, p. 76. Cambridge. 1938.

name of the Archduke, but in that of Queen Anne – an unscrupulous act which later caused a contributor to the *Encyclopaedia Britannica* to write, 'The captors had ostensibly fought in the interests of Charles, Archduke of Austria, but, though his sovereignty over the rock was proclaimed on July 24 [*sic*] 1704, Sir George Rooke on his own responsibility caused the English flag to be hoisted, and took possession in the name of Queen Anne. It is hardly to the honour of England that it was both unprincipled enough to sanction and ratify the occupation, and ungrateful enough to leave unrewarded the general to whose unscrupulous patriotism the acquisition was due. The Spaniards keenly felt the injustice done to them, and the inhabitants of the town of Gibraltar in great numbers abandoned their homes rather than recognize the authority of the invaders.'[1]

As to the morality of the proceeding, there can surely be no two views, for the Power which never tired of denouncing the wickedness of French designs upon Spain was thus the first to annex Spanish territory, and whether Gibraltar was captured in the name of Queen Anne or of the Archduke Charles as Charles III of Spain does not affect the issue. What does appear clear is that Rooke was determined from the beginning that there should be no doubt on the score of ownership. Even if the Archduke should make good his claim to the Spanish throne he would not be able to include Gibraltar among his possessions. That was the policy of the British government, and it was enforced by Rooke. From the moment of its capture, too, Bolingbroke attached the greatest importance to the retention of the place, and as he was the chief architect of the Treaty of Utrecht it is not surprising that its surrender by Philip should have been insisted upon in that settlement. Earlier in the negotiations the Dutch had expressed a desire that, to quote Bolingbroke, 'they should garrison Gibraltar and Port Mahon jointly with us', but he would not hear of it. On 29th March 1712 he wrote to Lord Portman, 'Gibraltar and Port Mahon will . . . be all we have left to show for those immense sums which we have expended, and for that blood which has been shed, in those parts.'[2] Whoever on the British side may or not have been in favour of returning Gibraltar to Spain, Bolingbroke was determined that it should remain a purely British possession,

[1] vol. X, p. 586. Edinburgh. 1879.
[2] Bolingbroke's *Letters and Correspondence*, vol. II, p. 243. London. 1798.

and in the last resort his was the word which counted at that time.[1]

So when peace was made at Utrecht in 1713 it was only to be expected that Article X should run as follows:

The Catholic King does hereby, for himself, his heirs, and successors, yield to the Crown of Great Britain the full and intire propriety of the town and castle of Gibraltar, together with the port, fortifications, and forts thereunto belonging; and he gives up the said propriety to be held and enjoyed absolutely with all manner of right for ever, without any exception or impediment whatsoever.

But that abuses and frauds may be avoided by importing any kinds of goods, the Catholic King wills, and takes it to be understood, that the above-named propriety be yielded to Great Britain without any territorial jurisdiction, and without any open communication by land with the country round about. Yet whereas the communication by sea with the coast of Spain may not at all times be safe or open, and thereby it may happen that the garrison, and other inhabitants of Gibraltar may be brought to great straits; and as it is the intention of the Catholic King, only that fraudulent importations of goods should, as is aforesaid, be hindered by an inland communication, it is therefore provided, that in such cases it may be lawful to purchase, for ready money, in the neighbouring territories of Spain, provisions, and other things necessary for the use of the garrison, the inhabitants, and the ships which lie in the harbour.

But if any goods be found imported into Gibraltar, either by way of barter for purchasing provisions, or under any other pretence, the same shall be confiscated, and complaint being made thereof, those persons who have acted contrary to the faith of this treaty, shall be severely punished.

And her Britannic Majesty, at the request of the Catholic King, does consent and agree, that no leave shall be given, under any pretence whatever, either for Jews or Moors, to reside and have their dwellings in the said town of Gibraltar; and that no refuge or shelter shall be allowed to any Moorish ships of war in the harbour of the said town, whereby the communication between Spain and Ceuta may be obstructed, or the coasts of Spain be infested by the excursions of the Moors. But whereas treaties of friendship, and a liberty and intercourse of commerce are between the British and certain countries on the coast of Africa, it is always to be understood,

---

[1] It is to be noted that the Spanish military reaction took place as early as September 1704, and the first siege lasted until March 1705: thereafter Gibraltar was blockaded until the conclusion of the Treaty of Utrecht.

that the British subjects cannot refuse the Moors and their ships entry into the port of Gibraltar purely upon the account of merchandizing.

Her Majesty the Queen of Great Britain does further promise, that the free exercise of their religion shall be indulged to the Roman Catholic inhabitants of the aforesaid town.

And in case it shall hereafter seem meet to the Crown of Great Britain to grant, sell, or by any means to alienate therefrom the propriety of the said town of Gibraltar, it is hereby agreed, and concluded, that the preference of having the same shall always be given to the Crown of Spain before any others.

The Treaty, of which the official text was in French and Latin, had been signed at Utrecht on 13th July, and was ratified by Anne at Kensington on 31st July 1713.

It had been of vital importance to Bolingbroke and his colleagues in the Tory administration that the War of the Spanish Succession should be brought to a close at the earliest possible moment, for the Queen's health was none too good, and they had to decide whether her successor was to be James Stuart or the Elector of Hanover.

Britain's principal enemy had been France, and it was therefore only natural that in the short time at their disposal they should have concentrated their attention upon the proposed terms of peace with that Power. In consequence the treaty with Spain would appear to have been somewhat loosely drafted, and especially was this the case with Article X, for it is by no means easy to reconcile 'full and intire propriety' with 'without any territorial jurisdiction'. There were subsequent infringements of other stipulations in the Article in question, but the contrast between these two phrases is most marked, and it cannot help raising a doubt whether the Treaty of Utrecht really gave Great Britain that right of full possession of Gibraltar which has commonly been supposed.

For the rest of his reign Philip V made repeated efforts to get the place back, and on more than one occasion he came very near to success. Indeed, had Elizabeth Farnese been less concerned with establishing her sons upon Italian thrones, and had paid more attention to the real interests of Spain, the Rock might easily have been restored to its original owners, for it was not until many years later that its retention became a cardinal maxim of British policy.[1] For example, in June 1721 George I wrote a personal letter to Philip expressing his readiness to satisfy the Spanish desire for the restitution of Gibraltar, and promising 'to make full use of the first opportunity of regulating the Article with the consent of Parliament'.[2] Philip and his advisers did not feel that this somewhat vague assurance took them very far, and they understandably regarded the letter as 'so darkly worded, and that which His Majesty promised so faintly expressed that it really and strictly engaged for nothing'.[3] This interpretation was the correct one. George's reference to Parliament was a mere subterfuge to gain time, for he was under no necessity to consult that body in the matter at all, while the state of British public opinion was such that in the spring of the previous year Stanhope had written to Sir Luke Schaud, the British ambassador in Paris, 'The public were moved with indignation on the simple suspicion . . . that we should cede that fortress.'[4] All the same something might have been effected had not Elizabeth Farnese turned the eyes of her husband and his ministers rather in the direction of Italy than in that of the Pillars of Hercules.

In 1725, as we have seen, Ripperdá brought about the short-lived agreement between Spain and the Empire. 'Choose', Elizabeth Farnese told Stanhope, 'between the loss of Gibraltar and that of your trade with the Indies', but the official British reply was not encouraging, for Townshend wrote from Hanover that 'the King thinks it not consistent either with his or the nation's honour, after the treatment both His Majesty and his people have received from the court of Spain, to lay His Catholic Majesty's demand for the restitution of that place before the Parliament; the late behaviour of Spain towards him and his kingdom having set him at liberty from any engagement His Majesty might have been under of doing it.'[5]

Even after the Spanish attempt to recover Gibraltar by force of arms in 1727 had failed, there yet seemed a reasonable chance that

[1] The theory that this was in deference to the views of the inhabitants came later still.

[2] *Parliamentary History*, vol. VIII, p. 695.

[3] cf. Baudrillart, A.: *Philippe V et le Cour de France*, vol. II, p. 460. Paris. 1890–1901.

[4] cf. Coxe, W.: *Memoirs of the Kings of Spain of the House of Bourbon*, vol. II, p. 260. London. 1813.

[5] R.O. MSS. State Papers, DOM G.I, bundle 64, no. 141.

it might be regained by negotiation. 'I see no daylight yet in the affairs of the congress,' wrote Stephen Poyntz, one of the British plenipotentiaries at Cambrai in June 1728, 'Only this much, that after we carry the point of Gibraltar, the Spaniards will leave no stone unturned to hurt our commerce, in order to distress us into a compliance upon the other point. The Queen of Spain may have other views, but the Catholic King and the true Spaniards are animated against us by this single consideration.'[1] The two leading members of the British government at that time were Sir Robert Walpole and Lord Townshend, and like Lord Stanhope before them, and the Elder Pitt later, they were quite prepared to surrender Gibraltar for the sake of a settlement with Spain. 'What you propose, in relation to Gibraltar,' Townshend accordingly replied to Poyntz, 'is certainly very reasonable; and is exactly conformable to the opinion which you know I have always entertained concerning that place.'[2]

At the same time the British ministers were afraid that their opponents at home might rouse public opinion against them if they surrendered Gibraltar, so they decided to tempt Elizabeth Farnese with proposals for the advancement of her family at somebody else's expense. This stratagem was brilliantly successful, for it will be remembered that Great Britain agreed that Spanish garrisons should be introduced into the Italian duchies, while in return the Queen ruthlessly sacrificed the real interests of Spain in every field, and the demand for the return of Gibraltar was waived in silence. A very favourable opportunity for regaining the fortress by diplomatic means had been lost.

A somewhat similar situation arose eighteen years later during the conference at Breda which was endeavouring to bring to an end the War of the Austrian Succession. On this occasion it was the Earl of Chesterfield, Secretary of State for the Northern Department, and the Earl of Sandwich, the British representative at Breda, who were prepared to restore Gibraltar to Spain, while the Duke of Newcastle, the Secretary of State for the Southern Department and future Prime Minister, took the opposite view. On 6th February 1747 Chesterfield wrote to Sandwich:

Were nobody here wiser than I, I confess I should be tractable upon

---

[1] cf. Coxe, W.: *Sir Robert Walpole*, p. 628. London. 1798.
[2] ibid., p. 631.

the affair of Gibraltar, rather than let the negotiation with Spain break off and throw the new King into the arms of France, from which I am convinced he is sincerely disposed to disingage himself. Nay, I am persuaded that, if we could, by the price of Gibraltar, purchase advantageous and unequivocal conditions for our commerce to America, the measure would be approved by all reasoning people.[1]

Newcastle, however, would have none of it. 'A peace with Spain,' he wrote, 'attended with a breach with our allies would as inevitably fling us into the power of France, as the purchase of it by Gibraltar and Port Mahon would expose us to the condemnation and resentment of the nation.'[2]

Sandwich himself then wrote to Newcastle from Breda.

In one of my former private letters I dropped a hint of the restitution of Gibraltar, and I must own that if we could at that price extricate ourselves out of the danger we are in hourly of being abandoned by our treacherous ally the Republick,[3] could secure the possession of Cape Breton, could regulate our commercial dispute with Spain upon an advantageous foot, and could put it out of the power of the French to force us to any terms but such as we would wish both for ourselves and our allies, I should think our friends in England could never charge us with having given up the maritime interests of our country.[4]

Newcastle, though not endowed with the higher virtues of statesmanship, was not an easy man to convince against his will, while both he and his brother, Henry Pelham, had their ears close to the electorate of those days, and they were convinced that public opinion would not tolerate the retrocession of Gibraltar.[5] In vain the representatives of Ferdinand VI asked for a secret article reserving the right of Spain, after peace had been made, to find some expedient for the recovery of Gibraltar, for the proposal was vetoed by the British government. Thus another European settlement, that of Aix-la-Chapelle, took place without Gibraltar being restored to Spain.

[1] This autograph letter is in the Sandwich Papers at Hinchingbroke.

[2] B.M. Add. MSS. 32,807, fo. 71.

[3] i.e. the Dutch.

[4] B.M. Add. MSS. 32,807, fo. 99.

[5] cf. Lodge, Sir. R.: *Studies in Eighteenth Century Diplomacy, 1740–1748*, p. 231. London. 1930.

Newcastle was equally intractable eight years later when, after Minorca had been captured by the French, there was a question of its being regained by Britain by the cession of Gibraltar. On the other hand the then Governor, Lord Tyrawly, reported to Pitt on 1st February 1757 that the place was a source of expense, and as ill-adapted as the Eddystone Lighthouse for the repair of a fleet. Pitt himself inclined to this view, and took no steps to improve its defences; in fact, he obviously regarded Gibraltar as a pawn in the game for the restoration of Minorca, to which he attached far more importance. When the next peace settlement was made, namely the Treaty of Paris in 1763, there was of course no question of the recovery of Gibraltar by Spain, for she had been the loser in the war against Britain, which she had been so ill-advised as to enter in support of France.

To return to the dilemma of Charles. The Spanish offer of mediation was rejected by London on the ground that it was inconsistent with the national honour to solicit the interference of a foreign Power until the views of France were known, whereupon Charles expressed his readiness to open a negotiation in a manner which should spare both parties the humiliation of making the first advances. He suggested that each government should transmit its conditions to Madrid, and that when this had been done he would draw up, from the offers and demands of both, a plan for the conclusion of a definitive treaty. In reply, Britain confined her requirements to one single article based on the principle of her right to treat with her own colonies independent of foreign intervention. She declared that if France would withdraw her assistance from the Americans she would readily agree to the re-establishment of friendly relations as in the past. France, on the contrary, required as a preliminary the acknowledgement of the independence of the colonies, and their evacuation by the British forces, naval and military. She also reserved the right to bring forward additional demands on the grounds of amending or explaining preceding treaties.

On examining these propositions Charles came to the conclusion that he would be justified in continuing his negotiations. The French proved to be the more difficult, though whether the British were sincere or were merely playing for time is, in the light of King George's letter to Lord North, not easy to decide. Anyhow, the French government refused to shift its position, on the ground that the honour of their crown did not permit them to withdraw from their commitments, while the colonists themselves had announced their resolution not to enter into any negotiation until their independence was acknowledged. Furthermore, the French ministers declined at this stage to specify what future claims they might put forward. London, now under the shadow of Saratoga, proved more accommodating, and the British Cabinet expressed a readiness to grant a general amnesty to the revolted colonies, at the same time treating them as confederating individuals for the restoration of constitutional government and the redress of grievances.

While these negotiations were taking their somewhat leisurely course there occurred a series of events of which the cumulative effect was to incline Charles more favourably towards the American cause and to co-operation with his French cousin in support of it. First of all there was the progress of hostilities which showed no sign of turning in favour of the British, who in June 1778 followed up the capitulation of Saratoga by the evacuation of Philadelphia. Nor was this all, for, as in earlier wars, the claims of the British Admiralty often proved incompatible with Spanish maritime interests, and caused bad blood between the two nations. Towards the end of the previous year there had been a change of French ambassador at Madrid, where old Ossun had been succeeded by the Comte de Montmorin, a young man under thirty, whose chief claim to distinction was that he was a friend of the new French King. He was short of stature, insignificant in appearance, and lacking in experience, but he made up in energy what he lacked in wisdom, and his influence on the American scene was by no means negligible.

Above all, there had arrived in the Spanish capital as early as 1777 a representative, unofficial as yet, of the United States in the person of thirty-six-year-old Dr. Arthur Lee, who was a much more attractive personality than his French colleague. Lee came of the old Virginian family of that name; he had been educated at Eton and Edinburgh University, and had graduated both in medicine and law. He kept a diary, and what he entered in it was by no means always flattering to his new-found Spanish friends, for he was most unfavourably impressed by the miserable conditions in which the aristocracy of Castille still lived, and he complained bitterly of the fleas and bugs which abounded in the

Spanish inns. At Burgos he met Grimaldi, who had already resigned but who, as we have seen, was carrying on his duties until the arrival of Floridablanca from Rome. The ex-minister had asked the American to wait at Burgos since he preferred that they should meet there, and so avoid the publicity attendant upon a meeting in Madrid. Grimaldi received Lee with the greatest courtesy, and his point of view was well expressed by the remark, 'The Spanish court is convinced that its dominions run much less danger if they have a commercial republic for a neighbour than an ambitious monarch.'[1] Whether at this early date Grimaldi also spoke for Charles is another matter, though the Americans were allowed to obtain credits for a large number of stores and equipment which they required.

In spite of all these events Charles still clung to his hope of effective mediation. He saw himself presiding over an international conference in Madrid which should have peace as its object. It would, so extravagant were his hopes, arrive at a settlement not only between Great Britain and her colonies, but also between London and Paris, and for his part in arriving at this agreement Spain should receive Gibraltar and Minorca. So, undeterred by the sarcasms of Versailles and the mutterings in Madrid itself, Charles continued in his thankless rôle of mediator.

He put forward three different proposals to the British government. The first was that there should be a truce between Britain and the American colonies for twenty-five years during which a permanent peace might be negotiated: the second was a truce with France and the colonies: and the third was an indefinite truce with the colonies and France, terminable only after a year's notice, during which the American, British, and French plenipotentiaries, including representatives from Spain, should meet in conference in Madrid. Whichever of these suggestions was adopted, the convention was to be signed by the American agents in Paris, that is to say Benjamin Franklin and his colleagues, on behalf of the United States, and their signatures the French government pledged itself to obtain. In the meantime the colonies were to enjoy freedom of trade and *de facto* independence, the British forces were either to be withdrawn altogether or greatly reduced in number, and in the latter case the position of those remaining in America was to be carefully defined.

[1] Tapia Ozcariz, Enrique de: *Carlos III y Su Epoca*, p. 320. Madrid. 1962.

In the prevailing climate of opinion in London, at any rate in royal and ministerial circles, these suggestions stood not the slightest chance of acceptance. Such a plan of peace, the British government observed, 'seemed to proceed on every principle which had been disclaimed, and to contain every term which had been rejected'. It was therefore declined on the ostensible grounds that, if compelled or reduced to grant such conditions, it would be more consistent with the dignity of the nation to concede them directly to the Americans themselves than through the intervention of France. This refusal, it may be added, was accompanied by expressions of the deepest respect for Charles himself.

By this time the King had begun to realize that mediation was hopeless, and he was also coming to have doubts whether the British were yet ready to make a negotiated peace, while evidence of their unfriendly attitude towards Spain kept mounting up. It was at this moment that Arthur Lee put in a well-timed and well-argued memorandum to the effect that this was the moment for Spain to break away from neutrality, and openly espouse the cause of American independence. There can be no doubt that this memorandum had great influence upon Charles, coming at the moment when his dominant feeling was one of exasperation against Britain, and also when the fortunes of war were going so strongly against her.

Accordingly in the middle of June 1779 Almodóvar handed to Lord Weymouth[1] a document couched in none too friendly terms. The opening paragraph emphasized the 'noble impartiality' of the King of Spain, but in its successors complaint was made that his efforts at mediation had been rejected, and further that he had several specific grievances. His territory had been trespassed on, his ships had been searched and plundered, his dominions in America were threatened, the British had encouraged the Indians to attack Louisiana, and hostile acts had been committed in the Bay of Honduras. Because of these unfriendly acts, the King 'found himself under the disagreeable necessity of making use of all the means that the Almighty has given him to do himself justice which he had in vain solicited'.

The British ministers replied in relatively pacific terms. Charles was informed that his mediation had only been rejected because the French conditions were inadmissible; that as Spain had been

[1] Temporarily the sole Secretary of State.

harbouring American privateers it had been difficult to avoid mistakes in captures at sea, but full reparation had been made when such mistakes were proved; that the setting of the Indians against the Spanish possessions was denied; and the supposed acts of hostility in the Bay of Honduras were now heard for the first time. By now, however, the sands had run out, and on 16th June 1779 Spain declared war on Britain.

XII

THE WAR OF AMERICAN INDEPENDENCE:
EUROPE

WITH the outbreak of hostilities it was clear that in Europe the main task of the Spanish army would be the capture of Gibraltar and Minorca, and for that it was by no means ill-prepared, since it had recently been modernized and its efficiency considerably increased. It is, fortunately, possible to obtain an accurate idea of it from the description of Commander W. Dalrymple, who had travelled all over the Peninsula three years previously, and left a fairly detailed, and not unfavourable, account of the Spanish soldier and the conditions under which he lived.[1]

The levies were based on the traditional system of raising drafts, improved by a recent order specifying the occupations exempt from military service, which was for eight years with the colours. To the English critics who objected to the method of exemption among the urban classes Dalrymple replied that by the exclusion of a great many tradesmen and artisans the authorities ensured that the army would have a peasant basis, namely that it would be recruited from that very class of the community which displayed the greatest patriotism, and that in consequence the Spanish army was much superior to that of so many countries where the ranks often contained a large proportion of drunks and wasters of various sorts. He found the soldiers well clothed and well fed: half of each regiment was given leave during the four months of harvest; desertions were rare; and discipline was good, while the barracks were, in general, clean. Dalrymple visited the recently founded Military Academy at Avila, and also inspected the regiment garrisoning that town, both of which met with his approval.

He summed up his impressions by saying that the units he had seen consisted of fine young men of whom the majority were

[1] *Travels in Spain and Portugal.*

183

under thirty. Possibly the general effect would not have been to the taste of an English regimental sergeant-major of the old school, but Dalrymple was of the opinion that the Spanish troops could be relied upon to give a good account of themselves, particularly if well led.[1] In view of this expert opinion there is no reason to believe that on this occasion at any rate the attack on Gibraltar was undertaken with troops of inferior quality: the responsibility for the failure, as we shall see, must be sought at a higher level.

With the Spanish navy the situation was somewhat different. Its principal home bases were at Ferrol, Cadiz, and Cartagena, and there were some sixty ships of the line ready for service: ship for ship the Spanish men-of-war were almost certainly better than the British, but the naval personnel were not of a high order. On the other hand the British fleet was reduced in numbers through the usual neglect in time of peace, and the coast was badly defended. Furthermore, although Portugal was in theory England's oldest ally, the skilful diplomacy of Charles and Floridablanca kept her neutral in the War of American Independence, and so the British were deprived of an associate and of a base of operations which had proved of inestimable advantage in previous contests. What went a long way to counterbalance these advantages was that the three main armaments of the Bourbon Powers, that is to say the Franco-Spanish Home Fleet, the Franco-Spanish fleet in the West Atlantic, and the American army never worked in close co-operation. If, from the beginning, the combined fleets in home waters had used their great strength to prevent British squadrons from putting to sea, while at the same time the French fleet in America had acted in close co-operation with Washington's army, the British government would have been hard put to it to adopt effective counter-measures: only once was close co-operation attempted, and then British dominion over the American colonies came to an end.

Even before war broke out it had been arranged that the French and Spanish Home Fleets should combine in that event, but this did not take place as speedily as had been anticipated in Madrid or Paris. There were long delays which are, indeed, unavoidable when the fleets of two nations attempt to co-operate

[1] It was Ferdinand V who said that Spanish troops required a very strong hand.

without previous practice together or carefully thought-out arrangements in peace time. The almost insuperable difficulties that arise from the organization and administration of ships of two nations in one fleet also made themselves felt. Nor was this all, for the French and Spanish governments had different ends in view: for Charles and his ministers the main objective was the recovery of Gibraltar and Minorca, while France hesitated between various schemes such as an invasion of England itself and the landing of fourteen thousand troops at Waterford under Patrick Wall, a native of County Carlow, who had been wounded fighting for the Stuarts at Culloden.[1]

A partial junction of the two fleets took place on 2nd July, but it was not until 23rd that it was complete with the arrival of the main Spanish squadron from Cadiz. By this time alarm in the south and west of England had become general, and anticipated in its main outlines that of the summer of 1940. On 9th July a Royal Proclamation was issued which instructed the people of the southern counties to drive all horses and cattle from the coast in case of invasion. Booms were placed across the entrance to Plymouth Harbour; orders were sent to prepare vessels for sinking across other harbour entrances; and a large number of troops were encamped on the south coast. Steps were also taken to strengthen naval defences, and small squadrons and flotillas were organized and stationed at different parts of the south coast to act against transports.

The result was anticlimax. With fifty thousand men collected at Le Havre and St. Malo for the invasion of England the great Franco-Spanish armada of sixty-six sail of the line with innumerable small craft sailed up the Channel, under the command of the French Admiral d'Orvilliers, flaunted its presence off the English coast until the beginning of September creating alarm and despondency wherever it appeared, and then dispersed to its home ports. The whole operation thus came to an end without a man being landed or a shot fired. All the same, however, something had been attained, for the loss of the command of the sea had prevented the British from interfering with the arrival of the plate fleet from America, and it had deprived the armies that were

[1] cf. James, W. M.: *The British Navy in Adversity*, pp. 171–173. London. 1926; also Hayes, R.: *Biographical Dictionary of Irishmen in France*, p. 304. Dublin. 1949.

fighting Washington of the reinforcements which they so urgently required.

Meanwhile the major Spanish effort was being prepared against Gibraltar, and for this Charles's astute diplomacy had prepared the way, for just as it had been of the first importance to secure the neutrality of Portugal, so it was vital to ensure that of Morocco. 'Your Majesty comprehends better than any other person,' Floridablanca wrote to the King, 'how great would have been our embarrassment, if, by omitting to form this connection in time, England had incited the Moors to attack Ceuta or Melilla, or by piratical cruises in the Straits, to damage all our measures for the blockade of Gibraltar, and the transport of provisions to our camp.' The Sultan, Mohammad I, was completely won over, and he not only opened his ports to Spanish ships, but he also deposited a large sum of money in Spain as a pledge of his sincerity. These arrangements had the further advantage of enabling the Spanish government to reduce its establishments on the coast of North Africa.

The siege of Gibraltar, which now became the main feature of the war in Europe, began in a very leisurely manner. The authorities on the Rock had for some time noticed an unaccustomed reserve on the part of those in La Linea, but it was not until the outbreak of hostilities that the latter place began to be thronged with workmen improving the defences of the camp, and by October there were more than fourteen thousand of them. On 21st June General Mendoza had notified the Governor that he had received orders to cut all communications by sea and land between Spain and the British garrison. At this time the garrison of Gibraltar totalled five thousand four hundred, including five line regiments, three battalions of Hanoverians, and three companies of artillery, but several months passed before there was any fighting worth the name. In the interval both sides made preparations for what was clearly going to be a long siege. The Spaniards were digging themselves in by degrees, opening up the earth in all directions to make trenches, approaches, casemates, dugouts, and breast works; they were also to be seen sawing up heavy tree trunks that were dragged along with teams of mules, and mounted guns which were brought to the spot in wagons with much difficulty. The British, inside the fortress, for their part were reorganizing, enlarging, and increasing the number of their batteries, putting the civil inhabitants on reduced rations, and evacuating many of them by night to the Moroccan coast.

Throughout the siege the Governor was George Eliott of Stobs, later Lord Heathfield, and one of the heroes of British history. In some ways he was the prototype of Sir William Dobbie, who defended Malta in the Second World War. A born sapper, Eliott had been in every fight since Dettingen. He was a Scot, but although he was a vegetarian and a teetotaller he possessed a sense of humour, and it is unquestionably due to him that Britain continued to hold the Rock. Leadership of a like calibre on the Franco-Spanish side was conspicuously lacking. To quote a recent Spanish writer:

The responsibility for the failure must be sought at a higher level (*i.e.* than the quality of the troops or a shortage of material): in the guiding plan and in lack of technical ability, especially the latter, and above all in the failure to make full use of the fleet, a factor of primary importance in an operation of this kind. The use which was made of the combined fleets of France and Spain could not have been less skilful or more incomprehensible; though they did at first serve to reduce communications with North Africa they did not prevent the arrival of large convoys or play an important part in the principal bombardments; indeed, despite their superior numbers and greater freedom in manœuvring (since they were operating from their own base at Algeciras and had not to protect convoys as their adversaries had) they did not in the end have either the resolution or the luck to force the enemy to give battle at the critical moment. A clear augury of such unskilful use of a navy was the pretentious threat of invasion of the British Isles by the French Admiral d'Orvilliers as soon as war broke out, which he handled so strangely that it remained no more than a threat.[1]

The actual hostilities seem to have been carried on with greater courtesy on both sides than the more recent controversy regarding the possession of the fortress. Captain John Drinkwater, for instance, noted on 4th December 1779, 'The enemy beat a parley, and sent in a mule (belonging to Colonel Green, the chief engineer) which had strayed to their lines; an instance of politeness which we did not expect.'[2] This incident was by no means

---

[1] Plá, José: *Gibraltar*, pp. 78–79. London. 1955.
[2] *A History of the Siege of Gibraltar, 1779–1783*. London. 1846.

exceptional, for from time to time a Spanish or French bugle sounded to attention so that letters and parcels sent by their friends could be handed over to members of the garrison. This was done originally at the strip of no-man's-land on the isthmus, but later it took place in the bay for fear of spying.

Very soon there were deserters from both camps, and those from the Spanish were mostly foreigners from the Walloon Guards. Occasionally, one of the besieged allowed his tongue to wag with more noise than discretion, with consequences related by Captain Spilsbury – 'It seems one of the 58th[1] was heard saying that if the Spaniards came, damn him that he would not join them; the Governor said he must be mad and ordered his head to be shaved, to be blistered, bled and sent to the Provost on bread and water, wear a tight waistcoat, and to be prayed for in church.'[2]

Although there was no serious fighting in these early days of the siege food before long began to run short because the British government had quite inexcusably neglected to provision the place before the outbreak of war. At first this was not felt to any great extent because in spite of the Moorish Sultan's arrangement with Charles, his subjects were not above slipping across the Straits by night, and discharging the cargoes of their boats at Europa Point under cover of darkness. Before long, however, the blockade was tightened, and there came days when there was no bread at all, and the civil population was extremely hard pressed. At this point the profiteer made his appearance, and none of the necessaries of life were procurable except at exorbitant prices in the black market. This stimulated the inventiveness of the besieged, and a Hanoverian soldier discovered a way of artificially incubating the eggs which were smuggled in by the Moors. By using damp rags slowly heated at a candle flame, he managed to hatch out chickens, which he placed in charge of a handy capon to bring up. To persuade the male bird to devote himself to his maternal duties, Captain Drinkwater has left on record, 'the feathers were plucked from his breast and belly; he was then gently scourged with nettles and placed upon the young hatch, whose downy warmth afforded such comfort to the bared and smarting parts that he from that period reared them up, with

[1] Later the Northamptonshire Regiment.
[2] *A Journal of the Siege of Gibraltar, 1779–1783*. London. 1908.

equal care and tenderness as if they had been his own offspring'.

In spite of the growing shortage of provisions the garrison, never more than seven thousand strong, inspired by Eliott's example, had been very active in defence. The artillery had kept the besiegers at a distance, while it had been found possible to mount a 24-pounder gun at the highest point of the Rock. Yet by the close of the year 1779 provisions were running very short indeed, with flour at a shilling a pound, chickens at fourteen shillings each, and turkeys at two guineas, while there was no fresh meat at all. That the Spanish blockade was so effective was due to a squadron of fifteen cruisers commanded by Don Antonio Barcelo, which operated under the shadow of a squadron of ships of the line at Algeciras and the main fleet at Cadiz: they were unhampered in their work, and seized all vessels bound for Gibraltar. At the beginning of the war the Spanish land forces took up a position two miles from the outer works of the fortress, and there they remained.

As 1779 passed into 1780 scurvy began to make its appearance, but early in the New Year the garrison obtained a temporary relief with the appearance of Admiral Rodney. His is one of the outstanding names in British naval history, and at this time he was sixty-one years of age. In the Seven Years' War he had proved himself a fine dashing officer, though perhaps a little too prone to attach undue importance to the acquisition of prize-money when selecting his object of attack, and his services in that conflict had won him a baronetcy. Since the Treaty of Paris he had fallen upon evil days, for he had ruined himself by gambling, and was actually taking refuge in Paris from his creditors when the War of American Independence broke out. In the French capital he had been greatly aided by his friend, the Maréchal Duc de Biron. By this time the Admiral was a martyr to gout and a wreck of his old self, but he was soon to prove that the fires could be rekindled in an emergency, and that he possessed considerable powers as a fleet commander. Such was the man who was now appointed to the command of the Leeward Islands Station.

The deteriorating conditions on the Rock were well known to the British government, so Rodney was reinforced, and told to relieve Gibraltar. He was much delayed by contrary winds and administrative difficulties, and he complained to the Secretary of State for the American Colonies that 'the almost total loss of naval discipline is almost beyond comprehension'. On 29th December 1779 he put to sea with twenty-two ships of the line, fourteen frigates, and a vast number of store ships. On his way to Gibraltar he fought two actions, and was successful in both. In the first he was merely concerned with some Spanish frigates escorting a convoy which he captured, but in the second he had to deal with a squadron of eleven ships of the line and two frigates under the command of Admiral Juan de Lángara. The Spaniards fought with great gallantry, but they were handicapped by their slow rate of fire, and were soon overwhelmed by the well-served British broadsides. Lángara in particular distinguished himself, for although severely wounded, and with his masts shot away, he bore the fire of four enemy ships during the greater part of the battle, and did not strike until his flagship was reduced to a complete wreck.

In addition the Franco-Spanish strategy on the occasion left a great deal to be desired. It was obvious that the effort would be made to revictual Gibraltar, but there was no attempt from Brest to interfere with Rodney on his way south. At Cadiz lay Don Juan de Córdoba with twenty Spanish and four French ships of the line, but he made no effort to leave the harbour, and he excused his inactivity on the score of the inefficient state of the Spanish ships and their bad sailing qualities; but after the battle Rodney wrote to his wife that 'the Spanish men-of-war we have taken are much superior to ours'. Lastly, no frigates or small craft were ordered out to patrol and give early warning of the approach of hostile vessels, with the result that Lángara's squadron was surprised by a superior force. After his capture Lángara was taken into Gibraltar, where he seems to have made himself popular, until he was released on his promise not to serve against Britain again in the war.

The joy of the beleaguered garrison at the sight of Rodney's fleet may be imagined. On 15th January 1780 a ship flying a British flag was seen entering the harbour, and before long news was passing round the men on watch at their guns that a relieving force was approaching. That night another ship arrived with stories of the capture of a large Spanish convoy, and three days later the garrison's cup of joy was filled when a frigate ran in with the thrilling news that part of the Spanish main fleet had been destroyed. Don Antonio Barcelo did not attempt to disturb the operations, but took the wiser course of ordering his fleet of cruisers and smaller craft to anchor under the fortifications of Algeciras, where he laid booms and mounted a number of additional guns to guard the anchorage. Finally, on 22nd January British men-of-war and merchant ships were seen making for the harbour.[1]

While these events were taking place an effort was being made, though unofficially, to bring hostilities between Britain and Spain to an end. In November 1779 Floridablanca received information from Commodore Johnson, the British commander on the Lisbon Station, to the effect that Lord North might be willing to purchase peace by the cession of Gibraltar. An Irish priest called Father Hussey, who had been Almodóvar's chaplain at the Spanish embassy in London, was chosen as an intermediary. He came to England, where he made contact with one Richard Cumberland, who was secretary to Lord George Germain, then Secretary of State for the American Colonies.[2] The negotiations both in Madrid and London dragged on for months, though how serious was either party to them is not easy to say. Charles, for his part, was perfectly willing to break with France if he could obtain Gibraltar, for he was in any case none too pleased with the fiasco of d'Orvilliers' Channel cruise; but the British government could not bring itself to discuss the surrender of a fortress which was holding out so gallantly.

In both capitals the hawks and the doves were much under the influence of outside events. Rodney's victory over Lángara had considerably depressed the more bellicose spirits in Madrid, and they remained depressed during the early months of 1780, until in June there arrived the news of the outbreak of the Gordon Riots in London,[3] which were interpreted as heralding a revolution, but even better news was in store. The Spanish intelligence service obtained information to the effect that the united fleets conveying supplies and goods to the East and West Indies were about to sail from England under a weak escort, and Florida-

---

[1] cf. Spinney, D.: *Rodney*, pp. 296–316. London. 1969.

[2] As Lord George Sackville he had in the previous reign been found by a court-martial 'unfit to serve His Majesty in any military capacity whatever' for his behaviour at the battle of Minden.

[3] cf. Petrie, Sir Charles: *The Four Georges, A Revaluation*, pp. 146–152. London. 1946.

blanca conceived the idea of intercepting them at the point of separation off the Azores. He obtained the reluctant consent of the King, who was doubtful on the score of risk, and the task was entrusted to Córdoba, who executed it brilliantly. Accordingly one day in August the citizens of Cadiz were treated to the sight of a captive fleet of nearly sixty sail, a train of civilian prisoners of every rank and station, eighteen hundred officers and men of the royal or East India Company's army, and nearly two million pounds' worth of goods entering the harbour.

'Córdoba's success has so changed affairs that I retreat from my confidence and coincide with your suspicions', Cumberland wrote to Germain, and although the negotiations with Britain dragged on for several months they never looked like achieving anything, and they finally petered out in February 1781.[1] One advantage, however, they did have from the point of view of the King and Floridablanca and it was that as the news of them leaked out in Paris the French government became frightened that Spain might make a separate peace with Britain, and so Louis XVI began to bestir himself to keep in Charles's good books.

The Spanish monarch's diplomacy was, indeed, particularly active at this time. In the early months of 1781 Mohammed I was induced to lease, for the sum of £7,500,000, the ports of Tangier and Tetuan to the Spanish government, and thus were closed the only remaining sources of supply of provisions for the beleaguered garrison of Gibraltar. Further afield it was Spain which played the pre-eminent part in the formation of that armed neutrality which caused the greatest inconvenience to Great Britain by drawing up its own list of contraband, and refusing to accept the British interpretation of the right of search.

To quote Floridablanca's memorial to the King:

To deprive our enemies of every maritime alliance which might incommode us in case of a rupture, by order of Your Majesty I cultivated a good correspondence with the court of Russia, with which some causes of coldness and want of confidence had arisen,

[1] A full account of them may be found in Coxe, W.: *The Bourbon Kings of Spain*, vol. III, pp. 423–437. London. 1813; also cf. Cantillo, Alejandro de: *Colección de Tratados, Convenios y Declaraciones de Paz y Comercio que han hecho con las Potencias Extranjeras Los Monarcas Españoles de la Casa de Borbón*, pp. 576 et seq. Madrid. 1843; and Bemis, S. F.: *The Hussey-Cumberland Mission and American Independence, passim*. Princeton. 1931.

in regard to the etiquette and treatment of an Imperial crown, and to the ceremonies and pretensions of that court. France entered into similar ideas, and we not only prevented Russia from uniting with England during the war, but even prevailed on her to send us purposely two of her frigates, charged with naval stores, at a time when the war prevented the transport of them for the equipment of our fleet. We also succeeded in inducing the Empress of Russia[1] to place herself at the head of almost all the neutral nations to support the honour of her flag, a confederacy which has been called 'the armed neutrality'. Thus was England deprived of the resources she might have drawn from the Maritime Powers, not excepting even Holland, her ancient ally.

By the summer of 1781 Russia, Denmark, and Sweden had no fewer than eighty-four ships of war in commission, so it was clear that the Armed Neutrality held the whip hand over Britain.

Meanwhile Gibraltar remained blockaded, for although Rodney's arrival had brought temporary relief it had by no means raised the siege. The stores he had landed were long since exhausted, and as far back as October 1780 the garrison had been put on short rations. The French were of the opinion that the Rock could best be starved out by a Franco-Spanish fleet sweeping up the Channel once more, and thus preventing any further attempt at relief, but, as we have seen, Charles was very sceptical regarding anything of this nature after the previous failure of d'Orvilliers, so it is not surprising to find the French ambassador in Madrid writing to his government on 24th April 1781, 'Spain's latest decision is absolutely contrary to a junction of the forces of the two nations in Europe. However disagreeable this decision may be, I am passing it on as promptly as I can; I know how important it is that you know on what you can count. I have foreseen this issue for a long while past.'[2]

It was clear that by now Britain had to relieve Gibraltar again or lose it, and as soon as the Spanish strategical decision was known in London it was decided, if possible, to repeat Rodney's manœuvre. The admiral selected for this purpose was George Darby, who sailed from Spithead on 13th March 1781, and after calling at Cork to pick up the victuallers he arrived off Cape Spartel on 11th April with twenty-eight of the line, ten frigates,

---

[1] Catherine II.
[2] French National Archives B.4, 189.

four fireships, and ninety-seven merchant vessels, the various 'trade' convoys having parted company at selected positions.

At this point it may well be asked why the navies of the two crowns allowed him to get there at all. During his passage from Cork the British admiral had to pass by Brest and the principal Spanish ports; it was known that a large French fleet was at Brest; and Córdoba commanded over thirty of the line at Cadiz. Earlier in the year the French had pressed the Spaniards to come north, and when news of the relief expedition reached Madrid the Spanish government urged the French to come south, equally without response. If the two Powers had really been working in harmony a French squadron would have been sent to join Córdoba, with the almost certain consequence that Darby would have been decisively defeated, and the vast assemblage of merchants ships captured. In that case Gibraltar must have fallen, and the war might easily have been ended at one blow.

Juan de Córdoba, however, seems to have been a good deal of a defeatist, and the only offensive action which he took was, as we have seen, on the orders of Charles and Floridablanca. Very different, it may be noted, was the conduct of the French Commodore La Motte-Picquet, who, on hearing that Darby was well to the south relieving Gibraltar, slipped out of Brest, rounded up a British convoy sixty miles west of the Scillies, and returned to harbour with twenty-two captured merchant-ships, whose cargoes were valued at nearly five million pounds. Córdoba's strategy affected the morale of those under his command, and all the evidence goes to show that the personnel of his fleet were suffering from the depression which is always the result of inactivity.

It has, on the other hand, been held that Córdoba was more sinned against than sinning, and that he was handicapped by a shortage of money and provisions. 'It is six months since the King has given me as much as a quarto', wrote a subordinate officer, 'and he does not think of doing it. . . . Every evening I am ordered to take information to the Admiral as regards the daily happenings, and thus I am deprived of the sole means which are at my disposal to reduce my expenses, which is to remain on board ship. . . . Twenty-two millions have arrived, and nevertheless there is not a real in the Naval Treasury nor any hope of receiving anything for a long while past. Orders have just been given to use the money in the convoy, which has lately been captured, to pay for provisions of the several Captains.'[1]

The French ambassador in Madrid had no high opinion of Córdoba or his fleet, for he wrote to his government, 'The Spanish fleet returned to Cadiz on the 27th. I must confess I am more easy knowing it to be there than if it was in the Straits. I was not at all anxious that it should meet with the British, and am much relieved to know that it is in safety. In the present circumstances a defeat would have the most disastrous consequences in every way. I am quite aware there is no glory in entering harbour when the enemy approaches, but at any rate there remain thirty battleships in fairly good condition, and if it becomes possible to divert them towards a good object we may still be able to make good use of them.'[2]

Defeatism, however, was not peculiar to Córdoba, for Captain Duro quotes one of the officials at the Ministry of Marine as opining that 'it is neither advisable nor necessary that our fleet should attack that of the British, and it would even be disadvantageous to do it and advantageous to avoid it, for it is impossible to prevent the arrival of help to the besieged town, or to hinder, during the fight, the entrance of the frigates attending the convoy. . . . The King should preserve his fleet so as to cover the seas and guard the coasts, protect trade to the Indies, and carry out, when the British have left, some of those other projects he proposes to undertake.' Truly a lamentable document.

The low morale of the Spanish High Command, at any rate at sea, renders it impossible not to wonder whether any responsibility attaches to the King himself. We have already seen his reluctance to consent to the one offensive action which was taken at this time, and he would certainly have been justified in superseding Córdoba. In this latter connection one cannot forget his disinclination to get rid of old servants, and it may have been this weakness that prevented him from dismissing Córdoba. It has also been suggested that Charles was primarily interested in the Americas – this charge was to be made when the Treaty of Versailles was being negotiated – and did not regard Gibraltar and Minorca of the first importance. Whatever the reason it must

[1] Quoted by Captain Duro, *Armada Española*.
[2] French National Archives B.4, 189.

be admitted that he did nothing personally to combat the defeatism so rife among his admirals.

To the besieged garrison of Gibraltar these considerations of high policy meant nothing, and they welcomed Admiral Darby's relieving squadron with the same enthusiasm with which they had greeted that of Rodney in the previous year. To quote Captain Drinkwater: 'At daybreak, on the 12th of April, the much-expected fleet, under the command of Admiral Darby, was in sight from our signalhouse, but was not discernible from below, being obscured by a thick mist in the Gut. As the sun, however, became more powerful, the fog gradually rose, like the curtain of a vast theatre, discovering to the anxious garrison one of the most beautiful and pleasing scenes it is possible to conceive. The convoy, consisting of near a hundred vessels, was in a compact body, whilst the majority of the line of battle ships lay-to under the Barbary shore, having orders not to enter the Bay, lest the enemy should molest them with their fire-ships. The ecstasies of the inhabitants at this grand and exhilarating sight are not to be described. Their expressions of joy far exceeded their former exultations. But alas! they little dreamed of the tremendous blow that impended, which was to annihilate their property, and reduce many of them to indigence and beggary.'

What happened was that the first great act of war since the outbreak of hostilities was launched. About fifteen gun-boats suddenly came out of Algeciras and attacked the convoy, with the support of the shore batteries, but they inflicted relatively little damage, as the ships composing it were able to take refuge under the guns of Gibraltar. This was followed by a cannonade from the various pieces of artillery collected by the besiegers on the isthmus; but again no great damage was done, and once Darby had completed his task of getting supplies into the town he was able to sail away without serious inconvenience.

From then until August the garrison was submitted to a continuous bombardment of shot and incendiary bombs, but in August this stopped as suddenly as it had begun, and the Spaniards then limited their activities in this line to three rounds a day, which were irreverently dubbed The Father, The Son, and The Holy Ghost by the British soldiers. However, it is proverbially an ill wind that blows nobody any good, and the fires started by the shelling gave the troops an opportunity of avenging themselves on the profiteers who had hoarded their wares during the days of famine so as to raise the price. The men detailed to put out the fires sacked the shops and warehouses instead, and then started to quarrel among themselves, even to the extent of throwing up barricades against the pickets sent to control them. As Captain Drinkwater put it, 'Some died of immediate intoxication, and several were with difficulty recovered, by oils and tobacco water, from a dangerous state of inebriety.'

The extremely severe penalties ordered by the Governor were of no avail, for the cannon-balls used to destroy ruined buildings opened up all sorts of *caches* full of food and cases of wine and spirits, upon which the riotous soldiers fell with avidity. On this point Captain Spilsbury reinforces the evidence of Captain Drinkwater when he says that 'such a scene of drunkenness, debauchery, and destitution was hardly seen before'. In one of these unbridled moments a group of drunken men stumbled upon a mutilated image of the Virgin in the ruins of a church where it had lain hidden since Gibraltar was first conquered. At once there was an outbreak of that public-house Protestantism never far below the surface in an eighteenth-century Englishman, and the soldiers formed themselves into a burlesque court martial to sentence the statue to the usual punishment of the whirligig in the market place.

Thereafter nothing worthy of mention happened until late in the spring of 1782, with the exception of two well-planned sorties by the garrison to relieve the pressure on the landward side, in the second of which José Cadalso, the author whose works remind the English reader not only of Goldsmith but also of Addison and even of Swift, was killed while in command of a troop of horse. Why Charles should have allowed the siege to be conducted in this languid manner is not easy to decide. He was a merciful man, and it may have been due to a desire to keep the casualties down, and in the belief that in due course hunger would cause the garrison to surrender.

If these were Charles's motives they had been a success in the case of Minorca, which was the only British base in the Mediterranean. It was not until the summer of 1781 that Floridablanca persuaded his master to authorize an attack on the island, for which the preparations were made in the utmost secrecy. Instead of the usual and natural ports of embarkation in Catalonia and

Murcia being used the preparations were made at Cadiz as if the expeditionary force were destined to operate against Gibraltar or the West Indies. Even the French court was kept in ignorance of what was intended until everything was ready, which was in July 1781, when a Franco-Spanish fleet set out from Cadiz conveying 15,000 men under the command of the Duc de Crillon. The British forces defending the place were not more than 2,700, and they were commanded by General James Murray, of Canadian fame.

The expedition effected a complete surprise, and landed without opposition. One division under the Marqués de Aviles took possession of Ciudadela, and another under the Marqués de Penafiel occupied Fornells. The principal body of the invaders moved into positions near Port Mahon, where they seized the arsenal, and the British were compelled to withdraw into Fort San Felipe. So sudden and well-combined was the attack that according to Floridablanca nothing but the delay caused by the uncertainty of the wind prevented San Felipe, also, being carried by assault. The local inhabitants greeted the Franco-Spanish forces with enthusiasm, for one of Crillon's first acts was to proclaim in the name of Charles the restoration of all their privileges. Nevertheless the failure to take San Felipe by storm had disconcerted Crillon's plans, for he had no siege implements with him, and was consequently reduced to a blockade with the assistance of a small fleet under Don Bonaventura Moreno. It was not until 11th November that he was in a position to open his batteries, and the real siege began: by this time he had been heavily reinforced with men, as well as supplied with artillery and munitions.

Murray put up a resistance worthy of Eliott in Gibraltar, but the odds were heavily against him. Not only were his men numerically inadequate, but even their small numbers were continually being depleted by disease, in particular by scurvy. Nor was this all, for an enemy shell set fire to a magazine which contained their medical stores, so that by the end of January 1782 only six hundred of the garrison were in any degree fit for duty, and for the majority of these the proper place was the hospital. On the fourth of the following month Murray surrendered, and what then ensued has been well described by Dr. Beatson in his *Naval and Military Memoirs*.

Perhaps a more noble, nor a more tragic scene was never exhibited, than that of the march of the garrison of St. Philip's, through the Spanish and French armies. It consisted of no more than six hundred old decrepit soldiers, two hundred seamen, one hundred and twenty of the Royal Artillery, twenty Corsicans, and twenty-five Greeks, Turks, Moors, Jews etc. The two armies were drawn up in two lines, the battalions fronting each other, forming a way for us to march through; they consisted of fourteen thousand men, and reached from the glacis to George Town, where our battalions laid down their arms, declaring they had surrendered them to God alone, having the consolation to know the victors could not plume themselves in taking a hospital.

Such were the distressing figures of our men, that many of the Spanish and French troops are said to have shed tears as they passed them; the Duc de Crillon and the Baron de Falkenhayn declare it is true. I cannot aver this, but think it very natural: for my own part, I felt no uneasiness on this occasion, but that which proceeded from the miserable disorder which threatened us with destruction.

Thanks to the Almighty, my apprehensions are now abated; the humanity of the Duc de Crillon, whose heart was sensibly touched by the misfortunes of such brave men, has gone even beyond my wishes in providing everything which can contribute to our recovery. The Spanish as well as the French surgeons attend our hospitals. We are greatly indebted to the Baron de Falkenhayn, who commands the French troops. We owe infinite obligations to the Duc de Crillon; they can never be forgot by any of us. I hope this young man never will command an army against my sovereign, for his military talents are as conspicuous as the goodness of his heart.

As the recovery of Minorca was one of the main Spanish objects in the war in Europe, this success placed Crillon high in Charles's favour, and the Frenchman was appointed to command the Franco-Spanish army besieging Gibraltar, while Don Bonaventura Moreno was also ordered to assist in the operations. A further reinforcement of twelve thousand French troops was also dispatched, and they were accompanied by a host of notabilities from all over Western Europe. The Comtes de Provence and d'Artois, brothers of Louis XVI and themselves subsequently Kings of France as Louis XVIII and Charles X, had long sought permission to go to America with the French expeditionary force, but it had been refused them, for the monarchs of France viewed their brothers with an almost Turkish suspicion. On this occa-

sion, however, the Comte d'Artois was given leave to participate in the siege of Gibraltar, and on 19th August 1782 Crillon
is found writing to Elliot:

His Royal Highness the Comte d'Artois, who has received permission from the King his brother to assist at the siege, as a volunteer
in the Combined Army, of which their Most Christian and Catholic
Majesties have honoured me with the command, arrived in this
camp on the 15th inst. This young Prince has been pleased, in passing
through Madrid, to take charge of some letters, which are addressed
to persons belonging to your garrison; His Royal Highness has
desired that I should transmit them to you, and that to this mark of
his goodness and attention I should add the strongest expressions
of esteem for your person and character. I feel the greatest pleasure
in giving this mark of condescension in this august Prince, as it
furnishes me with a pretext, which I have been anxiously looking
for for these two months that I have been in camp, to assure you of
the highest esteem I have conceived for Your Excellency, of the
sincerest desire I feel of deserving yours, and of the pleasure to
which I look forward of becoming your friend, after I shall have
learned to render myself worthy of the honour, by facing you as an
enemy. His Highness the Duc de Bourbon, who arrived here
twenty-four hours after the Comte d'Artois, desires also that I
should assure you of his particular esteem.

Permit me, Sir, to offer a few trifles for your table, of which I am
sure you must stand in need, as I know you live entirely upon
vegetables: I should be glad to know what kind you like best. I shall
add a few game for the gentlemen of your household, and some ice,
will not be disagreeable in the excessive heat of this climate at this
season of the year. I hope you will be obliging enough to accept a
small portion which I send with this letter.

The Governor replied equally politely, but suggested that
Crillon, if he thought fit, should abstain from making gifts of
vegetables since, although these were certainly in short supply,
the garrison were able to cultivate them in sufficient quantities
during the periods of leisure left them between the bombardments.

By this time it was clear both to Madrid and Paris that if
Gibraltar was to be taken other measures must be adopted than
those hitherto employed, and the leading Spanish and French
experts in siege warfare were consulted, while ministries and

embassies were inundated by an enormous mass of plans, many of which were fantastic to the point of madness. 'Some of them', wrote Bourgoing, the councillor of the French embassy in Madrid, 'I received myself. One proposed quite seriously to erect opposite the line of San Roque a huge mountain higher than Gibraltar, with the object of depriving the fortress of its chief advantage. The author of this scheme had calculated the number of cubic feet of earth, the man power and the time required for a work of this magnitude, and proved that it would work out cheaper and less destructive than the prolongation of the siege. Another proposed filling grenades with some substance so noxious that when they exploded within the walls they would either poison the besieged or force them to take to flight.'[1]

The plan finally adopted, and much favoured by the King of Spain, was that of a French engineer, one Michaud d'Arçon, and it provided for the building of floating batteries with a roof of thick hides, wooden sides, and a special water system for dealing with the red-hot shot used by the defenders' artillery. In Madrid there was now general confidence as a result that Gibraltar was at last about to fall, and Charles was heard muttering, 'It will soon be ours', during the weeks of preparation. Crillon, on the other hand, was sceptical of the scheme from the beginning, and before taking over the command, he deposited the following statement in Madrid:

On leaving for Gibraltar I declare that I accept the command which His Majesty has done me the honour of conferring upon me, to carry out the plan with the floating batteries against that fortress. I promise to assist M. d'Arçon by every means until the moment when the batteries have begun their attack. I have endeavoured to lay before His Majesty my objections to the execution of this plan which appears to me contrary to the prosperity and honour of the forces of the King. I therefore declare that if, contrary to my opinion, the fortress is taken by the effect of the said batteries and the assault following on their action, all the glory of this feat of arms shall go to M. d'Arçon, the French engineer who is author of the plan. I also declare that, should the floating batteries not prove successful, no reproaches can be made to me, since I have taken no part in the project.

I charge the Señores de Marco only to open this letter on the

[1] *Tableau de l'Espagne Moderne.*

arrival in Madrid of the courier whom I shall send to inform the King that the attack has begun. In this way the people of Madrid will be informed of the matter twenty-four hours before fate has spoken, the result being made known by a second courier whom I shall dispatch to the King twenty-four hours after the first. I also certify herewith that the present declaration has been made with the formal permission of the Conde de Floridablanca, Minister of State, and with the approval of His Majesty.[1]

When a number of these floating batteries had been completed preparations were made for a grand attack: a thousand pieces of ordnance were mounted afloat and on shore, and eighty-three thousand barrels of gunpowder were collected. The fleet consisted of forty gunboats with heavy artillery, bomb vessels with 12-inch mortars, ten ships of the line, three hundred large landing-craft, and a vast number of frigates and xebecs. This force was further increased just before the attack by the arrival of the Franco-Spanish fleet.

The assault took place on 13th September 1782, and from the beginning everything went wrong for the attackers. The floating batteries, unable to struggle against the current, lay at unsuitable points and distances, while the device for preventing fires proved to be useless. The British surpassed themselves in the accuracy and rapidity of their fire, and the showers of red-hot shot and bombs caused the greatest havoc among d'Arçon's contrivances. During the night the floating batteries caught fire one after another, and to make the confusion worse confounded they were suddenly attacked by a flotilla of British gunboats. To quote the official version of the disaster in the *Madrid Gazette* of 24th September:

When the English had made sure that the floating batteries could not fire, they flung into the water some of their gunboats, with which they seized several of our passing craft, thus overpowering the last remnants of troops or sailors who still remained in the batteries awaiting their turn to be rescued; so that by this means at dawn they had taken prisoner three hundred and thirty-five persons (including various wounded, whom General Eliott is known to have

[1] One is reminded of the action of Sir John Moore, who, on his appointment to the command in the Peninsula in 1808, said to Castlereagh, 'Remember, my Lord, I protest against the expedition, and foretell its failure.'

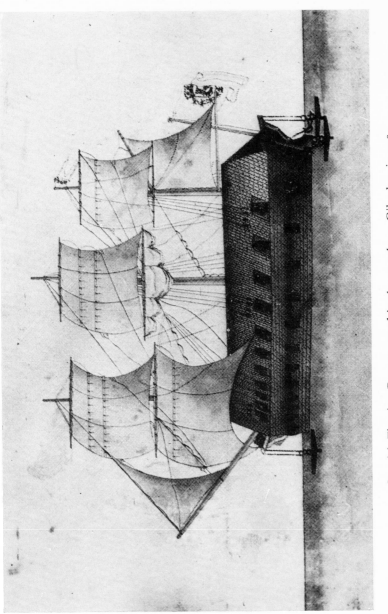

Spanish Floating Battery, used in the attack on Gibraltar in 1782

Charles III, by Velasquez

treated with the greatest humanity and kindness). The floating batteries blew up after that, with the exception of three which were completely consumed by fire even to the planks on the surface of the water.

The great attack had not only been beaten off but completely crushed.

In these circumstances it is small wonder that a recent Spanish historian, Don José Plá, should have put the blame fair and square on 'the extremely bad naval commanders of the day. Confused in their strategy, slow to make use of superior resources and of the immense advantage afforded by the proximity of naval bases, remiss in collaboration with their allies and careless of where they moved – a magnificent double-decker dashed herself to pieces against the English batteries – tardy in manœuvring and without a spark of daring, their behaviour, which surely presages Trafalgar, was, though it grieves us to record the fact, utterly deplorable.'[1]

Meanwhile preparations were being made in England for a third relief of Gibraltar, this time by Admiral Lord Howe, and they were successfully put into effect on 14th October without serious interference from the Spanish fleet. The operations afford another striking instance of failure due to the lack of offensive spirit, for Córdoba was far superior in numbers, Howe was hampered by a convoy on the outward voyage, and after the relief took up a challenging position to leeward of him, yet the Spanish admiral did absolutely nothing. It may be added that during these operations a British ship carrying the wives of the officers of the relieving regiments was captured by the Spaniards who promptly restored the ladies to their rightful lords and masters.

For all practical purposes this ended the siege of Gibraltar. Desultory fighting against the fortress continued for some time, but it was now in a good state of defence, thanks to fresh troops, provisions, and ammunition. Early in February 1783 news arrived of the signing of peace, and on the sixth of that month the gates were opened for the first time for three years, seven months, and five days, while in due course Eliott was created Lord Heathfield.

[1] *Gibraltar*, p. 83. London. 1955.

XIII

THE WAR OF AMERICAN INDEPENDENCE: AMERICA

GEOGRAPHICAL, as much as political, considerations weighed heavily with the British, French, and Spanish commanders both on land and sea in the American theatre of war, for during the eighteenth century trade with their overseas possessions was of vital importance to Great Britain, France, Spain, and Holland. In the case of France it has been calculated that thirty per cent of her imports and thirty-five per cent of her exports represented trade with the West Indies. None of these islands was self-supporting, and their revictualling from time to time was essential to their existence, but it often caused a deflection of strategy.

In this area Spain held Puerto Rico, San Domingo, and Cuba, all to leeward of the British eastern chain of islands, while in Havana she possessed a fine harbour with shipbuilding facilities. Now that she was allied with France she had the use of the French bases which to the eastward, or windward, were St. Lucia, Martinique, and Guadaloupe, and to leeward Haiti, with its good Harbour at Cap François: in the western area the French had the advantage of position over the British, for Haiti was well to the windward of Jamaica. Thus, though the islands were fairly evenly divided between the three countries, France and Spain had a considerable advantage in the matter of good anchorages and ports of refit. British ships could undergo minor repairs at English Harbour, Antigua, and at Barbados, it is true, but the anchorage at the latter island was a bad one. There were facilities at Jamaica for heaving ships down to clean and examine their bottoms, but no admiral would willingly send ships a thousand miles to leeward. There were some facilities at New York, which remained in British hands throughout the war, for ships of under sixty-four guns, and also at Halifax, Nova Scotia, but ships in need of serious repairs had to return to England.

Indeed, Great Britain was at a decided disadvantage in every way compared with her rivals in this theatre. Her West Indian possessions consisted of a chain of islands running from St. Kitts to Tobago, Barbados – a hundred miles to the eastward of this chain, and Jamaica a thousand miles to the westward. The position of these bases also had a special significance on account of the route taken by craft sailing to the Indies, for there were no alternative routes. West-bound ships clearing from British ports worked their way south to the latitude of Madeira in order to pick up the trade wind, and ships bound for the East Indies, via the Cape, took the same course for the first part of the voyage. They were thus in a danger-zone until well clear of the latitude of Gibraltar, and their safety could only be assured by the adoption of a convoy and escort system.

The governing factor for the seamen of all nationalities was the wind. The prevailing one was north-easterly, which meant that it was an easy matter for, say, ships to sail from the Windward Islands to Jamaica, but a very long and arduous operation to make the reverse passage. For this reason outward-bound convoys from England made their landfall at Barbados, where ships with cargoes for the various Windward Islands parted company, and the remainder went on in convoy to Jamaica. For the homeward voyage the ships with cargoes from the Windward Islands collected at St. Kitts, the most northerly of the British islands, and made their way north to about the latitude of Bermuda to pick up the prevailing west wind to carry them home to the Channel. On the other hand homeward-bound ships clearing from Jamaica, instead of beating to the eastward, took advantage of the Gulf Stream, and, after passing through the Yucatan Strait, made their way north until they felt the west wind.

The hurricane season, which lasted from July to October, was the determining factor in the duration of naval operations and the convoy programmes, for no big ships put to sea during these months, and convoys were timed to arrive from Europe not later than June or earlier than January, while homeward-bound convoys sailed in May or June, and sometimes in November.

The weakness of Britain's position is thus obvious, and her senior officers responsible for the direction of operations in West Indian waters had many difficulties with which to contend. The windward position, once surrendered, could only be recovered by days or weeks of laborious work. The campaigning season was a short one, and ships involved in operations and far from good shelter when the hurricanes commenced would be courting disaster. The revictualling of the island populations from time to time was vital to their existence. The defence of the convoy assembly ports at certain fixed dates took precedence of all other operations; and there were few facilities for the docking and up-keep of the fleet, or for the repair of damaged ships. In this respect Spain and France had a distinct advantage.

In spite of this, in the New World the Spaniards displayed a great deal more activity on land than they did on sea, possibly because there they were not under French command, which, with one or two exceptions, displayed little initiative. As soon as he received notification of the outbreak of war Don Bernardo de Gálvez, governor of Louisiana and nephew of the Minister for the Indies, mobilized a force of two thousand men, officially recognized the independence of the United States, and with New Orleans as his base struck at the British possessions to the north, first of all capturing Baton Rouge, and then proceeding up the Mississippi as far as Natchez. In this way he had by the end of 1779 become master of some twelve hundred miles of enemy territory. Having cleared the area to the north Gálvez moved against West Florida, and in the opening months of 1780 he moved against Mobile, but his operations were handicapped by bad weather. By the beginning of March, however, he had over-come his worst difficulties, and he proceeded against the place, which was badly defended, in the normal manner of those days. Approaches were formed, and a heavy battery opened against the garrison with such effect that the besieged proposed a capitula-tion: this was accepted, and they surrendered prisoners of war. The British luck was certainly out on this occasion, for at the very moment that they were being marched out Brigadier-General Campbell, the military governor of the province, appeared at the head of a relieving force. It was too late, and as the fort had im-mediately been occupied by the victors Campbell did not venture to risk an attack, but fell back on Pensacola. The remainder of the campaigning season was spent in some spasmodic fighting of no particular importance, while Gálvez was preparing his attack on Pensacola itself.

This was eventually made in October 1781, but was not a success as storms scattered the Spanish fleet, and the decisive operations had to be postponed until March of the following year. By this time reinforcements had arrived from Spain, and among them was the Hibernia Regiment. It was not the first occasion on which this unit had served in the Americas, for it fought against the Portuguese on the River Plate, this being the most southerly point in which Irish troops in the Spanish service had ever been in action.

On 9th March 1782 Gálvez anchored in his seventy-four-gun flagship, *San Ramón*, in Pensacola Bay, and with him were 1,315 troops from Cuba. This force was augmented within a fortnight by a further 2,253 men from Mobile and New Orleans, and on 19th April by another detachment of some 1,300 Spaniards. By the end of the month the first siege parallels were begun against Fort George. The Hibernia Regiment was present with the besieging force with a strength of 580 officers and men. The commanding officer, Lieutenant-Colonel Arturo O'Neil, was a man of some note. He had been born in Ireland about 1737, and had originally been a cadet in the Irlanda Regiment, but had transferred to Hibernia. After the siege Gálvez was to promote him to full colonel, and later he became Governor of West Florida. By the time he retired O'Neil was a Lieutenant-General.

At first it looked as if the siege was likely to be protracted, for Gálvez had a formidable opponent in his old adversary General Campbell. When the fighting had been going on for over a fortnight Campbell sent a two-hundred-men sortie by night against an outpost held by the Mallorca Regiment and the grenadier company of Hibernia. The raid was a complete success, for six guns were spiked, and thirty-eight Irishmen and Spaniards were killed or taken prisoners. Among the latter were two officers of Hibernia, one of whom died of his wounds and was buried by the British with full military honours. The siege was still in progress at the beginning of May, but on the seventh a Spanish shell landed in the British powder magazine, and the resulting explosion killed over a hundred of the garrison, while demoralizing the rest. Gálvez ordered an immediate assault, and stormed the key position, Queen's Redoubt. Campbell then realized that further resistance was useless, and ordered a flag of truce to be hoisted, the hostages exchanged being Lieutenant Meggs of the 69th Regiment[1] for the British, and Lieutenant Kenny of Hibernia for the Spaniards. The fighting cost the British ninety killed and forty-six wounded, while the Franco-Spanish forces lost ninety-six dead and over two hundred wounded, of which sixteen of the dead and twenty-seven of the wounded came from Hibernia. With the fall of Pensacola the whole province surrendered to Gálvez.

In retrospect one can see that this may well have been one of the decisive battles of history. Had the British managed to hold Pensacola it is more than likely that they would have kept Florida at the Treaty of Versailles, in which case the United Empire Loyalists would have flocked there after the war, and remained in the British Empire. In these circumstances, when the Civil War came the Confederacy would have had a long neutral border across which it could have exported its cotton and imported munitions of war: with the Federal naval blockade thus ineffective the result of the conflict might well have been very different.

Meanwhile there had been fighting in Central America. Sir Peter Parker was the British admiral in command of the Jamaica Station, and his fleet consisted of five small ships of the line and fourteen frigates; among the latter was the *Hinchingbrook*, twenty-four guns, commanded by Captain Horatio Nelson. As soon as hostilities began Parker sent a Captain Luttrell to look into the port of San Fernando de Omoa, in what is now the Republic of Honduras, where he had reason to suppose that a convoy was to be found. Luttrell dispatched a schooner to obtain the required information, and she reported that there were three ships at anchor under the fort, but that the defences did not appear to be particularly strong. This intelligence proved to be incorrect, for when Luttrell arrived he soon found that they were too formidable to attack from the sea. He accordingly withdrew, but by chance he encountered a sloop which was escorting a small convoy consisting of a detachment of the 18th Foot[2] and some Mosquito Indians under Major Dalrymple. With these, and a number of British logwood cutters whom he recruited, Luttrell decided to assault Omoa, this time from the landward side, which he accordingly did.

The operation was as successful as the similar Japanese one at

[1] Later the Welch Regiment.
[2] Later the Royal Irish Regiment.

Singapore in the Second World War, and for the same reason, namely that the defenders were taken by surprise. The Spanish governor formally surrendered to Dalrymple, and the cargo on board the ships was found to be of considerable value. The action was fought in the chivalrous spirit which characterized the Anglo-Spanish encounters in this war, and we are told of a British seaman who scaled the walls of Omoa with a cutlass in each hand. Suddenly he encountered a Spanish officer who was unarmed, so he gave him one of the cutlasses, saying, 'I will not take advantage of you – now we are on the same footing.' Which of them won the ensuing duel history does not record.

That was in October 1779, but the British triumph was short-lived. Luttrell left an insufficient garrison in Omoa, and the climate soon began to take its toll. On 25th November the Spaniards reappeared, and the hard-won conquest was at once abandoned to them. The whole affair was typical of the lack of foresight only too often displayed by the British commanders, both naval and military, in the War of American Independence. Either the fort should have been destroyed and evacuated immediately after its capture, or the garrison and fleet should have been maintained at sufficient strength to hold the place against any possible attack.

In the following year there was a further British attempt to secure a foothold in Central America, and on this occasion no less a person than Nelson himself was involved. The scheme, as planned in London, was indeed grandiose, for the orders were to obtain command of Lake Nicaragua, 'which for the present may in some degree be looked upon as the inland Gibraltar of Spanish America', and 'after that first conquest', and the capture of the rich cities of Granada and Léon, the expedition 'was to force a passage to the Pacific, thus cutting off all communication between North and South'. The Governor of Jamaica was little short of lyrical on the subject, for he went so far as to declare that 'by these different movements, I do not see how we can fail to bring about that grand object, a communication between sea and sea'. The objectives of the expedition, as so often on these occasions, were more impressive than its numbers, for it consisted of no more than four hundred regulars from the 60th and 79th Foot,[1] two hundred Jamaican volunteers, and a few marines. It had been hoped that a

[1] Later the K.R.R.C. and the Cameron Highlanders.

large number of Mosquito Indians would join them, but they proved singularly reluctant to do so since they were firmly convinced that the sole object of the British was to carry them off as slaves to Jamaica. It is little wonder that Nelson's comment should have been, 'How it will turn out, God knows.'[1]

It turned out very badly indeed. Nelson, in the *Hinchinbrook*, convoyed the troops successfully as far as San Juan del Norte, but when they proceeded inland their real troubles began. The expedition had arrived at the end of the dry season, so that before long it was overtaken by torrential rains. The banks of the river up which the invaders were advancing were at this time of year entirely composed either of unwholesome mud, submerged during the rainy season, from which after sunset arose a lethal miasma, or of decaying leaves and vegetables which had never seen the full light of the sun. It is true that there was no lack of medical supplies, but these got no further than the base, for priority was given to ammunition where transport was concerned. Snakes were a further occupational hazard to the fighting man in these parts, especially those dangling from trees, and such was the climate that the body of one soldier who fell out on being bitten under the eye was already putrefying by the time that the stretcher-party reached him.

The invaders did in due course, largely owing to the impetuosity of Nelson, capture the fort which was their immediate objective, but after that they rapidly dwindled away largely owing to the inroads of yellow fever. By the end of the year the fort had been blown up, and Nicaragua evacuated. The expedition was, in short, a badly organized and badly conducted affair, a dissipation of force, and a waste of valuable lives, while its only redeeming feature was the chance it gave the young Nelson of proving himself.

These, however, were the side-shows of the War of American Independence, for the real blows were being struck further north, and particularly at Yorktown, where Cornwallis capitulated to the Americans on 19th October 1781 to the not inappropriate tune of 'The World Turned Upside Down'. This event has been described as 'one of the decisive battles of the world',[2] and rightly so. In

[1] cf. Oman, Carola: *Nelson*. London, p. 31. 1947.
[2] Fuller, J. F. C.: *The Decisive Battles of the Western World*, vol. II, p. 331. London. 1955.

every struggle there comes a moment when one of the rival commanders begins to impose his will on his opponent. It may take a
long time; it may be from the outset; but the moment always
arrives and can be detected. Wolfe and Montcalm planned and
executed operations against one another at Quebec for a long
time before either attained a psychological superiority, but the
moment arrived when Montcalm's movements became dependent on those of his opponent, and from then he was a defeated man.

So it was with Clinton and Washington. Up to a short time
before Yorktown it was always Clinton and Cornwallis who
planned offensive operations, whilst Washington and his generals
did their best to hamper the execution of their projects, yielding
here, advancing there, attacking with guerilla bands. Neither had
established a superiority; neither was definitely imposing his will
on the other; but the psychological moment came when Washington and Rochambeau joined forces, and Clinton was set wonder-
ing what they were going to do. From the day when the British
commander-in-chief ceased to work out offensive plans for himself, and thought only of what the enemy was doing, the initiative
passed out of his hands, and then the war was lost.

All the same it took some time to wind it up. In London North's
administration did not collapse immediately on receipt of the
news of Yorktown, though it had the effect of bringing the
Cabinet to a decision that the war in America should cease to be
'continental', but should become merely a matter of clinging on to
what was still in British hands. On this ground Ministers successfully survived adverse motions on the Address in both Houses of
Parliament, and passed the army estimates with a large majority.
Over Christmas, however, the country gentlemen began to
change their minds, and when Parliament met again in the New
Year the government majorities on the continuance of the war
steadily fell, until in March 1782 North resigned, and was
succeeded by the Marquess of Rockingham, who took office on
condition that the independence of the United States should be
acknowledged. Somewhat languid negotiations towards this end
ensued, but Rockingham died at the beginning of July, and a
further delay took place until a new ministry was formed under
the Earl of Shelburne. In this administration Lord Grantham,
who had been British ambassador in Madrid, was Secretary of
State for Foreign Affairs.

The general situation when this new government took office was favourable to a continuation of the negotiations. All the belligerents were tired of the war, but its conclusion might have been long postponed had not the French tried to be too clever by half. Between Franklin and Vergennes relations were amicable, but the other two American representatives in Paris, Adams and Jay, were profoundly distrustful of French intentions, and before long it was proved that their attitude was not without justification. A letter from Marbois, the French chargé d'affaires in America, to Vergennes was intercepted, and in it Vergennes was recommended to resist certain of the American claims to territory in the valleys of the Mississippi and the Ohio. On reading this letter the Americans rightly came to the conclusion that the French were playing fast-and-loose with them, so they decided to make a separate peace, although this was contrary to the terms of their alliance. Accordingly on 30th November 1782 provisional articles of peace were signed between the United States and Great Britain.

The attitude of the Spanish King in these circumstances has not always been understood.[1] He had no desire to embark on wars of conquest, but he did see that American Independence was a heaven-sent opportunity of regaining the possessions which had been lost during his father's reign. Indeed, had the British government been prepared to meet him before he entered the conflict Spain might have remained neutral. By the time that the Americans had come to terms with the British he had attained several of his objectives. Minorca had been regained, and the Gulf of Mexico was once more a Spanish lake. Gibraltar still eluded him owing chiefly to the proved incompetence of the Franco-Spanish High Command, and the reconquest of Jamaica would necessitate a separate expedition on a considerable scale. Such being the case, he and his ministers decided to concentrate upon obtaining Gibraltar as part of the peace settlement, and in this he had at any rate the outward support of France.

Accordingly, both the Spanish and French governments in the negotiations which now took place pressed Britain hard to agree to some exchange for the Rock, and at first they were far from encountering serious opposition from official circles in London,

[1] cf. Ferrer del Rio, A.: *Historia del Reinado de Carlos III en España*, vol. III, pp. 360–361. Madrid. 1856.

where, as on previous occasions in the past, there was considerable difference of opinion. George III and Shelburne were quite prepared to let Gibraltar go if adequate compensation could be found elsewhere; only the Duke of Richmond and Viscount Keppel felt strongly in the opposite sense.[1] As the discussions continued it became clear that there were really only two practical alternatives. Either Spain should have Gibraltar back and keep one of the Floridas, ceding to Britain in compensation the island of Minorca, the Bahamas, and Puerto Rico, with the option, if the French agreed, of replacing Puerto Rico by the principal French possessions in the Leeward Islands and Trinidad; or Britain would keep Gibraltar and the Bahamas, in which case Spain would have Minorca, both the Floridas, and the British-occupied coasts of Yucatan and Honduras. In the light of later events it is not uninteresting to note that there was no suggestion by the British government that the inhabitants of Gibraltar should be consulted as to their fate.

There can be no doubt that Charles was most reluctant to abandon Gibraltar, and on 23rd November 1782 Floridablanca wrote to Aranda, 'It appears that the only difficulty in the way of peace is Gibraltar. I will not conceal from Your Excellency that the King wishes to support this solution (*i.e.* the first alternative) with all his might at the best possible moment; nevertheless, His Majesty would wish to know what advantages Spain would derive from the treaty if for any reason she should make such a sacrifice as to abandon the solution.' Aranda showed this letter to Vergennes, who asked if he might communicate it to the British government, and received the reply that 'in communicating this document my Court no doubt places it at your disposal'.

At this point it is difficult to avoid the conclusion that Charles was double-crossed by Vergennes, though whether Aranda was party to the French manœuvre it is impossible to say. What happened was that the French Foreign Minister at once told the British government that the demand for Gibraltar would be abandoned if agreement were reached on the sovereignty of Spain over Minorca and the two Floridas: these conditions were at once

[1] cf. Fitzmaurice, Lord Edmond: *Life of the Earl of Shelburne*, vol. III, pp. 305 and 312–314. London. 1875–76; also the *Autobiography and Political Correspondence of the Duke of Grafton*, edited by Sir William Anson, pp. 346 and 350. London. 1898.

accepted by London. That the King of Spain was by no means pleased with Aranda's attitude is proved by a letter he wrote on 2nd January 1783 to Louis XVI in which he said, 'Although my ambassador, knowing my heart's tender sentiments for you, has allowed himself to exceed my orders and pursue peace negotiations without insisting on the cession of Gibraltar . . . I do not wish to drive Your Majesty to extreme vexations for himself and his subjects.' In short, there was nothing the Spanish government could now do, and so the King, being a realist, put the best face he could upon it. The most recent critic of Vergennes is that distinguished British diplomatist, Sir Nicholas Henderson, who has quoted the American historian, Stetson Conn, to the effect that 'The French minister did not want to make the sacrifice of territory to accomplish the exchange; nor did he wish to weaken the ties that bound the Bourbon powers by removing the greatest single obstacle to a reconciliation between Spain and England.'[1] If such were the case Aranda's conduct becomes suspicious in the extreme.

Yet when all is said and done Charles and Floridablanca were surely right to accept what was in fact a *fait accompli*. There can be no question that the cession of the islands in question would have been tantamount to handing over to the British the outposts of the Antilles, to the grave peril of the trade and the security of the Spanish Empire, while there was no particular point in hauling down the Union Jack on Gibraltar only to hoist it immediately on Minorca. In effect, it is to be feared that the criticisms levelled at Charles and his ministers have been influenced by a strong dash of anachronism, which has made the critics take the line that, as the whole of Spanish America was to become independent in the next generation, the advantages which Spain obtained in the New World at Versailles did not greatly matter, but neither the King nor Floridablanca had any foreknowledge of this.

The preliminaries of peace with Britain were signed on 20th January 1783, and were followed by the definitive Treaty of Versailles concluded on 3rd September of the same year. Spain retained Minorca and West Florida, and East Florida was now ceded to her. On the other hand she surrendered Providence and the Bahamas which she had occupied without bloodshed in 1782, and which had since been recovered by Britain with equal ease.

[1] *History To-Day*, November 1968, p. 766.

Spain also guaranteed the right of the British to cut logwood in the Bay of Honduras. These terms were not as favourable to Spain as the course of the war might appear to have justified, but the position of Great Britain had been enormously strengthened by the United States having concluded a separate peace with her largely due to the over-cleverness of Vergennes.

XIV

THE LAST YEARS

THE reincorporation of Minorca in the Spanish dominions presented no great difficulty, but it was otherwise where Florida was concerned. Very wisely Irishmen were used for this purpose, for being fluent in both Spanish and English they helped to smooth over minor differences, and made the transfer of authority go the more easily. The new governor, too, was ideally suited to the task with which he was entrusted. Vincente de Zespedes was a veteran soldier of wide experience, and he was equally notable for his ability and honesty. He had been born in La Mancha c. 1720, had served in North Africa, and more recently he had been stationed in Cuba, where he had done much to raise the standard and morale of the Spanish forces. In effect, he was typical of the public servants whom Charles put in posts of responsibility both in the Old World and in the New, one or two Service chiefs excepted.

Zespedes landed at Saint Augustine on 27th June 1784, accompanied by Colonel William O'Kelly, Captain Edward Nugent, and four hundred and sixty soldiers of the Hibernia Regiment. On 12th July the Union Jack was replaced by the Lions and Castles on the Castillo de San Marcos, and Florida passed under Spanish rule. The governor then had time to look around him, and to size up his position, which was complicated by the fact that during the war thousands of United Empire Loyalists had fled to Florida, but they were now on the move again, this time to Canada or the West Indies, as they had no desire to live under any except British rule. There was also a small colony of Minorcans, together with a few Irish and English Catholics, as well as several hundred Negroes and mulattos, who, however, were quite prepared to accept the new dispensation.

None of these presented any great problem: more serious were the outlaws who haunted the Georgian borderland, for in that difficult area there had collected during the war pirates, smugglers, renegade Indians, runaway slaves, army deserters, and other undesirables. One of the leading gangs among these reprobates was that of Dan McGirt, and his favourite method of enriching himself was to steal Negro slaves on one side of the border and sell them on the other at cut-rate prices to customers who were not too particular about bills of sale or other legal formalities. Zespedes early came to the conclusion that to send a punitive column against these outlaws would only be asking for trouble, so he decided to use diplomacy rather than force. Captain Charles Howard, of Hibernia, was therefore sent to offer a free pardon to all who would promise to behave themselves in future. Howard was an experienced officer with twenty-three years' service in North Africa, Portugal, Brazil, and San Domingo, but it is to be feared that he was not wholly successful in his present mission.

Meanwhile Saint Augustine itself was settling down under Spanish rule, and as between victors and vanquished the same courtesy was displayed that had earlier marked the conduct of hostilities. There was much entertaining for the departing British, though occasionally there were incidents which would have been better avoided. For example, during the course of a ball given by Zespedes a messenger ran in with the news that the McGirt gang had rustled eight Negroes from the nearby plantation of one James Farley, and as Farley was present at the ball this information struck rather a discordant note. More serious was a blow to the governor himself during a dinner which he gave to the British officers when he was informed that his favourite daughter had eloped with a young Irish officer.

What had happened was that the young lady, taking advantage of the confusion caused by the dinner-party, had sneaked out to the house of the Chief Engineer, whose wife was clearly in the plot, and awaiting her there was Lieutenant John O'Donovan. The next to appear was the regimental chaplain, Father Miguel O'Reilly, who had been summoned on a false sick call, and was horrified when in front of him the young couple proceeded to hold hands and exchange marriage vows. The priest then rushed off to Zespedes, told him what had happened, and defended himself against any charge of complicity in the plot. As might be expected, the governor exploded, poured the vials of his wrath on Colonel O'Kelly, and O'Donovan was placed under close arrest. All the same, to save his family honour Zespedes compelled the unhappy chaplain that very evening to marry the lovers, who were then at once separated until a decision could be obtained from Spain with regard to the possibility of an annulment. The result was in the nature of anticlimax, for in due course the governor relented, and allowed O'Donovan to be posted to Cuba. By 1787 all was forgiven and forgotten, O'Donovan was back with his regiment, and reunited with his bride. Hibernia returned to Spain that same year.[1]

Meanwhile, the ink was hardly dry upon the Treaty of Versailles before Aranda put a very daring scheme before Charles. It was nothing less than the division of the Spanish dominions in the New World into three kingdoms—Peru, Mexico, and Costa Firma—each to be ruled by an Infante with the King of Spain as Emperor: commercial ties and matrimonial alliances to bind these new states together. Aranda was strongly of the opinion that some reorganization of the Spanish empire was essential if it was to make headway against the new Power which had come into existence to the north. 'This Federal Republic', he wrote, 'is born, so to speak, small; and before it could establish its independence it had to have the support of nations as powerful as France and Spain. The day, however, will come when it will be gigantic, and a formidable colossus in these regions; then it will forget the benefits which it has received from both Powers, and will think of nothing but its own aggrandisement.'[2]

Charles rejected the proposal, mainly on two grounds: one was that it might easily lead to the break-up of the Spanish Empire, and the other that there were not three Infantes capable of filling the new thrones. In this connection it is not uninteresting to note that at the time of the introduction of the Royal Titles Bill in Britain in 1876 the propriety of creating the Prince of Wales Prince Imperial of India, and his second and third brothers Princes of Canada and Australia, was canvassed between Queen Victoria and the Prime Minister, Disraeli, but the proposal was

---

[1] cf. Mullen, Thomas J.: *The Hibernia Regiment of the Spanish Army, The Irish Sword*, vol. VIII, pp. 218–225. Dublin. 1968.

[2] cf. Tapia Ozcariz, Enrique de: *Carlos III y Su Epoca*, pp. 361–362. Madrid. 1962.

Count d'Aranda

Count de Floridablanca, engraving after Goya

strongly opposed by the Prince of Wales and was wisely dropped without ever being submitted to Parliament.[1]

While the War of American Independence was still raging there occurred in Peru the last and most serious Indian rising against Spanish rule. Its leader was one José Gabriel Condorcanqui, a descendant of the Incas, and a man who, as befitted his birth, kept up a considerable state. In 1770 he went to Lima to establish his claim to the marquessate of Oropesa which had been granted to his family by Philip II. In this he was successful, and he was duly recognized by the Real Audiencia as eighth in lineal descent from Manco Inca, being the heir at law of Tupac Amaru, who had been put to death in 1571. This task accomplished the young man dropped his name Condorcanqui and assumed that of Tupac Amaru. For a time he seems to have been on the most friendly terms with his Spanish neighbours, but he was always a strong nationalist, and he never hesitated to champion the cause of his fellow-Indians. Such being the case it was more than a little unfortunate that his immediate superior the *corregidor* of Tinta, Don Antonio Aliaga, should have been a colonial administrator of the worst type, being cruel and avaricious, with the firm conviction that the only good Indian was a dead Indian.

As in the case of so many revolutionaries Tupac Amaru would appear to have been for a time content to advocate reform, and in particular he wished that the creoles would obey the regulations which Madrid had laid down for the protection of the Indians. At this stage of his career he professed loyalty to the throne and devotion to the Catholic Church, but before long he lost patience, and proceeded to resort to force. This first took place on 4th November 1780, being the name-day of the King of Spain.

To celebrate the event the *cura* of Yanaoca gave a dinner at which both Tupac Amaru and Aliaga were present, but the Inca left early on the pretext that he must return home because he was expecting a visitor from Cuzco. He then placed himself in ambush with a number of his dependents, and when the *corregidor* made his appearance he was thrown from his mount, securely bound with ropes, and taken to his captor's town of Tungasuca, where he was placed in close confinement. Tupac Amaru's next step was

[1] cf. Buckle, G. E.: *The Life of Benjamin Disraeli, Earl of Beaconsfield*, vol. V. p. 466. London. 1920.

to compel his unfortunate captive to sign an order to his cashier at Tinta to hand all the money in the provincial treasury over to the Inca, who in this way acquired twenty-two thousand dollars, some gold ingots, seventy-five muskets, and a number of horses and mules. Aliaga had now served his purpose, so a scaffold was erected in the square of Tungasuca, round which the Inca's recruits were ranged in three ranks, of which the first was armed with muskets, the second with pikes, and the third with treble-loaded slings. The execution took place on 10th November, but the hangman—a Negro slave of the Inca—bungled the job, and the *corregidor* had a painful death in consequence.

Having thus thrown down the gauntlet to Madrid by the execution of Aliaga, the Inca proceeded to widen the breach by a speech of extreme bitterness. He was a good deal of a showman, so he delighted the astonished multitude on horseback, attired in the princely costume of his ancestors, and described his present conduct and future intentions. He exhorted his audience to lend an attentive ear to the legitimate heir of their ancient sovereigns, he promised to abolish all forced labour, and to punish all cruel and extortionate *corregidores*. Needless to say his audience, being Indian, wildly applauded his sentiments, and rallied to him. From the beginning the rising was thus an Indian revolt against Spanish rule, and it is difficult to believe that it owed anything, as is sometimes alleged, to the example set by George Washington and his colleagues in British North America. With few, if any, exceptions, the creoles would have nothing to do with it, but espoused the cause of the Spanish government.

The Indians, however, saw in Tupac Amaru their liberator, and flocked to his standard, so that the revolt was soon spreading like a prairie fire. In due course the Inca found himself at the head of six thousand men, of whom half were armed with muskets and the rest with pikes and slings: he was also in possession of a few small field-pieces. At first all went well, and Tupac Amaru led his followers in the direction of Cuzco, the capital of his ancestors. News of the rising reached that city on 12th November 1780, and created a panic for the place was very poorly defended. Nevertheless in spite of their inferiority in numbers the Spaniards decided that offence was the best form of defence, and they marched out to do battle with the enemy. The clash came at a place called Sangarara, and after a desperate struggle the Indians won, and their victory served to fan the flames of revolt all over Peru.

Tupac Amaru now gave convincing proof of the fact that although he might be a spell-binding orator he was no soldier, for there is little doubt that had he pushed on he could have carried Cuzco by storm, so demoralized were the Spaniards by their defeat. Instead, he formed an encampment near Tinta, and contented himself with issuing proclamations setting out his own case and denouncing Spanish rule. December saw him extending his activities all over the countryside, and by the middle of the month he was at Azangaro, an important town to the north of Lake Titicaca. At every village he entered he addressed the people from the church steps, and declared that he had come to remedy abuses and punish the *corregidores*. He also detached his cousin, Diego Tupac Amaru, to the east with six thousand men to occupy the provinces of Calca and Paucartambo. While the Inca was campaigning in this manner, his opponents were mustering their forces, and with such effect that by the end of the year he felt it advisable to threaten Cuzco again, and once more the heights of the Andes were alight with his camp fires.

The next few weeks were marked by sporadic fighting outside Cuzco, and by a curious, if ineffective, exchange of proclamations. At the beginning of January 1781 the Inca addressed letters to the municipality and Bishop of Cuzco. To the former he said that, as heir of the ancient Kings of Peru, he was stimulated to endeavour by all possible means to put an end to abuses, and to see men appointed to office who would govern in accordance with the laws of the King of Spain.[1] He further announced the object of his movement to be the abolition of cruel exactions, and the establishment of an Indian judge in each province with a court of appeal in Cuzco within reach of the people. To the Bishop he said that he came forward on behalf of the whole nation to put an end to the robberies and outrages of the *corregidores*. He promised to respect the clergy, all ecclesiastical property, and all women and proved non-combatants if and when he captured Cuzco.

By now events were moving towards a climax. The Viceroy,

---

[1] It does not appear that he ever proclaimed himself a sovereign, independent of Spain, and the draft of an edict beginning, 'José I, by the Grace of God, Inca King of Peru', is almost certainly a forgery, cf. Markham, C. R.: *A History of Peru*, p. 203. London. 1892.

Don Agustin Jáuregui, had remained at Lima, but he had appointed as *visitador* with extraordinary judicial powers Don José Antonio de Areche, while the force to crush the rising was entrusted to General José del Valle. By the end of February there were collected in Cuzco troops to the number of some fifteen thousand, of whom a large part appear to have been Negroes and mulattos, and their morale was raised about this time by the arrival of news of a Spanish victory over the Inca's brother at Yucay. In these circumstances one would have thought that Tupac Amaru would have endeavoured to strike some telling blow before his enemies had completed their concentration, but he does not seem to have realized that a rebellion on the defensive has already failed, and he fell back upon his favourite resource of a long memorandum, which he sent to Areche. In this he once more stated what may be described as the Indian case, and suggested the opening of negotiations to discuss it. Areche would have none of this, and contented himself with telling the Inca that if he surrendered at once the harshness of his mode of execution would be mitigated.

The Spaniards marched out of Cuzco on 12th March 1781, and the final clash with the rebels took place on the sixth of the following month, after a brief campaign in which both sides displayed the maximum incompetence. Areche neglected the commissariat arrangements, so that in this mountain warfare his men suffered severely, while although in the decisive battle near Checaupe the Inca did indeed choose a position defended by a ditch and rampart he omitted to provide any defence for his flanks. After some desperate fighting the Indians were driven from this position back to the outskirts of Tinta, where a Spanish bayonet charge settled the day. For all practical purposes this marked the end of the rising, though there was sporadic fighting, some of it quite heavy, all over Peru, until the beginning of the following year, and in it, as we have seen, the Viceroy at Buenos Aires was involved.

The severity of the sentences meted out by the victors to the vanquished is evidence of the fear which the rebellion had instilled into the creoles, for Madrid cannot be blamed for the atrocities which followed. The fate of the Inca himself was peculiarly hard, for he was first of all compelled to witness the executions of his wife, his son, his uncle, his brother-in-law, cousins, and senior officers; then his tongue was torn out; and finally, his limbs having been secured to the girths of four horses pulling in different directions, the animals were set in motion until he was torn to pieces: his body was then burned on the heights of Picchu, his head stuck on a pole at Tinta, and his arms and legs displayed in a similar manner in four other towns. Yet Tupuc Amaru and his colleagues did not die in vain, for once Charles had had time to study the reforms which they had advocated most of them were put into force.[1]

Nearer home, the War of American Independence having freed his hands the King turned his attention once more to North Africa where the Barbary corsairs were again carrying matters with a very high hand, but the methods which he adopted were not sufficient to ensure a permanent cure. In 1784 Spain, Portugal, Naples, and Malta sent a combined fleet to Algiers, but the vessels of which it was composed were too small for the purpose and nothing definite was achieved. However, by the end of his reign treaties had been extorted by force or diplomacy from the Sultan of Morocco, the Dey of Algiers, and the Bey of Tunis in which those rulers not only pledged themselves to refrain from attacking the ships and coast of Spain, but also to grant freedom of worship to Spanish subjects. A treaty of peace was also made with their suzerain, the Ottoman Sultan Abdul Hamid I, and one of the last official acts of Charles's life was to receive his representative at La Granja in July 1788.

If, during his reign, the King succeeded in raising both at home and abroad the prestige of the crown to a point which it had not known since the days of Philip II, like that monarch he had, as we have seen, been unfortunate in his family, and his misfortunes on this score pursued him to the grave. It is said that just before his death the dying Philip remarked, 'God, who has given me so many kingdoms, has denied me a son capable of ruling them. I fear that they will govern him.' Charles might with equal truth have made the same observation about the Prince of Asturias.

The younger Charles had been born in Naples in 1748, and in his late thirties was clearly putting on weight: fairly tall, he possessed a small head, regular features, round eyes, a ruddy complexion, and the long nose, so often found to be among the

[1] cf. Tapia Ozcariz, Enrique de: *Carlos III y Su Epoca*, p. 369. Madrid. 1962.

Bourbons, which overhung a weak mouth and a protruding chin. The whole effect was, according to his admirers, an air of majestic benevolence, while those who did not think so well of him described it as one of stupidity. Indeed, physically, he recalled his mother's Saxon rather than his father's French forbears. It would be an exaggeration to say that he was feeble-minded. He was, in fact, a good-natured man with a fair memory, and he was nowise deficient in judgement once his interest had been aroused, but his development was what is known as somewhat 'arrested'. In more ways than one the Prince of Asturias resembled his contemporary and relative Louis XVI, for like the French monarch he was exceedingly fond of hunting, and he was a great collector of curious clocks, of which no inconsiderable number are still to be seen by visitors to Aranjuez.

Apart from the chase his chief hobby was carpentry. He was also more at home in the stable than in the drawing-room, and he preferred the society of grooms, with whom he was not above enjoying the odd bout of wrestling, to that of statesmen and courtiers. It is to be feared that his father was not always able to conceal his contempt for his heir, who having just enough intelligence to realize his mediocrity thus came to be driven in on himself, and to take refuge in a state of mental inactivity. Had his mother lived he might have developed along different lines, though that is admittedly doubtful. As it was, his sole objective was tranquillity so far as he personally was concerned, and anyone who would relieve him of the necessity for taking a decision was his friend. To this passion for tranquillity he was in the end, decent and well intentioned as he was, to sacrifice his authority as a prince, his dignity as a husband, the interests of his country, and, finally, his crown. Yet the Prince of Asturias was far from being uncultured, for he protected Goya, whom he made his painter-in-ordinary, and he was extremely fond of music, like his uncle, Ferdinand VI. He even played the violin passably, and could take his part in a chamber quartet. His besetting sin was laziness, and in a monarch this can have as evil consequences as cruelty or vice.

A very different character was the Princess of Asturias, by whom he was completely dominated. Maria Luisa of Parma was her husband's first cousin, being the daughter of Philip, Duke of Parma, and she had been born in 1751. In some of Goya's port-

raits she is little short of repellent, and one finds it very difficult
to believe that anyone could have been foolish enough to have
placed the least confidence in her. Yet we are told by those who
knew her that her manners combined the highest dignity with the
most perfect ease, and that she was endowed with great charm,
while she dressed superbly. Her enemies declared that she was
ruthless, cruel, and vicious, while Napoleon, no mean judge of a
woman, said, 'Maria Luisa has her past and her character written
on her face: it surpasses anything you can imagine.'

She and her husband had been married in 1765, and for some
years she would seem to have behaved herself, at any rate out-
wardly, for as late as 1783 we find a French observer writing,
'Madame the Princess of Asturias, whose kindness, wit, and
natural graces have an irresistible charm, spends her whole time
in her apartment where almost her only pleasures are conversation
and music.'[1] However this may be, it would seem that her esca-
pades had already begun, and, what is more, had reached the ears
of her father-in-law, who had little sympathy with the weaknesses
of the flesh. Maria Luisa was given a severe scolding, and in
future Charles kept a close eye upon her extra-marital activities.
The moment information reached him that a young man seemed
to be getting on too well with his daughter-in-law, the unfortunate lover would find himself condemned to an exile often of an
Ovidian nature: four members of the high aristocracy in due
course met this fate.

In these circumstances Maria Luisa came to the conclusion that
the best way to escape the King's notice would be to seek sexual
satisfaction rather lower in the social scale, so she turned to the
members of the Bodyguard who had the double advantage of
being young and reasonably anonymous. In this way she met
Manuel Godoy, but how or where is by no means certain. It was
probably through his elder brother who had been her lover until
Charles discovered their intrigue and sent him into exile, but
there were many other explanations running round Madrid as the
old King's reign came to a close. One was that Godoy was presented to the Princess by a lady-in-waiting, and that he whiled
away her boredom by his skill with the guitar; another was that
he deliberately fell from his horse as his troop was filing past her
window; while yet a third was that her attention was called to

[1] cf. Chastenet, J.: *Godoy, Master of Spain, 1792–1808*, p. 21. London. 1953.

him by the offhand manner in which he dropped a statue that he had been ordered to carry in a procession.

Manuel Godoy had been born in Badajoz in 1767 of a very ancient but extremely impoverished family, and he came to Madrid in 1784 as an ordinary Gentleman of the Bodyguard. Few men in their lives have occasioned such violent controversy. A modern writer says that he 'was an accomplished man of affairs', and that he 'kept Spain, and even the Indies, secure and peaceful: such a task required a remarkable man'.[1] Lord Holland was predisposed in his favour, and wrote of him:

Godoy's manner, though somewhat indolent, or as the French term it nonchalant, was graceful and engaging. In spite of his education, which I presume was provincial and none of the best, his language appeared to me elegant, and equally exempt from vulgarity and affectation. Indeed, his whole demeanour announced, more than that of any untravelled Spaniard I ever met with, a mixture of dignity and politeness, of propriety and ease. He seemed born for a high station. Without effort he would have passed in any mixed society for the first man in it.

As for Maria Luisa, there was no limit to her admiration. 'Your fame and memory will end only when the world is burnt to ashes, and then they will after that be rewarded in glory.' On the other hand we have Richard Ford, the traveller, who wrote of him as 'a foul beast of prey always craving and swallowing', while the future Ferdinand VII, admittedly not an unprejudiced witness, talks of 'the black and cancered conscience of this tiger'. Finally, there is Napoleon, who changed his mind more than once on the subject of Godoy, but who declared at St. Helena, 'That man was a genius.'

The *naïveté* of the Prince of Asturias where his wife's infidelities were concerned is almost unbelievable. Whether the King knew of her intrigue with Godoy is doubtful, for had he been aware of it the handsome guardsman would have been exiled like his brother, but he warned his son against potential rivals of that sort; only to be met with the reply that princes were in little danger of wifely unfaithfulness, for princesses would certainly not consort with men of inferior rank, while men of their own were few and far

[1] Voltes, Pedro: *Carlos III y Su Tiempo*, p. 194. Barcelona. 1964.

between. On hearing this inane observation Charles exclaimed, 'What a complete fool you are, my son.'[1]

The other children, apart from Philip who had been excluded from the succession for reasons which have already been noticed, and Ferdinand, the King of The Two Sicilies, were:

> Gabriel, who was born in 1752, married Maria Ana of Portugal, but they both died a few weeks before Charles himself.
>
> Pedro, Antonio, and Francisco Javier who all died before their father.
>
> Maria Josefa who was deformed, and never married.
>
> Maria Luisa, who married the Archduke Leopold, Grand Duke of Tuscany, subsequently the Emperor Leopold II.

Charles was devoted to all his children, and he saw that they received an education above the standard usually given to royal personages, but it is universally agreed that his favourite was Don Gabriel, who was gifted in many ways, being a classical scholar and no inconsiderable musician. It has even been suggested that at one time the King was considering in favour of Don Gabriel a modification of the order of succession laid down by his father.

In the international field the last years of the King's life were spent in a successful struggle to keep the peace of Europe unbroken. The death of Frederick the Great, the continued dissensions between Britain and France, and the disturbed state of the Netherlands all furnished elements of strife which, but for the prudent handling of Charles and Floridablanca, could easily have led to war. In old age the King reverted to the pacific policy of his predecessor, Ferdinand, and refused to be drawn into foreign complications or entangling alliances.

In his private life the old routine persisted. Charles was circumspect by nature, and the events of 1766 rendered him more cautious than ever, especially when it came to interference with the ingrained prejudices and habits of his subjects. For example, he was, like more than one of his predecessors on the Spanish throne, averse to bull-fighting, but caution prevented him from taking any steps to abolish it, so popular had it become with the

[1] cf. Tapia, Enrique de: *Carlos III y Su Epoca*, p. 402. Madrid. 1962.

mass of the people. Mr. Henderson has taken the view[1] that the King 'had stronger feelings for animals than human beings', and he was certainly devoted to his dogs, whom he fed himself. For the rest, his life went on in the same old way, for he was a creature of habit in all he did, and he never acted precipitately either in public or in private. He ate the same things every day, and drank the same wine which was very little, merely one glass of Canary at midday, and another in the evening. He carried out all his public functions at the same hour and with great precision, for like his great-grandfather, Louis XIV, he insisted that punctuality was the courtesy of kings. With absolute regularity he moved at the same time each year from one palace to another – the Pardo in January; Aranjuez at Easter; La Granja in July; the Escorial in October; and back to Madrid in December.

To the end of his life Charles retained Floridablanca as his chief minister, and the two men worked together as a team for the reorganization and reform of Spain. There was no aspect of public welfare that did not receive attention, and hospitals, asylums, poor-houses, and free schools sprang up all over the country, thanks to the initiative of the monarch. Savings-banks, benefit societies, and philanthropic institutions were established, whilst vagrancy and mendicancy were put down with a stern hand. Men of science and learning, skilled organizers of industry, and experienced craftsmen were brought from abroad in large numbers, and under their guidance new industries were founded and fostered by the government. The glass factory at La Granja, the porcelains of the Buen Retiro, the cotton velvets of Avila, the fine leathers of Seville and Córdoba, and the machinery, watches, optical instruments, and fancy goods of Madrid all became both famous and profitable under Charles's patronage. Public credit was raised and funds procured for these reforms, as well as for the repayment of old loans, by the establishment of the national Bank of San Carlos, and the issue of interest-bearing government bonds for 800 millions of reals, which were freely circulated at par. The *alcabalas* and 'millions' which had killed Spanish industry were reduced from 14 per cent to 5 per cent in Castille, and suspended altogether in the case of manufactured goods or produce sold in the place of origin, while the deficit was made up by a 5 per cent tax on incomes from land, and a 2 or 3 per cent one on the rental

[1] cf. *History To-Day*, November 1968, p. 767.

of holdings. Thus the great project of the single tax was abandoned in favour of this system of graduation, and the *alcabalas* ceased to have the disastrous effect which they had exercised for so long.

It must not, however, be supposed that these reforms made the King and Floridablanca popular—far from it, for far too many vested interests are adversely affected, not least in aristocratic and ecclesiastical quarters. Among the minister's critics was, surprisingly enough, Aranda, but he was probably actuated by personal jealousy, and O'Reilly. Satires, pasquinades, and newspaper attacks rained upon Floridablanca, and at one point he tendered his resignation, but Charles stood by him, and passed him on as chief minister to his son at his death.

As the autumn of 1788 passed into winter this event was clearly approaching. The King was now in his seventy-fourth year, and throughout his life his health had been remarkably good, chiefly, no doubt, owing to his regular and temperate habits, but now it began to break down. The death of his favourite son, Gabriel, also hit him very hard, and matters were not helped by a severe chill, of which he could not get rid. For the first time since he came from Naples the King took to his bed. As usual at this time of year the Court was at the Escorial, but on 1st December it returned to Madrid as usual, and Charles took up his residence in the new Palacio de Oriente which had been built on the site of the old Alcazar in which he had been born. For a day or two he rallied, but not for long, and it became clear that the fever which gripped him would soon prove fatal. To the end Charles remained singularly composed, and when during the reading of his will Floridablanca showed signs of emotion, the King asked, 'Did you think I was going to live for ever?' When on his deathbed a bishop asked him whether he pardoned his enemies, the reply came, 'How should I wait for this pass before forgiving them? They were all forgiven the moment after the offence.' At dawn on 14th December 1788 he died—one of the best, greatest, and most patriotic monarchs that Spain has ever known.

In his first interview with the President of the Council of Castille on his accession to the throne Charles said, 'I want to apply the law so far as possible to favour the poor', and during the whole of his reign he did his best to hold the balance evenly between all classes of the community, which probably explains his annoyance with the populace of Madrid for its apparent ingratitude during the riots in 1766. A man's origins meant nothing to him – what mattered was his efficiency, and there was nothing exclusive about those who administered Spain during his reign, while the importance of birth was not regarded at all – in marked contrast with the state of affairs obtaining in contemporary London and Paris. Perhaps Charles's greatest achievement was that he brought about, if only temporarily, a national revival in all spheres of activity, which was no mean task when it is remembered that the French 'image' had been the dominant feature in Spain, not least in literature and art, for at least two generations.[1] With a successor of equal ability his country might have continued happy, prosperous, and powerful, but it was not to be, and it was the Spain of Godoy that had to face the turmoil of the Napoleonic era.

---

[1] cf. Ximénez de Sandoval, F.: *La Piel de Toro*, pp. 230–235. Madrid. 1968.

APPENDIX

THE WALLOON GUARDS

The Regiment was created by Royal Decree on 17th October 1702, and consisted of two battalions, each of thirteen companies, one of which was in each battalion a grenadier company. Each company consisted of:

1 Captain	2 Sergeants	5 Second Corporals
1 Lieutenant	2 Drummers	38 Other Ranks
1 Ensign	3 First Corporals	

The Staff establishment was:

1 Colonel	2 Under A.D.C.s
1 Lieutenant-Colonel	1 Q.M.
1 Major	1 Commissaire
2 A.D.C.s	1 Drum Major

The original officers were all members of the Belgian aristocracy, and the privilege of the Regiment was that it had seniority over all other corps except the Spanish Guards: the Colonel had to be a Grandee of Spain, and he had personal access to the King. Recruiting for the ranks was limited to natives of the Netherlands. There was a depot at Liége until the French Revolution, and recruiting was at the rate of 500–600 a year. Recruits had to be 17–40 years old, 5 ft. 3 in. tall, and of honourable family. Enlistment was for six years in time of peace and five in time of war.

The number of battalions varied, for the Regiment was soon raised to six, and although it was reduced to four in 1716, it soon returned to six, and at that figure it remained during the reign of Charles III.

INDEX

Tuscany, Grand Duke of (Gian
Gastone Medici), 21. 22–3, 25,
26, 31

Ulloa, Antonio de, 148–9
United Empire Loyalists, 208, 216
Ursins, Princess des, 5–6
Utrecht, Treaty of, 2, 7, 8, 19,
26–7, 30, 32, 35, 59, 67, 74, 75,
115, 172–4

Velletri, battle of, 52–4, 101, 159
Vergennes, Count de, 168–9, 170,
212, 213–15
Vernon, Admiral, 69
Versailles, Treaty of, 1756, 83;
1783, 195, 208, 214–15, 218
Vertiz y Salcedo, Juan José de, 144
Viceroyalties of Spain in New
World, 90–3, *and see* America,
Spanish dominions in
Vienna, Treaty of, 1725, 11;
1739, 30–1
Villars, Marshal, 25–6
Voltaire, xix, 45

Wall, Richard, 64, 77–8, 79, 81,
85, 87, 97, 99, 100, 104, 105,
112–14
Walloon regiments, 53, 54, 101,
231; and Squillaci riots, 119–20,
121, 188
Walpole, Horace, 76
Walpole, Sir Robert, 19, 68, 69,
176
Washington, George, 186, 211, 220
Wellington, Duke of, 184
West Indies, 67, 68, 88–9, 102, and
American War of Independence,
204–6; Spanish possessions in,
204; British possessions in,
205–6
Westminster, Treaty of, 83
Weymouth, Lord, 181
William III, of England, 113 n1,
156, 171

Yorktown, battle of, 210–11

Zespedes, Vincente de, 216–18